ABOUT THE AUTHOR

Adam Fergusson was born in Scotland in 1932. He graduated in history at Cambridge, and later became a journalist with the *Glasgow Herald*, the *Statist* and *The Times*. He has been a Member of the European Parliament, a Special Adviser at the Foreign Office, and a consultant on European affairs for international industry and commerce. He has written five books, including three novels; many articles and pamphlets; three musical comedies; and much light verse. He is a Fellow of the Royal Society of Literature, and lives in London.

First published 1975 by William Kimber & Co. Ltd.

This edition published 2010 by Old Street Publishing Ltd
40 Bowling Green Lane, London EC1R 0NE
www.oldstreetpublishing.co.uk

ISBN 978-1-906964-44-3

10 9 8 7 6 5 4 3

A CIP catalogue record for this title is available from the British Library.

Printed and bound in Great Britain.

WHEN MONEY DIES
The Nightmare of the Weimar Hyper-Inflation

ADAM FERGUSSON

To my Mother

Contents

Note to the 2010 edition   vii

Prologue   ix

1 Gold for Iron   1

2 Joyless Streets   17

3 The Bill Presented   27

4 Delirium of Milliards   39

5 The Slide to Hyperinflation   61

6 Summer of '22   80

7 The Hapsburg Inheritance   92

8 Autumn Paper-chase   108

9 *Ruhrkampf*   129

10 Summer of '23   158

11 Havenstein   1   70

12 The Bottom of the Abyss   186

13 Schacht   205

14 Unemployment Breaks Out   218

15 The Wounds are Bared   233

Epilogue   248

Bibliography   259

Index   261

Note to the 2010 edition

When this book was first published in 1975, as its prologue observes, comparison of contemporary prices and values with those of half a century earlier was of limited advantage. Thirty-five years on, when currencies have continually merged, diverged, depreciated or disappeared, and when costs and wages have risen and fallen with so little uniformity, the exercise sheds no more light. True, statisticians have reckoned that the pound sterling of 1923 would do the job of £623 today; and that the 1923 dollar might now buy $220 worth of goods and services. However, rather than be burdened with interesting but highly speculative comparative calculations, the reader is invited to accept the text as it was written.

In dealing with the stupendous figures with which Germany wrestled in the Weimar period, the book maintains the same numerical designations as were used then and as appeared on her banknotes. That is to say, when a milliard meant one thousand million, when a billion was still a million times a million, when the term billiard was coined to indicate a thousand times more, and a trillion was 1,000,000 cubed. To have converted these words to the more modern usage, when a billion boasts only nine noughts and a trillion a mere twelve, might, I fancy, have added to what a German minister of the 1920s justly called 'the delirium of milliards'.

Prologue

When a nation's money is no longer a source of security, and when inflation has become the concern of an entire people, it is natural to turn for information and guidance to the history of other societies who have already undergone this most tragic and upsetting of human experiences. Yet to survey the great array of literature of all kinds – economic, military, social, historic, political and biographical – which deals with the fortunes of the defeated Central Powers after the First World War is to discover one particular shortage. Either the economic analyses of the times (for reasons best known to economists who sometimes tend to think that inflations are deliberate acts of fiscal policy) have ignored the human element, to say nothing in the case of the Weimar Republic and of post-revolutionary Austria of the military and political elements; or the historical accounts, though of impressive erudition and insight, have overlooked – or at least much underestimated – inflation as one of the most powerful engines of the upheavals which they narrate.

The first-hand accounts and diaries, on the other hand, although of incalculable value in assessing inflation from the human aspect, have tended even in anthological form either to have had too narrow a field of vision – the battle seen from one shell-hole may look very different when seen from another – or to recall the financial extravaganza of 1923 in such a general way as to underplay the many years of misfortune of which it was both the climax and the herald.

The agony of inflation, however prolonged, is perhaps somewhat similar to acute pain – totally absorbing, demanding complete attention while it lasts; forgotten or ignorable when it has gone, whatever mental or physical scars it may leave behind. Some such explanation may apply to the strange way in which the remarkable episode of the Weimar inflation has been divorced – and *vice versa* – from so much contemporary incident. And yet, one would have thought, considering how persistent, extended and terrible that inflation was, and how baleful its consequences, no study of the period could be complete without continual reference to the one obsessive circumstance of the time.

The converse is also true: except at the narrowest level of economic treatise or personal reminiscence, how can a fair account of the German inflation be given outside the context of political subversion by Nationalists and by Communists, or the turmoil in the Army, or the quarrel with France, or the problem of war reparations, or the parallel hyperinflations in Austria and Hungary? How can one gauge the political significance of inflation, or judge the circumstances in which inflation in an industrialised democracy takes root and becomes uncontrollable, unless its course is charted side by side with the political events of the moment?

The Germany of 1923 was the Germany of Ludendorff as well as of Stinnes, of Havenstein as well as of Hitler. For all their different worlds, of the Army, of industry, of finance and of politics, these four grotesque figures stalking the German stage may equally be represented as the villains of the play: Ludendorff, the soulless, humourless, ex-Quartermaster-General, worshipper of Thor and Odin, rallying point and dupe of the forces of reaction; Stinnes, the plutocratic profiteer who owed allegiance only to Mammon; Havenstein, the mad banker whose one object was to swamp the country with banknotes; Hitler, the power-hungry demagogue whose every speech and action even then called forth all that was evil in human nature. In respect of Havenstein alone the description is of course unjust; but the fact that this highly-respected financial authority was sound in mind made no difference to the wreckage he wrought.

Or one may say that there were no real human villains; that given the economic and political cues, actors would have been in the wings to come on and play the parts which circumstances dictated. Certainly there were many others as reprehensible and irresponsible as those who played the leading roles. The German people were the victims. The battle, as one who survived it explained, left them dazed and inflation-shocked. They did not understand how it had happened to them, and who the foe was who had defeated them.

This book presents a few new facts, but many forgotten facts and many hitherto unpublished opinions – most usefully of those who could observe events objectively because their purses, health and security were unaffected by what they were witnessing. The most bountiful store of such material is the records of the British Foreign Office, supplied originally by the embassy in Berlin where Lord D'Abernon prosecuted in those years one of the most successful ambassadorships of the age. His information was amply augmented by the consular service in every important city in Germany, as by reports from individual members of the Allied commissions concerned with reparations or disarmament. The documents in the Public Record Office, apart from being among the more accessible, are also probably the most important source available, not only because the British Embassy through D'Abernon was in exceptionally close touch at all times with Germany's senior politicians, but because the withdrawal of the United States presence at the start of 1923, and the almost complete interruption of any communication between Berlin and Paris earlier still, rendered sporadic or superficial what might have been information of comparable value. Supplemented by contemporary German material, I have not hesitated to draw as fully as seemed justified on those papers.

I have tried as far as possible to keep these actions, reactions and interactions in their proper historical sequence in the hope that this perhaps obvious order is in this case both a new and enlightening one, and the better to expose a number of important but little-noticed relationships. In relating the story, I have followed, and at times had to hang on grimly to, a special thread which wound through Austria, Hungary, Russia, Poland and France, too. It is one which the great authorities have sometimes seemed to lose touch with: the effect of inflation on people as individuals and as nations, and how they responded to it.

I have not, however, dared to draw hard and fast conclusions about humanity and inflation on the basis of what I have written here: the facts speak very well for themselves. Still less have I expounded any economic lessons or indulged in theoretical explanations of economic phenomena. This is emphatically not an economic study. Yet inflation is about money as well as people, and it would be impossible to tell the tale without introducing figures, sometimes vast figures, again and again. Vast figures were what the people of central Europe were assailed by and bludgeoned with for years on end until they could bear no more. The value of the mark in 1922 and 1923 was in everyone's mind; but who could comprehend a figure followed by a dozen ciphers?

In October 1923 it was noted in the British Embassy in Berlin that the number of marks to the pound equalled the number of yards to the sun. Dr Schacht, Germany's National Currency Commissioner, explained that at the end of the Great War one could in theory have bought 500,000,000,000 eggs for the same price as that for which, five years later, only a single egg was procurable. When stability returned, the sum of paper marks needed to buy a gold mark was precisely equal to the quantity of square millimetres in a square kilometre. It is far from certain that such calculations helped anyone to understand what was going on; so let the un-mathematical reader take heart.

Because of the varying ways in which nations express large amounts, I have tried to avoid notations such as billions and trillions upon which custom is confusingly divided. When I have departed from this practice, due indication has been given.

It has been harder in the writing to find enough simple epithets to describe without repetition the continuous, worsening succession of misfortunes that struck the German people at this time. It was a difficulty noticed and noted by Mr Lloyd George writing in 1932, who said that words such as 'disaster', 'ruin', and 'catastrophe' had ceased to rouse any sense of genuine apprehension any more, into such common usage had they fallen. Disaster itself was devalued: in contemporary documents the word was used year after year to describe situations incalculably more serious than the time before. When the mark finally dropped out of sight and ruin was all around, there were still Germans to be heard predicting *Katastrophe* for the future.

I have tried, therefore, to limit the number of disasters, crashes, cataclysms, collapses and catastrophes in the text, as well as the degree of crisis and chaos, to a digestible amount, to which the reader may mentally add as much more as his power of sympathy dictates.

In one other matter the reader must act independently. It has been necessary frequently to give the 1920s' sterling or dollar equivalents of the mark sums involved, in order to show the scale of the mark's depreciation. The continuing process of inflation in all western countries makes conversion to present-day values an unrewarding occupation. For the lowest range of conversions I have kept to the £sd system of 12 pence to the shilling and 20 shillings to the pound. At this distance, cost of living comparisons are fairly futile; yet it may be useful to reckon that in the middle of 1975 it was necessary to multiply every 1920 sterling figure by about 15 times to find an equivalent. Thus a wage of £200 in 1919 might be worth £3,000 today; a sum of ten shillings worth seven or eight pounds. For dollars, a multiplicator of six or eight could be enough. If a mark in 1913 would buy almost a pound's worth of goods and services in 1975 (some items, clearly, were much more expensive; others such as labour much cheaper in real terms than now), then a simple but rough conversion is available for sterling readers whom it amuses or vexes to imagine paying £148,000,000 for a postage stamp: for marks they should read pounds.

There is no constant rule of thumb for coping accurately with the later stages of the inflation. Until autumn 1921 the internal depreciation of the mark sometimes lagged far behind its fall abroad – making Germany such a haven for tourists. Later on (from the beginning of 1922), as public confidence in the mark dissolved, domestic prices adjusted themselves rapidly upwards in tune with the dollar rate, and at the end were even heftily anticipating the mark's fall. This was one more of the phenomena of the times which fatally confused the issue then and which exercised the interest of economists for many years afterwards.

This is, I believe, a moral tale. It goes far to prove the revolutionary axiom that if you wish to destroy a nation you must first corrupt its currency. Thus must sound money be the first bastion of a society's defence.

1: Gold for Iron

Just before the First World War in 1913, the German mark, the British shilling, the French franc, and the Italian lira were all worth about the same, and four or five of any were worth about a dollar. At the end of 1923, it would have been possible to exchange a shilling, a franc or a lira for up to 1,000,000,000,000 marks, although in practice by then no one was willing to take marks in return for anything. The mark was dead, one million-millionth of its former self. It had taken almost ten years to die.

The mark's fall began gradually. In the war years, 1914-1918, its foreign exchange value halved, and by August 1919 it had halved again. In early 1920, however, although the cost of living had risen less than nine times since 1914, the mark had only one-fortieth of its overseas purchasing power left. There followed twelve months of nervous fluctuation, but then the mark sped downwards with gathering momentum, dragging social misery and political disruption in its wake. Not until 1923 did Germany's currency at last go over the cliff-edge of sanity to which it had, as it were, clung for many months with slipping finger-tips. Pursuing the money of Austria and Hungary into the abyss, it crashed there more heavily than either.

The year 1923 was the one of galloping inflation when a kind of madness gripped Germany's financial authorities and economic disaster overwhelmed millions of people. It was the year of astronomical figures, of 'wheelbarrow inflation', of financial phenomena that had never been observed before. The death of the mark in November 1923 came as a merciful release, for the events of the preceding eight months had ensured that the old mark could never recover. They ensured, too, that Germany would have to undergo appalling rigours of financial reconstruction such as might otherwise have been escaped. The re-establishment of monetary sanity, which bankrupted thousands, robbed millions of their livelihoods, and killed the hopes of millions more, indirectly exacted a more terrible price which the whole world had to pay.

The inflation of 1923 was so preposterous, and its end so sudden, that the story has tended to be passed off more as a historical curiosity, which it also undoubtedly was, than as the culmination of a chain of economic, social and political circumstances of permanent significance. It matters little that the causes of the Weimar inflation are in many ways unrepeatable; that political conditions are different, or that it is almost inconceivable that financial chaos would ever again be allowed to develop so far. The question to be asked – the danger to be recognised – is how inflation, however caused, affects a nation: its government, its people, its officials, and its society. The more materialist that society, possibly, the more cruelly it hurts. If what happened to the defeated Central Powers in the early 1920s is anything to go by, then the process of collapse of the recognised, traditional, trusted medium of exchange, the currency by which all values are measured, by which social status is guaranteed, upon which security depends, and in which the fruits of labour are stored, unleashes such greed, violence, unhappiness, and hatred, largely bred from fear, as no society can survive uncrippled and unchanged.

Certainly, 1922 and 1923 brought catastrophe to the German, Austrian and Hungarian bourgeoisie, as well as hunger, disease, destitution and sometimes death to an even wider public. Yet any people might have ridden out those years had they represented one frightful storm in an otherwise calm passage. What most severely damaged the morale of those nations was that they were merely the climax of unreality to years of unimagined strain of every kind. Financially, for nearly four years, the ultimate cataclysm was always just round the corner. It always arrived, and there was always an even worse one on its way – again, and again, and again. The speeches, the newspaper articles, the official records, the diplomatic telegrams, the letters and diaries of the period, all report month by month, year by year, that things could not go on like that any longer: and yet things always did, from bad to worse, to worse, to worse. It was unimaginable in 1921 that 1922 could hold any more terrors. They came, sure enough, and were in due course eclipsed, and more than eclipsed, with the turn of the following year.

To ascribe the despair which gripped those nations entirely to inflation would of course be misleading. In the winter of 1918-1919 all three underwent political revolutions, following the deprivations of wartime and crushing military defeat: so that conditions were fundamentally unfavourable to any revival of national spirit not rooted in revenge, and would have remained so even had the peace treaties permitted the losers to struggle however gradually to their economic feet. It is not always clear what events – what popular uprising, or Allied ultimatum, or political assassination – contributed to the inflationary panic; or which were themselves directly or indirectly caused by the ceaseless depreciation of the currency and rise in the cost of living.

Undoubtedly, though, inflation aggravated every evil, ruined every chance of national revival or individual success, and eventually produced precisely the conditions in which extremists of Right and Left could raise the mob against the State, set class against class, race against race, family against family, husband against wife, trade against trade, town against country. It undermined national resolution when simple want or need might have bolstered it. Partly because of its unfairly discriminatory nature, it brought out the worst in everybody – industrialist and worker, farmer and peasant, banker and shopkeeper, politician and civil servant, housewife, soldier, merchant, tradesman, miner, moneylender, pensioner, doctor, trade union leader, student, tourist – especially the tourist. It caused fear and insecurity among those who had already known too much of both. It fostered xenophobia. It promoted contempt for government and the subversion of law and order. It corrupted even where corruption had been unknown, and too often where it should have been impossible. It was the worst possible prelude – although detached from it by several years – to the great depression; and thus to what followed.

That is to put the inflation of early 1920s back again in its historical setting. From there, very probably, it is unwise to try too hard to prise it. After all, no one would argue strongly that the German inflation directly caused the world depression, nor even that it alone spawned Nazi Germany. Unquestionably it made the one the more unbearable and, as a contributary cause, made much easier the coming of the other. However, it is the purpose in the pages which follow not to predict by analogy a similar destiny for any industrialised, democratic nation in the grip of severe inflation, but rather, by recounting an extraordinary story, to present some of the evidence of what inflation may do to people, and what in consequence they may do to one another.

The origins of the German inflation are in some ways fundamental, in some ways incidental, to this theme. They were both internal and external. Even during the war, Germany's financial arrangements were such as to permit the grossest monetary excesses by her national banking system. They were eventually to render post-war inflation uncontrollable, while the nature and presentation of the Entente's reparation demands – the indemnity for the war – encouraged the activities of the printing presses to the utter exclusion of other, more desirable policies. Nor may it be overlooked that Germany's industrialists ruthlessly drove their Government down the road to monetary doom.

Nevertheless, it was the natural reaction of most Germans, or Austrians, or Hungarians – indeed, as for any victims of inflation – to assume not so much that their money was falling in value as that the goods which it bought were becoming more expensive in absolute terms; not that their currency was depreciating, but – especially in the beginning – that other currencies were unfairly rising, so pushing up the price of every necessity of life. It reflected the point of view of those who believe the sun, the planets and the stars revolve with the moon around the earth.

In a lengthy interview many years afterwards with Pearl Buck, Erna von Pustau, whose father was a small Hamburg businessman who ran a fishmarket, made the same point: 'We used to say "The dollar is going up again", while in reality the dollar remained stable but our mark was falling. But, you see, we could hardly say our mark was falling since in figures it was constantly going up – and so were the prices – and this was much more visible than the realisation that the value of our money was going down ... It all seemed just madness, and it made the people mad.'

In other words, the causes of the mark's depreciation, which certainly escaped Germany's politicians and bankers as well, had little enough to do with how the people, individually or collectively, reacted to it. Most of them clung to the mark, the currency they knew and believed in, long after the eleventh hour had come round for the umpteenth time. Most had no choice; but all were encouraged or bemused by the Reichsbank's creed of *Mark gleich Mark* – paper or gold, a mark is a mark is a mark. If prices went up, people demanded not a stable purchasing power for the marks they had, but more marks to buy what they needed. More marks were printed, and more, and more. Inflation, already in its fourth year when revolution overthrew the old regime, added a new, overwhelming uncertainty to the many uncertainties that attended the birth of the Weimar Republic.

Although the German revolution originated as a military mutiny against the bungling of the Army's leaders, and was bent upon getting rid of the officer caste who had brought military disaster upon the country, it had distinguishable economic origins as well. Support for the Soldiers' Councils which were coming into being in every unit as the war drew to an end rested heavily on the personal financial calamities which so many of the soldiers and their families were already experiencing. Their frustrations had been eloquently aggravated by the arrival at the front in the spring of 1918 of a group of seasoned anti-war agitators – the leaders of the factory strikes which had ravaged the country after the Treaty of Brest-Litovsk with Communist Russia. The ruthlessly annexationist terms of that treaty were but another of the crass political mistakes – including the unrestricted submarine warfare that brought the United States into the battle, and the return of Lenin to Petrograd – which were made by the Great German General Staff of whom the Kaiser liked to regard himself the war lord. Through the late summer of 1918 defeatism and disaffection spread; and when defeat itself came the Army was torn in two, essentially between the professional soldiers and the conscripts.

The Supreme Command lost no time in exculpating itself in respect of losing the war. As the Kaiser fled to Holland, at least a week too late to save the monarchy in any form, and Ludendorff made off to Sweden, the odium of signing the Armistice was placed firmly on the head of the civilian authority. A month later, in December 1918, President Ebert at the Brandenburger Tor was welcoming the legions home with the words: 'I salute you, who return unvanquished from the field of battle.'

The myth of the *Dolchstoss*, the stab in the back of the Army by the craven politicians and treacherous intellectuals behind the lines, was thereafter to be cultivated to the point when democratic political evolution was poisoned at its heart. This was a heavy burden for the new civilian government to bear, thrown unprepared and with an untried constitution into the deep end of democracy. Finding itself accepting the responsibility for a devastating defeat, and weak in human and material resources, it was miserably equipped to set to rights the financial and fiscal legacy of the purely and arrogantly militarist establishment which had run the war practically to the exclusion of politicians and economists.

Now the new Republic was saddled with the hatred of the Officer Corps as well, permanently generating Right-wing discontent and disruption during a period when Left-wing agitation in the wake of the Russian revolution was already as much as the government could cope with. The German revolution, as that in Austria, was a comparatively tame affair. True, as the Armistice commission completed its task, Berlin was in revolt, loyal troops going over hourly to the revolutionaries. True, too, that all twenty-two of Germany's lesser royalty had been deposed even before the Kaiser's formal abdication, Ludwig III of Bavaria hustling from the palace of the Wittelsbachs out into the fog and exile, with four daughters at his side and a box of cigars under his arm – a Soviet republic had already been declared in his patrimony. But the revolution had no other goals beyond the expulsion of the old order. There was neither barricade to man nor gun-fire to march towards.

The immediate turmoil therefore was among the nobility and the Officer Corps itself, acutely aware of its loss of status as a result of its war lord's departure. The officers, who had once been a race apart, and were still outside the jurisdiction of civil courts, were to remember the revolution primarily as a popular outrage in which the nation's warriors were repudiated and insulted by those they had protected. They perceived the country close to chaos, the social institutions for which they had fought crumbling away, disorganisation, frustration, hunger and want everywhere. Worse, the Bolsheviks, infiltrating and subverting, seemed to be taking over. There were clashes between Leftist forces and Army units at Aachen, Cologne, Essen and many other places. In Braunschweig a Soldiers' and Workers' Council, greeting a squadron of hussars returning from the front, was ridden down for its pains.

The critical point in the Army's fortunes came a few hours before the Armistice was signed. The Spartakists – the German Bolsheviks who were to become the German Communist Party – were already massing in the streets of Berlin. The civilian power (in the person of President Ebert), already fearing that its democratic hours were numbered, struck a bargain with the German High Command (in the person of

General Gröner) to co-operate in the suppression of Bolshevism, to restore order, and to maintain military discipline. It saved the Army: the Republican government, technically the revolutionary regime, instructed the Soldiers' Councils to support their officers without reserve, and within three months the Weimar Assembly was meeting under military protection.

For a body of society who by its strategic ambitions and failures had brought Germany so low, the speed with which the Army effectually achieved the restitution of its privileged position of power was nothing short of remarkable. Although volunteer Free Corps were used both to protect the Weimar meeting and for the suppression of the Spartakist risings in March, by May 1919 the Army proper had been entirely reorganised, with 400,000 men trained in arms.

However, Germany's failure had not been only in battle. The nation which had learnt before all others to make a virtue of war, and to exalt her warriors above all other professions, was bound to seek scapegoats when the end came. The myth that the Army was undefeated in the field was believed not only because Germany wanted to believe it but because, other factors being equal, military defeat was not credible. If what Hindenburg was coolly to term 'the lamentable outcome of the war' was not the fault of the Supreme Command, then it had logically to be the fault of someone or something else. Yet when the war was over and recriminations began it genuinely did not seem to occur to the Supreme Command, who had kept the civilian government largely in the dark about the true war prospects throughout the summer of 1918, that the breakdown of the military machine – that complex synthesis of munitions, men and morale – stemmed as much from economic mismanagement as anything else.

It may have been true – there is no reason to doubt it – that a short, sharp war and a speedy victory in 1914 had been both hoped for and expected. Together with the prospect of eventual war indemnities extorted from the Entente, this would possibly have justified taking temporary liberties, even outrageous ones, with the known laws of finance. The spoils of conquest might well have outweighed the losses of running an autarky for a short time: it was Germany's stated intention to take over France's colonies. Nevertheless, the fact that the same monetary policies were pursued without serious change not only when it was evident that no quick victory was possible (a matter about which the financial authorities may have been broadly ignorant), but when peace came and for years afterwards, would seem to discredit any notion that the German inflation began with a temporary expedient. However, although paper notes had been legal tender since 1910, that was indeed how it did begin: in part the natural result of having a self-willed Army itching for war and a Federal Parliament which, though with limited power over the country's constituent states, still had to find the money to pay for it.

The first stage of inflation took place under the auspices of one Karl Helfferich, State Secretary for Finance from 1915 to 1917. Before 1914, the credit policy of the Reichsbank had been governed by the Bank Law of 1875, whereby not less than one-third of the note issue had to be covered by gold and the remainder by three-month discounted bills adequately guaranteed. In August 1914 action was taken both to pay for the war and to protect the country's gold reserves. The latter objective was achieved by the simple device of suspending the redemption of Reichsbank notes in gold. The former was contrived by setting up loan banks whose funds were to be provided simply by printing them. The loan banks would give credits to business, to the Federal states, to the municipalities and to the new war corporations; and, moreover, they were to advance money for war bond subscriptions. Loan bank notes, whose denominations ranged from one to 50 marks, were to be regarded as legal tender; and those not taken up by the Reichsbank were put into immediate circulation. However, the most ominous measure for the future was the one which permitted the Reichsbank to include three-month Treasury bills in its note-coverage, so that unlimited amounts could be rediscounted against banknotes.

Thus were the Government's plans drawn up, wilfully and simply, for financing the war – not by taxation, but by borrowing; and with the printing press as the well to supply both the needs of the Government and the growing credit demand of private business. Taxation was to play not the smallest part in meeting the costs of war before 1916. The Allied blockade of the Central Powers threw Germany, which over half a century had grown to be a foremost trading nation, fully back on her own resources for fighting the most devastating war in history. It was inevitable that those resources would be shot away to nothing: the question was when the bill would be presented, and who would pay it.

Germany's total war expenditure was 164,000 million marks; but as the mark's purchasing power during the war declined continually, that sum was the equivalent of only about 110,000 million pre-war marks (£5,500 million): *Mark gleich Mark* had already become a fiction. War loans were the most important source of this money, the eight issues providing three-fifths of it. The remainder was made up by the credit banks who willingly accepted Treasury bills (of which nearly 30,000 million marks' worth were still held outside the Reichsbank when the war ended); and by taxation.

This last seems still to have gone against the grain. Helfferich had actually announced to the Reichstag in March 1915 that the war was to be financed exclusively by borrowing – so that the small amount of tax revenue raised for the purpose, first with a war profits tax and a turnover tax, later with a coal and transport tax, was less than 8,000 million marks a year even in 1917. This amount covered neither the extra expenditure caused by inflation, nor even the interest burden on the war debt: so that war expenditures duly exceeded revenues, and the money in circulation increased in 1917 to five times what it had been in 1913. As essential supplies day by day grew scarcer the money available to buy them grew proportionately more plentiful. As war-profiteering began to flourish – the war profits tax was a political sop, and an ineffectual one, rather than a serious fiscal innovation – the influence of the banks on the general economy declined in proportion. Even without losing the war, Germany would have had a hard task after 1918 to straighten out her finances again.

Dr Hjalmar Schacht, who was later to pull the Weimar chestnuts out of the fire as President of the Reichsbank, and later still to organise the financial power of Hitler's Germany, thus described the mistakes of Helfferich:

> Germany tried to meet the colossal costs of the war by an appeal to the self-sacrificing spirit of the people. 'I gave gold for iron' was the slogan for the surrender of gold ornaments and jewellery. 'Invest in War Loan' ran the appeal to the patriotic sense of duty of all classes. Issue after issue of War Loan transformed the greater part of German private fortunes into paper claims on the State. Our enemies, especially Britain, took another line. They met the cost of war with taxes aimed primarily at those industries and groups to whom the war spelled prosperity. Britain's policy of taxation proved socially more equitable than Germany's policy of War Loans which lost their value after the war was over.

As the war machine lumbered expensively on, circumstances and policies combined to pull the wool over the financial eyes of the German people, not least those classes who had most to lose. Every German stock exchange was closed for the duration, so that the effect of Reichsbank policies on stocks and shares was unknown. Further, foreign exchange rates were not published, and only those in contact with neutral markets such as Amsterdam or Zurich could guess what was going on. It was never clear how much the steep rise in domestic prices was due to economy measures and war shortages rather than to inflation – and even the relevance of those prices was rendered dubious by the much higher black market rates. Only when the war was over, with the veil of censorship lifted but the Allied blockade continuing, did it become clear to all with eyes to read that Germany had already met an economic disaster nearly as shattering as her military one.

The scales may have fallen at last from German eyes with the coming of peace, but that did not mean that the difficulties and injustices created by war-time inflation had passed unnoticed. The activities of profiteers were only one source of growing social discontent. The upsetting of the old patterns of pay differentials did its share of harm. With the benefit of two years' hindsight, the *Vossische Zeitung* could print in August 1921:

> Our military defeat was due to the fact that for every 1,000 men we
> had in the trenches, double that number of deserters and embusqués
> remained at home. These deserters were activated less by military
> than economic motives. The rise in prices was mainly responsible
> for the poverty of the families of the enlisted men ... The first to
> suffer had to be those who did not share in the general increase in
> paper revenue, the soldiers who did not participate in the increase in
> wages, trading profits and war industries ... they realised that their
> situation and that of their families would be hopeless after the war.
> Hence the dull, often dismal attitude of soldiers on furlough from
> the front during the latter years of the war.

Even in the war years, in other words, inflation was taking its toll on national morale. 'There must be some people to whom the war is useful,' argued one of the young soldiers in *All Quiet on the Western Front*; and in the last pages the bitter comment came: 'The factory owners in Germany have grown wealthy: dysentry dissolves our bowels.' The newspaper went on to put the blame where some of it, at least, belonged:

> It must be admitted generally now that the cause of the depreciation
> of our currency and of the purchasing power of the mark was neither

the commercial balance during the war nor the estimate of our military situation abroad; but in the exploitation of our currency for the purpose of obtaining money for the Treasury, that is to say in a fictitious increase of our total income. In as much as the country issued milliards in the form of extraordinary levies, War Loans, Treasury bills, and so on, without withdrawing from circulation corresponding amounts in the shape of taxes, it created new paper income and wealth incessantly, while the real national wealth was steadily being diminished by the war.

War had been bad enough for the German economy. The Armistice first, and then the peace terms, shook it to the foundations. At Compiègne on November 11, 1918 the surrender of the German fleet, withdrawal from Alsace-Lorraine and the immediate evacuation of Belgium and France were all expected conditions. Bitterer pills to swallow were the handing over of Germany's African colonies and the occupation of the Rhineland by the Allies. However, the article which stipulated that the blockade of the Central Powers would go on until the peace terms were agreed and signed struck the people hardest. The German standard of living, it was estimated, had fallen to about half what it had been before the war. It is indicative that the first street demonstration of the revolution in Munich, where 100,000 people took to the streets on November 7, was set off by an increase of 6 pfennigs in the price of a litre of beer. Not only conscripted soldiers had lost patience.

With Ludendorff's sudden announcement in October 1918 that an armistice had to be obtained on virtually any terms, Germany's military dictatorship subsided and the coalition of Majority Socialists (SPD), Progressives and Centre which had held together in the Reichstag for the best part of two years found itself genuinely in charge, and therefore responsible for picking up the pieces. In the immediate anarchic conditions of that autumn, it was inevitable that this government should come under almost instant attack from all sides. It assumed its new role with trepidation, the government of the revolution, but not itself especially revolutionary. The proclamation of the Republic was in part a holding operation against the Bolshevist tide. To the Left, the Independent Socialists had been alienated by the SPD's repeated willingness to vote for war credits, while the Spartakists were pushing on from extreme to extreme, and did not believe in parliamentary rule at all. To the Right, there was no love for republicanism and, in any case, that Mathias Erzberger, leader of the Centre Party, had signed the Armistice had put him beyond the pale.

January 1919 saw the first elections to the Reichstag since 1912. Over 30 million voters (more than 80 per cent of those eligible) produced the coalition which was to face the peace terms presented by the Allies in June. The principal constituent was the new Democratic Party, and the Democrats were the main authors of the Weimar constitution which was completed in August. Sir John Wheeler-Bennett[*] has described the German people in 1919 as deprived of their physical and moral capacity for further resistance.

> They lacked the power to translate their hatred into active opposition. Instead they cherished it within their bosoms, warming themselves with its rancorous fire.

The coals for this fire were the Versailles peace terms. The Allies offered them without significant previous consultation, but the German Government was nevertheless bound to accept them under the threat of further heavy sanctions. Until that moment Germany had entertained the illusion that the peace would be based on President Wilson's famous 'fourteen points', and that the principle of national self-determination would mould the future shape of Europe. It was thought that the replacement of the old regime would itself have ensured reasonable terms from Germany's enemies; but that was reckoning without the determination of the French, founded on fear,

---

[*] In *The Nemesis of Power* (Macmillan, 1953), Part I, Chapter I (vii).

or the desire for vengeance, or the pursuit of retributive justice, that any German resurgence should be prevented.

The Treaty of Versailles separated Germany not just from her colonies but from one-seventh of her pre-war territory – north, south, east and west – as well as from a tenth of her population. Under its terms, Alsace-Lorraine was returned to France, and France was to occupy the Rhineland and to exploit the coal of the Saar for fifteen years, after which the Saar's future was to be settled by plebiscite. A plebiscite, too, was to determine the future of Upper Silesia in the east.

The implications of these truncations for the German economy were of course enormous: and so were those of the requirement to reduce the German army to a quarter of its size, for it meant that over a quarter of a million more disbanded soldiers were to be thrown on the labour market. Work had to be found for them at any cost, or so it was calculated. What spelt doom were the clauses that made Germany responsible for the war and demanded colossal reparations – in money and in kind – to meet the Allies' costs. As was evident again in 1945, war guilt had not previously impinged upon German consciousness. When the peace terms were published in Berlin in May 1919, reaction set in. The Ministry fell, and a new one bowed at last to the Allies' ultimatum. Although the first Weimar Parliament struggled on for another year, it was as though a landslide had crashed across the road to economic revival.

Thus within a few months of the Armistice the elements were present for the most devastating monetary collapse that any industrialised nation has ever known. Her industrial resources and manpower* heavily reduced, and hopelessly burdened with the insupportable weight of reparation payments stretching indefinitely into the future, Germany was required to regain her feet in those quicksands of her own making: the financial and fiscal arrangements of the Helfferich dispensation.

---

* The labour force in the confiscated territories apart, Germany lost 1.6 million dead and suffered 3.5 million casualties in the war.

The state of the mark, meanwhile, had become the barometer both of international confidence in Germany and of Germany's national despair. Before the war it had stood at 20 to the pound sterling. At the end of the war, in December 1918, it stood at 43. Before the terms of the Treaty of Versailles were accepted in June 1919, a pound would buy 60 marks. But when December came round again it would buy 185. Already the average annual war-time depreciation of about 20 per cent had come to resemble stability.

2: Joyless Streets

The Treaty of Versailles weakened and diminished Germany, but left her no less a whole nation. The parallel peace treaties of St Germain and Trianon not only dismantled the Hapsburg Empire in its entirety but respectively whittled down Austria and Hungary to fractions of what they had been, and much further than the principal of national self-determination for the empire's successor states demanded. Both lost enormous areas of territory and millions of their nationals – German Austria mainly to the new Czechoslovakia, Hungary mainly to Rumania. Vienna, once an imperial capital, found herself as a vast city without an adequate hinterland to support her; and the rump of empire was forbidden to make the one move which made economic sense, that of *Anschluss* with Germany. Revolution turned the Emperor Karl off the throne in Vienna and brought a Republican government to power. In Budapest the Bolshevik revolution of Bela Kun was succeeded by counter-revolution and, at the beginning of 1920, by the regency of Horthy.

The plight of the Austrians, and more particularly of the Viennese, was indeed pathetic after the war. Hungary, if only her peasants had been more willing to share their produce with the starving townspeople, would have been self-sufficient in respect of the necessities of life. That was not so of the remnant of Austria, where cold and hunger set in in earnest in the first post-war winter, and where the returning soldiers, defeated, angry and exhausted, were if possible more susceptible than in Germany to inflammatory talk. Often Vienna and its neighbourhood could exist only upon what Germany had to spare, which was not much. In consequence, the depreciation of the Austrian krone advanced during the first post-war years far ahead of that of the mark, and with even less chance of recovery.

Politically Austria was in desperate shape, and looked in vain to the new government to restore either order or prosperity. Mr G. M. Young, who arrived in Vienna in 1920, reported after 18 months to the British Treasury in a passage which had Lord Curzon, the Foreign Secretary, to whom it was passed, calling for more:

> Out of the capital and dynastic patrimony of a great empire, the Treaty of St Germain created a Republic. Nominally at least, it made this oddly mixed community of bankers and peasants responsible for the cost of a great war. In such a world of make-believe it is not always easy, even for a foreigner, to keep his mind fixed on the realities of the new position. For many native officials and politicians it has so far been impossible … Nearly all the Departmental buildings of the Monarchy are still in occupation, and are lighted, heated, cleaned and so forth for the officials of a Republic of only six million souls. A Roman who was born under Theodosius and died under Romulus Augustulus had seventy years in which to pass through the changes which Austria has seen in three.
>
> The Constitution of the country is a kind of super-democracy, contrived to ensure that as little authority as possible is exercised by anyone. The Provinces defy the Federation; the Federal Government dare not use the economic weapon which their bankruptcy puts into its hands. The President is a purely ceremonial figure: he opens flower shows and legitimates bastards. He does not appoint ministers (even nominally) and he cannot dissolve the House. Nor can the Government. Legally the Chamber is supreme: it appoints the Cabinet by vote; it decrees its own dissolution. Actually all business is done by standing committee, of which the public hears little, or preferably in the clubs and party meetings, of which they hear at any rate very little that is true … The political parties strike me as combining the worst parts of an Approved Society with the worst

parts of the British Medical Association, and I might add that the mental processes of the Pan-Germans constantly recall to my mind those of a certified midwife.

The truth is that Austria was quite unripe for the advanced parliamentary system which the revolution gave her.

That was the institutional background for an immense amount of human misery. At the outbreak of war the Austrian krone had been nearly on a par with the mark. By the war's end inflation had pushed them apart, to the krone's great disadvantage. Official prices in either case seldom reflected the true black market costs, and in Vienna where food shortage was acute the black market was for many the only sufficient source. Thus in 1914 in Vienna a kilogram of best wheat flour cost 44 heller (the equivalent of about 6d sterling); but in December 1918, with wheat flour unobtainable anywhere, the indefinable mixture which masqueraded as flour could be procured from an illicit dealer at 22 kronen a kilo – exactly fifty times as much.

In 1914 a pound sterling was worth about 25 kronen. By May 1922, when the pound could still purchase only 1,200 marks, it would have bought 35,000 kronen.

The force of such conditions on the Austrian bourgeoisie was vividly shown in the early Greta Garbo film *The Joyless Street*, made in Vienna by Pabst in 1925. As the symbol of untouchable purity in a milieu of want, greed and corruption, finally finding truth and happiness in the arms of an American volunteer, Garbo's role may lack persuasion today; but from the odious butcher insulting and taunting the food queues at his shop, refusing meat to women he found unattractive or unwilling, to the scenes of the unlicensed, gluttonous revelry of the nightlife of the speculator and profiteer, and to the ultimate attack by a starving, angry crowd on a café full of merrymakers – the film was a faithful reflection of the times.

A more telling contemporary account of the scourge of inflation in post-war Vienna is given in the diary, greatly overladen with explanatory translation for English-speaking readers, of Anna Eisenmenger. As the ex-Imperial Army drifted homewards, armed and in revolutionary mood, and as the food shortage of the war years turned to famine, this middle-class widow found herself progressively turning to illegal practices to keep her family going – a war-blinded son, a tubercular daughter, a son-in-law with amputated legs, a hungry grandson, and another son who had become a Communist. She began to resort at enormous expense to the *Schleichhändler* – the smugglers – for the most basic foods which, despite ration cards, the State could no longer supply. 'Hamstering' – hoarding – though an indictable offence, became no more than commonsense. Pitifully aware of her family's lowering standard of living and social status, Frau Eisenmenger was nevertheless lucky in having investments which in 1914 brought her nearly 5,000 kronen a year – equal to about £200.

She recorded that in October 1918 when she resolved to cash 20,000 kronen worth for immediate use, her bank manager advised her earnestly to convert all her money into Swiss francs. However, private dealings in foreign currencies were illegal, and she decided that to break the law against the hoarding of fuel and food was enough.

> I must make myself believe [she wrote] that I am really far better off than hundreds of thousands of other women. I am at least immune from material cares and can help my children since I have a small fortune, safely invested in gilt-edged securities. Thank God for that!

She also had a substantial quantity of her husband's cigars, which could be traded for meat or other food as the opportunity arose: an important enough means of survival even during the early months of the post-war blockade.

But the country was now deprived both of Czech coal and Hungarian food; and within a month of the end of the war Austrian currency began to lose its exchange value at a far greater rate than before. By December 1918, when all businesses were forced to employ an allocation of demobilised soldiers whether or not extra staff were required, bankruptcies were common. That month Frau Eisenmenger's legless son received 35,000 kronen in 'caution money', which he decided to keep safely until the value of the krone increased again; but in the meantime he converted it into War Loan. In December, too, as an anti-inflationary measure, all paper money had to be overprinted '*Deutschösterreich*'. Frau Eisen-menger, who took what remained of her 20,000 kronen to the bank to be stamped, recorded the first evidence she heard that ruin lay in front of her:

> In the large banking hall a great deal of business was being done ... All around me animated discussions were in progress concerning the stamping of currency, the issue of new notes, the purchase of foreign money and so on. There were always some who knew exactly what was now the best thing to do! I went to see the bank official who always advised me. 'Well, wasn't I right?' he said. 'If you had bought Swiss francs when I suggested, you would not now have lost three-fourths of your fortune'. 'Lost!' I exclaimed in horror. 'Why, don't you think the krone will recover again?' 'Recover!' he said with a laugh ... 'Just test the promise made on this ao-kronen note and try to get, say, 20 silver kronen in exchange'. 'Yes, but mine are government securities: Surely there can't be anything safer than that?' 'My dear lady, where is the State which guaranteed these securities to you? It is dead."

Discovering that her son's War Loan had already become unsaleable, Frau Eisenmenger was then induced to exchange her government securities for industrial shares. Her grandson developed scurvy. Two days after Christmas, the first food train arrived in Vienna from Switzerland. The prices of the new food, strictly rationed as it was, were four times as high as the previous official prices. Other food was hardly available for money, and could be obtained principally by barter. 'Panic bids defiance to all legal decrees', runs the diary entry for January 1, 1919.

Even the most respectable of Austrian citizens now breaks the law, unless he is prepared to starve for the sake of obeying it ... The fact that the future is so uncertain has led to stagnation in industry and public works, and swelling numbers of unemployed supported by the State ... yet it is impossible to get domestic servants or indeed any sort of workers ...

Heightened class-consciousness is daily being instilled into the manual workers by the Socialist government, and, in heads bewildered by catchwords, leads to an enormously exaggerated estimate of the value of manual labour. Only in this way could it come about that the wages of manual workers are now far higher than the salaries of intellectual workers. Even our otherwise honest old house-porter is demanding such extravagant sums for performing little jobs that I prefer to do the heavier and more unpleasant household work myself ...

I survey my remaining 1,000-kronen notes mistrustfully, lying by the side of the pack of unredeemed food cards in the writing table drawer. Will they not perhaps share the fate of the food cards if the State fails to keep the promise made on the inscription on every note? The State still accepts its own money for the scanty provisions it offers us. The private tradesman already refuses to sell his precious wares for money and demands something of real value in exchange. The wife of a doctor whom I know recently exchanged her beautiful piano for a sack of wheat flour. I, too, have exchanged my husband's gold watch for four sacks of potatoes, which will at all events carry us through the winter ... My farmer had hidden the sacks of potatoes under straw on top of which he placed some apples. The apples were duly stolen, but the potatoes reached me safely ... I had to give the porter half a sack as hush-money ... When the farmer's eyes rested on the grand piano at which Erni [her blinded son] was seated improvising, he took me aside and said: 'My wife has been wanting one of those things for a long time. If you'll give it to me, you shall have all you want for three months.

Although the misery of Austria was more immediately and directly the result of war, the pattern was to be repeated almost exactly in Germany. In both countries rapid inflation caused homegrown produce to be withheld from the urban markets, with hunger and anger the inevitable result. All Austrians, but especially those with savings, watched horrified as the value of their money fell, Frau Eisenmenger among them. She noted early in 1919:

> The State has been obliged to put 10,000 kronen notes into circulation – each equivalent to two years' income from my capital. A suit costs about six times what it was in 1913, but some things like food are a hundred or two hundred times as much ... Paper clothes are being sold. Never had I dreamed it possible that one could purchase so little for 10,000 kronen ... Jealousy and envy flourish in this atmosphere, and if one has procured some harmless article of food, one is careful to conceal the fact from one's fellow men. Hunger reigns inexorably and selects its dumb and uncomplaining victims above all from the middle classes.

Spring saw no alleviation of the troubles of those with no political leverage to bargain with. Not only Austrian peasants and profiteers took advantage of their helplessness. Furniture, fittings, pianos and carpets were being bought up wholesale by what were known as the 'gold-currency' people – the occupying Italians, the British, the Americans. The last valuables of countless houses flowed on to the market, no one warning their owners not to part with goods whose intrinsic value remained unimpaired.

> The Viennese [commented Frau Eisenmenger], handed a large bundle of kronen, still thinks he has grown richer, without taking into account the enormous rise in prices resulting from the Zurich quotations which come as a fresh surprise to him every day.

Where the German looked to the New York and London rates, Vienna's eyes were on the Swiss franc.

Twice a day we are all forced to await the quotation of the Zurich bourse. Every fresh drop in its value is followed by a wave of rising prices ... The confidence of Austrian citizens in the currency administration of the State is shaken to its foundation. The State which is perpetually printing new banknotes deceives us with the face value ... A housewife who has had no experience of the horrors of currency depreciation has no idea what a blessing stable money is, and how glorious it is to be able to buy with the note in one's purse the article one had intended to buy at the price one had intended to pay.

In November, a year after the Armistice, Frau Eisenmenger wrote that her position was alarmingly worse, the financial situation beyond her understanding. The krone, at 25 Swiss centimes the previous Christmas, was now quoted at one-twelfth of a centime. Her shares, however, were going up. Gambling on the stock exchange had become the fashion – the only way to avoid losing all one's money and perhaps to add to it. Many new bankers were giving people advice, the flight from the krone governing all transactions. 'Meanwhile,' Frau Eisenmenger wrote,

the large numbers of unemployed, their passions fermented by the Communists, are seething with discontent ... a mob has attempted to set the Parliament building on fire. Mounted policemen were torn from their horses, which were slaughtered in the Ringstrasse and the warm bleeding flesh dragged away by the crowd ... the rioters clamoured for bread and work ... Side by side with unprecedented want among the bulk of the population, there is a striking display of luxury among those who are benefitting from the inflation. New nightclubs are being opened. These clubs have the further effect of greatly intensifying the class hatred of the proletariate against the bourgeoisie.

On December 15 1919, Frau Eisenmenger recorded that, whereas the downward movement of the krone in Zurich had gone on, 'the value of my industrial investments is rising to an extent which seems to be incomprehensible and almost makes me uneasy ...' Her daughter was able to make two dollars a day at the American Mission, which could be exchanged for 400 krone, only 100 krone less than the monthly pension of a retired privy councillor.

> Former civil servants and officers are undoubtedly the poorest of the poor in Austria today. They are too proud to press their claims, can get no employment. Thus it happens every day, again and again, that elderly, retired officials of high rank collapse on the streets of Vienna from hunger.

Frau Eisenmenger let a room to the gentleman from the American Mission – just as Garbo's father in *The Joyless Street* was able to do – and received for it ten times the rent which, in accordance still with the wartime rent restriction Act, she herself paid for the whole flat. On a now slender quantity of negotiable cigars, on her daughter's earnings, on that rent, and on the diminishing real income from her burgeoning shares, she tackled the first months of 1920.

> Speculation on the stock exchange has spread to all ranks of the population and shares rise like air balloons to limitless heights ... My banker congratulates me on every new rise, but he does not dispel the secret uneasiness which my growing wealth arouses in me ... it already amounts to millions.

What was happening to Austria then was simply a foretaste of what was to come to Germany. The plight of Frau Eisenmenger and her family would be repeated a thousandfold in every town in both countries. The torture of Germany's middle classes, however, was more lingering, and more intense.

3: The Bill Presented

Signed on June 29, 1919, the Treaty of Versailles was denounced in Germany by all sides. Universal condemnation, however, produced no political unity. Its effect, on the contrary, was to give an easy stick to the Right – the Conservatives and the Army – with which to beat a government which had to abide by its terms. From then on the struggle was about whether or not those terms were to be fulfilled. The ones at issue boiled down to two: the future of the Army, which Versailles attempted to reduce to a toothless, token force; and the payment of reparations.

The Army was not destroyed, and indeed had a vital part to play in upholding the Republic as that fragile institution was rocked ever more fiercely by the inflationary storm and the political troubles which accompanied it. Nominally, certainly, the reduction of the Reichswehr from 400,000 of June 1919 to the 100,000 demanded by the following March proceeded more or less on schedule. General von Seeckt skilfully prised the Army away from the political arena – where by and large it remained, a highly efficient, highly trained, easily expandable military nucleus. In 1933 it was the last obstacle which might have prevented the onset of the Third Reich, in which matter it proved a broken reed.

Neither was what the Army stood for destroyed. Hindenburg duly resigned; but was accorded by the newly-elected President Ebert 'the inextinguishable gratitude of the German people'. When the Reichstag's commission of inquiry into the responsibility for the war opened – with the Cabinet hoping that the old military regime would be thoroughly discredited – the prestige of the old Officer Corps, and especially that of Hindenburg and Ludendorff, soared to new heights:

while the *Dolchstoss* legend was given wings, the onus of Germany's defeat was hoisted permanently on to the backs of the politicians then struggling miserably with its consequences.

As 1919 drew to its close, talk of a military coup, on the cards since the summer, became more frenzied. In January 1920, when the treaty came into force, an attempt was made to assassinate Erzberger, still regarded by the Right as one of the principal authors of Germany's shame. However, the spark which caused the explosion came from without: on February 3 the Allied Note was delivered presenting the first list of war criminals to be handed over, including the Kaiser, Hindenburg and Ludendorff. Only the extreme Left remained unmoved by what was regarded by all others as a callous threat to the nation's war heroes, most of whom had already been vindicated in German eyes by the commission of inquiry. It was a short step for the universal outrage to be translated into military deed – the Kapp *Putsch* of March.

This episode was primarily a trial of strength between the Right wing militarists, notably the Free Corps who had been suppressing Bolshevism brutally in the Baltic States, and the Republican government, with the Army proper sitting on the fence until the cat jumped. The Cabinet, in the shape of the Defence Minister, Herr Noske, were determined to enforce the Allies' demand to disband two Free Corps brigades (one already with swastikas on its helmets) outside Berlin. The reactionary General von Lüttwitz, the Reichswehr's senior commanding officer, knowing that his striking force was about to be taken away from him, gave the order to march, but without sufficiently warning Dr Wolfgang Kapp, no less a Right-wing, fanatic patriot, who was to take political control when the *coup* was complete. The lawful Cabinet fled to Dresden, but Kapp was unready to take its place, and the *Putsch* immediately began to collapse in a welter of incompetence and anticlimax.

Kapp's proclamation of himself as the new Chancellor was met by the Republican government with the counter-proclamation of a general strike. This proved decisive, because Berlin quickly ground to a halt, military enthusiasm for Kapp fell away, and von Lüttwitz was replaced by General von Seeckt. The *Putsch* was over, defeated by the unions. The brief period during which many of the Officer Corps actually imagined that the good old days had returned – ex-officers were seen to swagger about the streets to the rhythm of patriotic marches – passed away swiftly, and the Army's short dalliance with the idea of a new military dictatorship was ended. From then on the Army and the State were to work more or less in unison.

March 1920 was something of a watershed in terms of the war's aftermath in Germany. Although Right-wing revolt and subversion were to continue, especially in Bavaria where the Kapp *Putsch* had been echoed simultaneously by that of von Kahr, the immediate period of revolution and counter-revolution passed. Had other things been equal reconciliation and reconstruction might have followed. Although it is unwise to be too rigid in asserting which events most truly affect a society's behaviour, one may suggest that after the damp squib of the Kapp *Putsch* the demoralisation and distress of Germany owed less to the mortification of defeat in war than to the new, virulent economic and financial afflictions which had become the daily experience.

Some of the poison of northern militarism having, as it were, been drawn off, the disaffected, reactionary elements mainly took refuge in the hotbeds of the south. Bavaria then became the mainspring of Germany's 400 political murders, mostly unpunished, many unsolved, between 1919 and 1922: the militarist Right may not have been responsible for more than the lion's share of them, but those years were certainly an open season for the officials and supporters of the new Republic. Although the weaker minds of the Right still pined for old glories, fresh bursts of militancy were as likely to be caused by the economic mess the government was making of the peace as by post-war blues or bitterness.

The observed depredations of the Allies, especially the French, were no doubt made the reason for popular outbreaks; Hitler's rapid rise to influence in Munich was largely based on his attacks upon those who were felt to have betrayed the country in 1918; and the Left was still using the lessons of the immediate past to incite social turmoil wherever the opportunity was offered. Yet it was the five years of inflation before 1921 which made the soil so fertile for the agitator; and it was the continuing, worsening financial predicament in which so many classes found themselves which governed social and political development in the ensuing period.

Because the Kapp *Putsch* had been defeated by a general strike, it was widely supposed that the power of the working classes had finally been demonstrated, and that the advent of government by the proletariate was only a matter of time. On the contrary, however, the working classes who had indubitably established their power directly to interfere with the Cabinet's composition, if not in the conduct of affairs, allowed those advantages to go without resistance. The circumstances of the strike were of course exceptional, for it had stemmed from a government initiative and had the Cabinet's support. Yet it seemed that the parliamentary government had defeated its reactionary foe only by conjuring up a dangerous spirit which might have been better unroused. Such was not the case; and Lord Kilmarnock,* then British *Chargé d'Affaires* in Berlin, thought 'the proletariate had discovered that the misery resulting from such a strike fell largely upon itself'.

Misery, however, was already present in abundance, and the trade unions' energies were shortly to be directed almost exclusively at winning wage increases for their members in some way in line with the mounting cost of living: for the time being, a pliant government and an even more pliant monetary system seemed to be all they wanted. The facts of life, after all, were plain enough to them as Christmas 1920 approached.

The cost of living since the outbreak of the war had risen by nearly twelve times (compared with three times in the United States, almost

---

* Later 21st Earl of Erroll. From 1921-1928 he was British High Commissioner of the Inter-Allied Rhineland High Commission. Born 1876, died 1941.

four times in Britain and seven times in France). Food had accounted for half the family budget then, but now nearly three-quarters of any family's income went on it. The food for a family of four persons which cost 60 marks a week in April 1919, cost 198 marks by September 1920, and 230 marks by November 1920. Certain items such as lard, ham, tea and eggs rose to between thirty and forty times the pre-war price. On the bright side – in contrast to Austria – the official unemployed figure was low, and only 375,000 people were on the dole.

There was, on the other hand, the hope that things would get better. As business improved in the summer of 1920, a more tolerable standard of living for the working classes came into prospect. There had been resentment when strikes in the essential services were made illegal, and towards the end of the year there was considerable unrest among State employees, particularly in the post office and the railways: that unrest, indeed, led to more strikes and to uneconomic concessions by the government. None the less, a certain revival of the national spirit and a will to work was noticeable, even among Germany's miners. The idea of a better future in fact had substance to it. The standard of living in Germany had fallen steeply during the war, whereas in France and Britain it had actually risen a few percentage points. A small rise in German standards and a small fall in British standards, although leaving Britain still far in advance of Germany, would notwithstanding create discontent in Britain while leaving the Germans feeling better off.

The British consul in Leipzig, as one dispassionate observer, was optimistic. Although there was still 'much dissatisfaction in the working class' and Communist propaganda and agitation continued, he reported that discipline had returned, and that those same workers, now apathetic and weary of political dispute, felt some improvement in conditions of life.

> I am left with the impression [he wrote] that wages and the cost of living have now reached an equilibrium, and that the purchasing power of wages is nearly equal to that of before the war. But there

is still much insecurity of life and property, and acts of violence are frequently reported . . . The middle class, i.e. persons with fixed incomes from investments or pensions and government officials are perhaps the most hard hit, and it can readily be realised that what before the war had been a fair competence – I speak of incomes up to 10,000 marks a year – is now entirely inadequate for the barest necessities.

He reported finally that Saxon industry was in a very satisfactory condition, making a good recovery though working only the new eight-hour day, and with many orders in hand.

Indeed, the apparent health of industry was one of the factors which most effectively confused the inflation issue. Bolstered by a financial programme geared to subsidising in various vital ways an industrial front which continuous depreciation of the currency had already made highly competitive in foreign markets, the lot of German industry had materially improved over the previous twelve months. Industrialists, taking care to express the extremest pessimism to foreigners, were agreed that a reversion to the ten-hour day was essential in the circumstances; but in fact the miners, who with the support of their colleagues in Britain and France were not disposed to lengthen their shifts, were working well; and most workers, von Thyssen believed, had now realised that work rather than political dogma was the answer to their difficulties.

Alas, not only were the hopes of the German working classes shortly to be dashed: there were no such hopes at all for the broader spectrum of the German people who had no unions to protect their short-term interests and no stake in the monopoly power of organised labour. Two developments in 1920 were storm-cones for the future. The elections of June, although returning a central coalition to power under Herr Fehrenbach as Chancellor and with Dr Wirth at the Finance Ministry, demonstrated the political polarisation of the country in the meantime: the German National People's Party (DNVP) on the far Right trebled its vote, while that of the Independent Socialists on the far Left was doubled. The moderate coalition of the Democrats and Majority Socialists had lost much of the voters' confidence.

Secondly, there took place in July the Spa conference in Belgium, the first of the numerous post-Versailles meetings to discuss the payment of war reparations and kindred matters arising from the peace treaties. Reparations questions naturally directly affected confidence in the mark and, indeed, the whole question of the German economy, but they were postponed until a further meeting in Geneva. That conference also fell through, and the issue was remitted to yet another meeting in Brussels in December.

The uncertainties to which these postponements gave rise in large measure accounted for the wild fluctuations of the mark during the year. At the outbreak of war the paper marks in circulation in Germany had a total face value of 2,700 million marks (less than half of the value of the coinage which the population were encouraged to trade in in return for paper). After the war's end, in November 1918, the figure had risen to 27,000 million; and by November 1920 to 77,000 million. But the pound sterling now stood at 240 marks, the dollar at 60. During 1920 when the Allies' Reparations Commission began its work, the mark swung from 230 to the pound sterling down to 152 and back again. The low point was reached when, for almost the first and last time, the actual final amount due in reparations appeared to be reasonably settled.* As the mark improved, so unemployment rapidly rose, reaching 6 per cent of the work force in the summer of 1920 – a condition which a 'buyers strike' may have worsened. Full employment thereafter became a primary objective of both government and unions, at the mark's expense.

Lord D'Abernon, who was to be British Ambassador in Berlin for more than six years, arrived at his post in June 1920. A man more practically versed in money matters than most in office in that city, he dutifully recorded both in his diaries and in his despatches home

---

* M. Poincaré, soon to become Prime Minister of France, did not believe in a fixed sum and resigned the chairmanship of the commission.

the mark's precise course over the brink and far down into the depths. Enjoying the fullest confidences of German ministers wrestling with the twin problems of inflation and reparations, yet unable to influence their monetary policy to any important effect, he watched helplessly as, against every warning he could give, the chickens of unlimited deficit financing swarmed in to roost.

His warnings went as much to the Allies as to the Germans. The German budget barely balanced as it was, leaving nothing for war indemnities. To raise enough money to meet the level of reparations discussed in June would require almost twice the revenue which the latest tax proposals were expected to produce. 'It is altogether impossible to conceive that twice the new rate of taxation could be imposed,' wrote Lord D'Abernon, 'without producing a revolution.'

Inflation provided the answer to the equation. If a budget did not balance, the deficit had to be made good somehow. In October 1920 Germany's national debt stood at 287,800 million marks. At the old 1914 parities this sum equalled £14,400 million; but at the new it represented only £1,200 million.* A year before Germany's great inflation is generally thought to have started, Germany's national debt had all but been wiped out.

Whom did that benefit? D'Abernon speaking to two members of 'the old Imperial Foreign Office' found their attitude one of unmitigated gloom. All their banker friends were sending money out of Germany, a process which no amount of restriction could prevent. Non-payment of taxes, they said, was 'no longer a crime but a patriotic duty'. The President of the Reichstag, the Liberal-minded Loebe, was no less pessimistic, especially concerning the conditions of nourishment which he regarded as inviting action from the Left:

I know from the case of my own children how badly people are fed. You cannot get milk, and an egg costs 2¾ marks. The financial condition of the middle classes, the small employers and so on is

---

* Great Britain's national debt amounted then to £8,075 million.

even worse than that of the working class, to which I belong. Only today we had a memo from the lower officials in South Germany saying that if their pay was not increased they would wreck the till. Working-class wages have roughly been increased eight to ten times compared with pre-war; smaller salaries have only been increased two to four times. This makes an impossible situation when the cost of living has gone up tenfold.

The year 1920 ended with the Brussels conference, which met to consider Germany's capacity for payment of reparations. It led only to the Paris conference, at the end of January 1921, where France, herself not far from insolvency, began making demands on Germany which D'Abernon described quite simply as 'amazing'. The figures that came out of Paris for German consideration, although nowhere near what the French had demanded, provoked shock in Germany. That reaction in turn led in February to another conference in London, where Germany's counter-proposals were studied. In the course of these discussions which lasted until the second half of March, France lost patience with the Germans and, by way of sanctions under the peace treaty, the Rhine ports of Duisburg, Ruhrort and Düsseldorf were occupied by the Allies. On March 30, talks began in London again.

Already, though, the reparations question was bearing acutely on German economic life. A few days before the Rhine ports were occupied, the British High Commissioner in Coblenz reported to London that

> a large majority of the German people did not realise all that the Treaty of Versailles entailed. Probably by a large number of the lower classes it was not even read, and the result is that at the present time it has dawned on the population of Germany for the first time that the day of reckoning has arrived.[*]

---

[*] Lord Curzon wrote in pencil in the margin of this report: 'The idea of the "lower classes" "reading" the treaty is humorous.')

The new military sanctions produced a reaction at the other end of the social scale; and Lord D'Abernon remarked that there was 'a decided reversion to Junkerism, and I hear that in many of the officers' clubs quasi-penal lists are drawn up of those officers who associate with ex-enemies. The application of the military sanctions has not produced a normal or healthy reaction – it has turned the Germans sour.'

Feeling against France was particularly bitter. France's attitude under the premiership of M. Briand was acidly but accurately summed up by Lloyd George whom D'Abernon found in the Cabinet Room in Downing Street just before the reparation conference one morning, 'as usual, a roaring fire behind his back and an open window in front of him'. The French, said the Prime Minister, 'can never make up their mind whether they want payment or whether they want the enjoyment of trampling on Germany, occupying the Ruhr, or taking some other military action. It is quite clear they cannot have both.'

On April 27, 1921, the Reparations Commission fixed Germany's total liability at 132,000 million gold marks, equivalent to £6,600 million. The problem before the London conference was how, and over what period, that enormous sum should be paid. It was decided that Germany was to be asked to pay 2,000 million gold marks – £100 million – a year and, in addition, a sum equal to 26 per cent of her exports; and these terms were conveyed to Berlin accompanied by the threat of further sanctions – namely the occupation of the Ruhr which the French were pressing for – if compliance did not come within the week. This 'London Ultimatum', which drove the mark to 268 to the pound, caused the Fehrenbach government to fall. It was supplanted by that of Dr Wirth who, as the new Chancellor, just before the French Army started to roll again, accepted those terms knowing that heavy additional taxation would have to be imposed on the nation. The mark thereupon advanced to 232 to the pound as the atmosphere of financial uncertainty briefly retreated and the outlook for credit abroad improved. A further reason for optimism was that the plebiscite just completed in Upper Silesia, whose industries were of considerable importance to the German economy, had resulted in a palpable majority of the people in favour of adhering to Germany.* There was also general relief that a Communist-inspired armed rising by the miners of Mansfeld collapsed in ignominy – even causing Lenin in Moscow to despair of a new German revolution.

Unfortunately, as spring turned to summer, there was much more that was not well. The occupation of the Rhine ports continued. Worse than that, the money supply was growing more prodigiously than ever. 'So far from the printing press having stopped printing notes,' D'Abernon wrote to Curzon, 'it has recently resumed its activities to a quite undesirable degree.' The reason for that at a stage when the cost of reparations had still not begun to bite was quite simply that insufficient revenue was being collected:

'Taxation is enormous,' wrote Mr Howard Hodgkin.†

> To say that it is less per head than in England [Lloyd George's complaint] is simply misleading, if not absolutely untrue. The yearly deficiency in the railways alone is 17,000 million marks. The extravagance of the rich one hears of is very sad, but it is said to be largely due to high taxation, as they feel that unless they spend it the government will get most of it ... Unfortunately the persons from whom it is most difficult to collect taxes are those who most should pay, that is to say war profiteers and particularly traders in contraband goods who in many cases have not kept accounts.

A week after the London Ultimatum had been accepted, Mr Piggott, the Inter-Allied Rhineland High Commissioner at Cologne, reported a conversation with the *Oberburgermeister*, Dr Konrad Adenauer, who said that he had been offered the chancellorship before Dr Wirth had accepted it. Adenauer's conditions had been the return of the nine-hour day, an end to talk of socialisation and complete power

---

* More heads voted for Germany, but more communes for Poland.
† The Oxford historian, Provost of Queen's College, 1937-1946.

to select his ministers from whatever party he chose. It was his view that Germany needed a government with almost dictatorial powers capable of enforcing an intensive production programme and the strictest universal taxation. 'Dr Adenauer's personal ambition,' wrote Piggott, 'is well-known, and the idea of a dictatorial government with himself as dictator no doubt appeals to his imagination.' The proposal which kept Dr Adenauer out of power at this early date was apparently that of abolishing the eight-hour day. In any event, it meant that no government capable of competent tax-collection was in sight.

In June 1921, Dr Walther Rathenau, whose name was to become closely linked with the policy of fulfilment of the reparations demands, assumed office as Minister of Reconstruction. The first payments of £50 million in gold and Treasury bills were duly made to the Reparations Commission during the second week of the month. On June 21, Herr Gareis, a Socialist deputy in the Reichstag who had spoken out against the Free Corps, was murdered, part of the extreme Right's campaign to demoralise the Republicans. At the end of June, John Maynard Keynes was heard to prophesy that the mark would fall by an average of a point a day against the pound for the next two or three years. Otherwise that month, and July too, passed without serious incident, beyond some squabbling with Poland over the future of Upper Silesia, a matter which the Paris conference which sat during the first half of August referred eagerly to the League of Nations in Geneva. For almost nine months the mark had risen and fallen within 15 points on either side of 250 to the pound. July 1921, was the last month of even relative stability which the old mark was ever to experience.

4: Delirium of Milliards

'The delirium of milliards' was a phrase of Rathenau's coining. 'The majority of statesmen and financiers think in terms of paper,' he had written.[*]

> They sit in their offices and look at papers which are lying in front of them, and on those papers are written figures which again represent papers … They write down noughts, and nine noughts mean a milliard. A milliard comes easily and trippingly to the tongue, but no one can imagine a milliard.
>
> What is a milliard? Does a wood contain a milliard leaves? Are there a milliard blades of grass in a meadow? Who knows? If the Tiergarten were to be cleared and wheat sown upon its surface, how many stalks would grow? Two milliards!

Rathenau rightly diagnosed that delirium as an affliction not of the people in general – that was to come – but of those who were supposedly in control of the country's finances, who had raised the note circulation since the beginning of the year from 73 milliard marks to 80 milliard. The immediate blame for the latest fall in the mark, which by the middle of August had slid from June's figure of 261 to the pound to 310, was laid squarely by Rathenau (as by Wirth) on the reparation payments. The 1,000 million gold marks – money at the pre-war parity – due at the end of August had been found, but less than 60 per cent had been raised on realistic terms in foreign credits or otherwise. 'Next November, or next spring,' Rathenau said, 'whenever

---

* *Berliner Tageblatt*, February 9, 1921.

a large payment comes, exchange will fall again to a still lower level. This cannot go on.'

The mechanism of depreciation had many wheels, however. A close though unnamed confederate of Herr Hugo Stinnes, the industrialist, assessing the situation with great candour a few weeks later said that the real breaking point came immediately after the German government repaid the loan which had been arranged in England by Herr Mannheimer of Mendelssohn's Bank, 'the confidential man' of Dr Rudolf Havenstein, President of the Reichsbank since 1908. Mannheimer, instructed by his chief, went out in August 1921 and started to buy foreign currency at any price – 'for Germany had any amount of paper marks but no foreign currency'. This was the first signal of

> the absolute breakdown in the value of the mark. Since then, foreigners have not speculated to the same extent in marks and have kept their holdings, waiting for some improvement. The banks, on behalf of their clients and the industrialists, went further and not only sold their marks at any price but also started to speculate.
>
> There were four reasons for encouraging such a policy: to enable heavy industry to compete with foreign countries, to satisfy the workmen's demands by increasing their wages with worthless paper marks, to avoid political troubles and disturbances – and also to prove to the world that Germany could not fulfil the Versailles Treaty.

That assessment took a too blinkered view of the other events of that August. The virtual collapse of Austria, which had already cast a deep gloom over the Paris conference, thoroughly alarmed Austria's nearest neighbours. The krone, at 800 eighteen months before, had fallen to 3,000 to the pound, and was still falling steeply, now apparently in advance of the mark by a factor of ten. Confidence was in headlong flight. In Munich, the Bavarian capital, the gloomiest forebodings were entertained about the cost of living, deepened by the farmers' scandalous profiteering in milk and grain and the news that the Reich was to increase taxes again on sugar and beer. The farmers' associations in Lower Bavaria did their best to warn their members about over-charging or withholding their produce from the market, but the ill-feeling in the towns against the peasants was now thoroughly aroused. The government were unfortunately identified with agrarian interests, and were therefore bound to be blamed when the hard-pressed Munich municipality, in a flagrant vote-catching move at the beginning of the month, voted against dearer bread, *tout court*. Since dearer bread was already one of the facts of life, this action encouraged in advance the inevitable demands for still higher wages.

In the meantime the impatience, fear and prejudice of the Right became more openly expressed, reaching its summer climax in a nakedly political, anti-Republic display in Berlin on *Frontkämpf-ertag*, War Army Day. On August 24, 1921, Ludendorff took the march-past of 2,000 war veterans headed by the 39-year-old Prince Eitel Friedrich, second son of the Kaiser. They marched under an archway bearing the inscription '*In Kriege Unbesiegt*' (unbeaten in war), and past the royal box in *Paradeschritt*, Prince Eitel Friedrich throwing his heels as high as anyone else.

Then in front of 20,000 spectators there followed a sermon by the Army chaplain which suggested that Germany's greatness could only be recovered by military power, through the monarchy and the Hohenzollerns. There were speeches in the same strain by the three generals present, Ludendorff, Graf Waldersee and von der Goltz. Von der Goltz, who had commanded the Baltic Free Corps, was at pains to attack the 'Jew Government', and thus caused some anti-Semitic incidents in the crowd; but he stole the limelight in any case by producing telegrams of congratulations not only from Admiral Scheer and Grossadmiral von Tirpitz, but from Hindenburg and the ex-Kaiser himself. This last apparently caused '*rauschender Jubel*' and long, continued cheers for the Hohenzollerns. The arena in which the display took place was lined by two or three thousand youths and girls, two-deep, the precision of whose drill and military movements was (said one eye-witness) 'most striking'.

Such inopportune demonstrations were not confined to the capital, nor to the military. An honorary degree of doctor of medicine was conferred that same day on Ludendorff by the University of Königsberg. The diploma was presented in an unctuous tribute 'to the hero who with the sharp edge of his unbroken sword defended the German nation, hemmed in by a world of enemies all greedy for booty, till that nation, trustful of lying promises, abandoned its unconquered Army and its strong leader; to the German, whose picture, shining from the darkness of our present hour, gives us faith that the future will bring a Saviour and Avenger for our people ...'.

The Defence Minister, Dr Gessler, a civilian notoriously under the thumb of the Army, to his credit publicly described all this 'rattling of an empty scabbard' as ridiculous. The *Berlin Morgenpost* with some restraint said that the university's effusion 'ill befitted a body of professors in whose hands lay the education of German youth, and provided a commentary on the reactionary attitude of the *literati* of Germany in general and of East Prussia in particular'.

The Königsberg apostrophe must have read oddly indeed to those who remembered that at the moment when the sword of the German High Command lay, so to speak, broken to bits in the wood at Compiègne, Ludendorff was already in flight to Sweden, disguised in blue spectacles. It was certainly not the nation which had abandoned its leader. Perhaps the professors need not be judged too harshly. The academic class had suffered as heavily as any from the fall of the mark, and were unaccustomed to a situation in which (to quote a contemporary) 'the scholarly writer does not earn as much with a printed line as the street sweeper earns with two whisks of the broom'. They were as liable as any to blame their very considerable woes on the new order, and to do so to the advantage of the military clique who had run the country in the good old days. However, a convinced pacifist,

Herr von Gerlach, writing in *Die Welt* next day, did not hesitate to put them straight:

> Ludendorff, far from justifying the terms of the diploma, by his obstinacy and by his meddling in politics was responsible not only for the unnecessary prolongation of the war but also for the disastrous terms of the Treaty of Versailles.

Gerlach reminded the professors that Ludendorff had telegraphed to Berlin over and over again in October 1918, saying that a peace offer had to be made at once as the Army could not hold out another 48 hours.

> They put Erzberger at the head of the Armistice Commission – an insane choice, but remember that he first heard of the abdication of the Kaiser in the Bois de Compiègne, where he also got the wire from Hindenburg ending 'if you can't force these points through, conclude an armistice anyhow'.

Frontkämpfertag expressed a spirit of reaction that was rife in Germany from north to south. Flesh was being added to the skeletal myth of the *Dolchstoss*. Two days later, on August 26, Mathias Erzberger himself, to the Right the embodiment of civilian treachery, was murdered by Nationalist gunmen in the Black Forest. It is not fanciful to suppose that this deed was largely inspired by the speeches of the Nationalist (DNVP) leader Karl Helfferich, the wartime Minister of Finance under whose auspices the German inflation first got a grip. Erzberger was not only a civilian and a Republican but a Jew.

The outside world watched with deep misgivings. In an article in *Le Peuple*, a Belgian Socialist deputy remarked that

> assassination seems now to have become the rule in Germany, where militarist brutes, after having practised on thousands of Belgians

whom they massacred, continue to adopt this means of suppressing those in their way ... it is a very grave sign of collective criminal degeneration, which must strike all Germans who have retained feelings of respect for human life.

In Germany itself, the death of Erzberger, that most fearless exponent of Socialist taxation, let loose a torrent of abuse against the Right. In Berlin the Majority Socialists and the Independent Socialists joined forces in a demonstration to protest 'against the enemies of the Republic'. One Herr Harden, whom Lord D'Aber-non described as an acute if somewhat acid observer, explained to the British Ambassador that 'the followers of the Right were perpetually hunting for the old culprits responsible for the downfall of the empire and the old system, but instead of attacking the generals – Ludendorff and company – who were really the cause, or the old gang of princes and sycophants, they reviled the Jews and assassinated the leaders of the Left together with those who did not take their own perverted view'. More than three hundred assassinations among the leaders of the Left had been perpetrated since the Armistice, Herr Harden said, 'and no one is punished'. (He himself had had fifty telephone calls to warn him that he was next on the black list, and was leaving for America.)

The Chancellor, Dr Wirth, expressed to D'Abernon his confidence that public order could be maintained, although admitting that several newspapers, notably in Bavaria, would have to be suppressed, and that the working classes were 'extraordinarily excited'. The government's worries in fact were more for the economic crisis than for the political one, and although revenue appeared to be coming in quite well at that point, better was expected with the new taxation programme. It was hoped to reconcile the Left to the principle of indirect taxation by increasing again the taxation on capital. The recent fall in the exchange, Wirth concluded, and the consequent rise in the cost of living had forced him to grant new increases of salaries and wages of about 10 milliards.

The economic crisis, too, was behind the troubles in Bavaria, where agitation continued unabated against the rise in food prices, a development employed unhesitatingly by the Socialists as a weapon against the state government. 'The Socialist trade unions are to hold a mass meeting this evening,' reported the British Consul-General in Munich, Mr William Seeds,* on the day of Erzberger's murder,

> to protest against the increased cost of living and against the reactionary tyranny of Dr von Kahr's state government. The 'class-conscious workman' will be urged to carry out a gigantic demonstration through the streets undeterred by thoughts of the machine-guns and armoured cars of Herr Poehner, the Chief of Police. This official, with that curt firmness which makes him so obnoxious to the Socialists, has reinforced the government's warning with a terse little proclamation ending with these words: 'If you don't want to be hurt tonight, keep off the streets!'

In the event the mass meeting of about 50,000 people went off without serious disturbance. Poehner – one of the earlier converts to National Socialism – kept his men quiet, and only one demonstrator was killed and another wounded in a scuffle with the police late in the proceedings. 'The Socialists,' Mr Seeds subsequently reported, 'will find the proletariate a most dangerously useful tool where more material considerations than political agitation are concerned.' They had passed a resolution requiring wages to be fixed according to world rates, 'never forgetting the fact that the welfare of the people depends solely on the overthrow of the present capitalistic system'.

The signing on August 25, 1921 of the separate peace treaty between Germany and America, which neither mentioned the League of Nations nor sought to blame anyone for the war, might well have been a signal for universal relief and celebration. In the event, it did nothing to calm either fears or tempers, within Germany or without.

---

* Later Sir William Seeds, British Ambassador at Moscow 1939-1940.

The fact was that the new run on the mark was set off not merely by the irresponsible behaviour of the banks, nor in consequence of the government's inevitable failure by orthodox methods to raise the cash to pay the August reparations bill, but owing to a host of circumstances, including the murder of Erzberger, which undermined any remaining confidence that the German economy might be allowed to recover its health.

The international financial community was perhaps the first to appreciate the position. No help was available for the Reichsbank but on the most onerous terms. A September conference in Berne of bankers from Switzerland, Italy and Germany soberly concluded that it was impossible for Germany to continue her payments to the Entente and that sooner or later she would have to declare herself bankrupt, followed (they thought) by first France and then Italy. The mark, at 310 to the pound in mid-August, had sped downwards to over 400 by mid-September, and was still going down.

On September 20, 1921, Mr Joseph Addison,* Councillor at the British Embassy in Berlin, reported to the Foreign Office:

> The daily creation of fresh paper money which the government requires in order to meet its obligations both at home and abroad (services and goods which it is 'obliged both to render and deliver') inevitably decreases the purchasing value of the mark and leads to fresh demands, which in turn bring about a further decline, and so on *ad infinitum*.

Even progressive increases in taxation could not completely meet the situation, since new impositions meant an increased cost of living, which automatically reduced the purchasing value of the mark, and in turn brought about more inflation and budget instability.

'There is enormous speculation,' Addison continued.

---

* Later Sir Joseph Addison. He was Chargé d'Affaires in Berlin on several occasions. Born 1879, died 1953.

Millions of persons in this country are, I think accurately, reported to be buying foreign currencies in anticipation of fresh tax burdens, and to be hoarding foreign bank notes ... I hardly know a single German of either sex who is not speculating in foreign currencies, such as Austrian crowns, Polish marks and even Kerensky roubles. In as much also as a fall in the value of the mark is inevitably accompanied by a rise in the quotation of industrial shares, speculators are supposed to be operating systematically to depreciate the mark with a view to reaping the benefit of higher quotations in the share market.

There was every incentive for the ordinary citizen to take precautions against further tax liabilities. He found himself subject to four principal taxes, assuming that his business was such as to escape the corporation tax (*Korperschaftssteuer*) of up to 20 per cent. There was the once-and-for-all increment tax (*Vermogenszewachsteuer*) on the increase in value of all property acquired between 1913 and 1919, and the capital tax (*Notopfer*) on the value of all possessions after the increment tax had been paid. The unearned income tax (*Kapitalertragsteue*) of 10 per cent was becoming of lesser importance as the real value of unearned income shrank day by day, but the ordinary income tax (*Einkommensteuer*) naturally affected more seriously a wider and wider public as money wages rose to keep up with prices and brought more people into its thrall.

Income tax in 1921 started at 10 per cent on the first 24,000 marks earned, rose to 20 per cent on the next 60,000 marks, and so on in steps upwards until a maximum of 60 per cent was paid on all income over 395,000 marks a year, a sum equivalent in September 1921 to about £1,000 or $4,200 – a substantial salary in the 1920s. In the autumn of 1921 the minimum income necessary for the existence of a family of four – two adults and two chidren – was just less than 24,000 marks (or about £60) a year. As the mark fell and as wages rose, the taxation of real income became proportionately greater.

Lord D'Abernon's diary entry for September 30 noted, however, that compared with the year before the feeding and clothing of the people, especially children, had markedly improved. In his official hat he observed with misgivings that the privations of the war must have given the Germans a distinct competitive advantage over populations whose nourishment and consumption of luxuries were still near the pre-war standard. It was a fortuitous addition to the other substantial benefits that German industry already enjoyed: various government subventions whose effect was to cheapen production. Coal was available below cost price in Britain. Bread was sold considerably under its open market price. Railway transport was offered at less than working costs. The German budget suffered to the immense and continuous gain of German commerce and industry.

Not all German traders and industrialists had yet given up hope for the mark, but few were not doing their best to protect their businesses in advance – a protection which could only be bought at the expense of the State and thus made their fears self-fulfilling. Where possible, they tried to create credit balances abroad, usually by direct arrangement with their customers or commercial friends: they would under-invoice their exported products sold (for example) in The Hague and buy in return imports for which they were over-invoiced. Such manoeuvres had the extra advantage of avoiding taxation in Germany.

Carried on on a large scale, this kind of thing would have tended towards the mark's inflation. If continued, the eventual outcome would be insolvency for Germany as a country although its subjects might hold considerable assets outside. The process was particularly reprehensible not simply because the exporter's profit was the country's loss, but because part of that loss was in the substantial subsidies – of workers' food and of industry's rail costs – which ensured the competitive prices of Germany's manufactured exports.

In practice the business of under- and over-invoicing was probably not wide-spread, simply because all a German exporter had to do, provided he had no need to bring his profits home, was to pay his foreign balances into a foreign bank where the tax authorities could not get at them. In any case, so long as plenty of foreign currency was received and enough of it returned, the net effect on the mark was likely to be beneficial. Mr F. Thelwall, the British Commercial Secretary in Berlin, found more worrying symptoms of Germany's troubles. German workmen's wages, he reported in mid-October, as the mark approached 500 to the pound sterling, were too low, and the workers were not being fairly treated:

> The present labour unrest is caused by the fall of the mark and the impending new taxation, both of which send the cost of living up. The German manufacturer and trader is making a lot of money, both in Germany and abroad, while the State is getting ever nearer bankruptcy. But I do not think this is due so much to the fact that the German exporter is accumulating a vast fortune in foreign countries as to the wrong financial system of the German government with regard to its own budget and to the fact that the government has obligations imposed on it too heavy to meet.
>
> The German system of taxation has two chief faults. One is that on paper it is too heavy, and therefore places before the citizen the alternative of either being ruined or not paying his taxes, and he has no hesitation as to which course he will choose; and the other, that it has involved such a large amount of reorganisation of the executive apparatus that it will probably be some years before it will become really effective.

In October 1921 the state of the budget was sombre. In terms of paper marks, the sum of the government's ordinary expenditure (including the recent 10 milliard wage increase) and the estimated payments to the Allies in reparations and occupation costs was 113 milliard marks. The revenue from the previous budget and from the new taxation proposals of July would amount to less than 90 milliards. These calculations were based on a conversion ratio of one gold mark to 13 paper marks

– but already the true rate was 22 to one. The reality was that the total due by Germany for contributions to the Allies alone already equalled the total real receipts from the ordinary and extraordinary budgets, which would themselves be in balance only if Chancellor Wirth's 15 new tax schemes could be brought effectively into force. Under the prevailing political conditions, and using the current fiscal system, this was the most dubious proposition. A capital levy, for example, which had been demanded by the Socialists in July in the hope of tapping real property values, failed to produce any substantial amount of real revenue because of the lapse of time between assessment and payment. Effectively, therefore, any reparations payments at all would unbalance the budget again, with the inevitable effect on the mark.

'The prospect,' the British Ambassador informed Lord Curzon, 'is of a somewhat alarming character. There has been no real determination to stop the printing press, there is little efficiency in the tax-collecting system, and there is very great timidity in putting a stop to doles and subventions … If a really able and powerful Finance Minister could be entrusted with the direction of Germany's finance I imagine he would soon put a different aspect on the position.' He advanced two desiderata: that any increased direct taxation ought not to synchronise with higher prices, and that the taxpayer ought not to realise too clearly the destination of his contributions, particularly when they were due to foreign creditors.

For a fortnight, Wirth's government had been undergoing a severe fit of nerves and had been on the point of resignation. The straw that was to break it was the announcement on October 17 of the League of Nations' decision on the future of Upper Silesia – that the former imperial province be partitioned between Germany and Poland. Indignation was universal and acute, as much out of national pride as because the loss of another highly important slice of Germany's industrial areas would make economic recovery still less likely. The League's decision was one of the principal reasons which for years made Germany's own membership impossible. The Chancellor was obliged to resign, but October 26 found him back in power again, leading the coalition of Majority Socialists and Democrats which accepted, though under protest, the Allied Note which delivered the news from Geneva. Meanwhile the mark hit a new low of 600 to the pound.

Dr Wirth was not short of advice about how to carry on. On October 25 the Bavarian state Finance Minister, while professing himself not unopposed to reparation payments so far as they were possible, warned the Berlin Government in a speech that 'there is a limit to taxation if the economic life of the nation is not to be paralysed'. He drew attention to the flood of new revenue legislation pouring in upon the tax officials, which (he said) could have produced milliards more if the revenue officers had had time to go after the profiteers and others who evaded taxes.

The public were angry, but they were in the main not yet as depressed or pessimistic as the politicians. Berlin shops were selling huge quantities of goods to Germans as well as to foreigners. Share prices moved upwards as the dollar improved against the mark. The banks were so full of stock exchange orders that some were days behind in opening letters in the stock departments.

'Of course the rise is unhealthy and feverish,' wrote Lord D'Abernon.

> We cannot be very far from a panic. As soon as inflation ceases to increase and deflation sets in, there will be the devil to pay. Behrenstrasse here, which corresponds to Lombard Street, reminds me of San Francisco after the Earthquake. Almost every bank is being increased or rebuilt, and one can hardly get along the roadway. Something like the South Sea Bubble.

It must have been very hard for the ordinary man with little knowledge of finance to determine whether the outlook was good or bad. The truth, no doubt, as the Ship of State steamed headlong downstream towards the cataract, was that it was good for some and bad for others. At any rate, people knew whom to blame if, despite some of the trappings of prosperity, the nation's survival was in danger. The *Berliner Tageblatt* pointed out on November 9, 1921:

> We still import more than we export. And yet we must surrender 26 per cent of the gross value of our exports [in reparation payments]. Foreign countries, frightened by our rivalry, are constructing barbed-wire fences. Obligations are forced on us for decades to come, and nothing is done to stabilise the mark by any international action. When the [London] Ultimatum was accepted the dollar was at 60 marks. Today it is 180 or more.

The newspaper complained of the 'quite small capitalist upper class' making huge profits by taking advantage of the exchange fluctuations, while foreigners were using the discrepancy between the home and foreign values of the mark 'to purchase our goods *en masse*'. It demanded that profits on exchange and dollar speculations be taxed intensively, and went on:

> The tax on corporations produces the minimum revenue because all kinds of expenditure are deducted ... including the cost of the private motor cars of the owner or directors and so on ... The assessment of all our taxes is so behindhand that hundreds of thousands of the wealthy classes have not yet paid their taxes for the year 1920. The whole tax edifice, a house of cards in Babel, is tottering. Social democracy demands an immediate visible sacrifice of the producing classes in the form of taxation of real values. Industry has sought to parry the thrust by its readiness to facilitate the payment of the next gold milliard by a credit action.

More and more astounding estimates were by then circulating in regard both to the amount of German banknotes held physically abroad, against what eventuality it was not clear, and the amount of

German capital deposited or invested or retained abroad in order to escape taxation. A newspaper article by Arthur Eichhorn commented authoritatively on the flight of capital, observing in the first place that the amount of exported capital was unknown even approximately, although it had certainly been extensive since the end of the war:

> Evasion of taxation, fear of socialisation, and inflation have combined to drive capital out of countries with a depreciated currency into countries where the currency is sound or at a premium ... This has nothing to do with international trade or with normal credit operations, but merely increases the chaos of exchange rates.

Dollars, Swiss francs and guilders were the favourite objects in this scramble for conversion, but others, including the Czech crown, were coming into favour. The credits in Dutch names in Swiss banks were out of all proportion to the trade between Holland and Switzerland, and the assumption was that these were 'Swiss credits of German speculation camouflaged as Dutch'. A curious side-effect of the rush for Swiss francs was that the market rate for short-term money in Switzerland was at less than 3 per cent while long-term was at over 10 per cent.

With capital escaping, the budget unbalanceable, and no one wanting to hold marks, the inevitable happened; and by the middle of November 1921 a dollar would buy 250 paper marks, and a pound sterling 1,040. The mark had sailed past another traumatic milepost in its downward progress. Germany now needed to find 500 million gold marks before the end of February to pay the Allies, and knew that she faced sanctions by France – the occupation of the Ruhr – in case of default. Default would come unless London helped. The London bankers, however, refused to give the necessary credits unless Germany put her financial house in order and unless French demands became more reasonable. Since no condition could apparently be met without the fulfilment of the others as its preconditions, German bankers now began to fear that the mark might fall to Austrian levels.

On the face of it, three urgent measures were needed: a balancing of the budget to permit the shutting down of the printing presses; the end of subventions to industry made through the subsidy of food, the inadequacy of rail freight rates, and the insufficiency of the coal tax (even a 100 per cent tax would only have brought Germany's cheap coal up to 550 marks a ton, a small fraction of the world price); and the revision of customs duties coupled with an efficient system of tax collection. Given the power of the industrial lobby, none of these departures looked likely or even possible.

The rising cost of living was by now causing considerable industrial unrest in the Ruhr, where even the new wage tariffs were failing to keep pace with it. The factory owners loudly held that the high prices were the result of a financial blockade by the Entente, of which the partition of Upper Silesia was the latest episode. It was special pleading which moved the wage-earner little. The British Vice-Consul in Essen reported:

> The present prices of food are liable to be increased still more, assisted by an utter lack of organisation from the executive point of view. Although this town has a special office for dealing with profiteering, and although each week the punishments meted out are published in the local press, comparatively few of the delinquents are adequately punished. For example, a man arrested for selling white flour obtained illicitly was tried and imprisoned, but was able to sell the flour again on his release ... Not only are prices of incoming commodities increasing daily, but the prices of old stocks are increased within the twenty-four hours.

On November 22, Sir Basil Blackett,* Controller of Finance at the British Treasury, presented the Foreign Office with a sobering memorandum on Germany's problems. He had been much struck

---

* Later a Director of the Bank of England. He joined the Treasury in 1904. Born 1882, died 1935.

on his tour of inspection by the contrasting positions of Britain with nearly two million people out of work and Germany with scarcely any unemployed at all.

> In spite of his robust common sense, the man in the [German] street is beginning to believe what some interested industrialists are telling him, so that he seems almost readily to subscribe to the false doctrine that it is good for trade that a government, by inflationary finance, should habitually spend more than its income; and that it is necessarily bad for a country to receive a large income from abroad 'by way of an indemnity …
>
> Even the German industrialist knows that the present activity of German industry (destroying the export trade of its neighbours) is a sign of fever and not of prosperity. But, as usual, each class in Germany thinks that the burden of taxation should fall on some other class or classes … Even the best disposed are inclined in a fatalistic way to let things take their course and wait for the world to recover its reason. The big industrialists are attempting to save something from the wreck by turning all the paper marks they can into foreign currencies or, failing that, into real things – land, machinery, and so on, which have an independent value … The incentive to saving is gone just when saving is of vital necessity to the State.

The fall in the mark, the memorandum continued, was gradually-wiping out the middle classes, the value of whose investments was quickly disappearing. A holding of 1 million marks in German War Loan, which had corresponded at the time of purchase to about £45,000 of British War Loan, now had a sterling value of about £1,000, 'and even its internal purchasing power is not more than £3,000 and is rapidly falling'. A German pensioner with an income of 10,000 marks before the war compared favourably with an English pensioner with an income of £500. Now, the sterling value of his pension was £10 and its purchasing power less than £30. Insurance policies, furthermore, were worth less to the holder or his widow than the annual premium which he had put by each year out of his hard-earned savings.

Blackett noted that the rent restriction Acts hit much the same classes, who were 'forced to starvation in order to subsidise the German workman's wages and the employer's profits'. The bread and rail subsidies, financed by inflation, combined with the rent restriction, enabled the foreigner to buy German goods well below world prices and, if he lived in or visited Germany, to travel, eat and occupy houses at ridiculously cheap rates. 'A gradual process of buying up and carrying off Germany's movable capital, secondhand furniture, pianos, etc., is taking place at the expense of Germany as a whole.'

Foreigners were also buying up real property and interests in factories and all kinds of businesses. To some extent this was at the expense of the workman whose wages lagged behind the climbing cost of living, but it was mainly at the expense of the middle classes whose capital was destroyed and largely exported. The exporting industrialists could just keep their heads above water, Blackett thought, but the others making goods out of partly imported material could not possibly replace it with a continually rapidly falling mark.

The report ended:

> The one real temporary advantage is that Germany's workmen are in employ, but even this is mainly due not to successful exporting but to the misdirected consumption of holders of paper marks who want to get rid of them, and therefore to misdirected production, which actually interferes with the proper flow of exports and to some extent increases the amount of luxury imports.
>
> That the government has been or is deliberately pursuing a policy of inflation so disastrous for any government that adopts it is sufficiently disproved. It is partly weakness and inexperience which have prevented greater success.

Blackett's assessment, with which D'Abernon would entirely have agreed, contrasted sharply with the French government's belief, or affected belief, that Germany was bluffing, manipulating the exchanges to her own advantage, and in reality rapidly increasing her prosperity. In fact, the evidence of what was happening to the German economy was ready to hand in the Allied occupied zones beside the Rhine.

The British Consul-General in Cologne, Mr Paget Thurstan, writing on November 23, 1921, observed that the shops there were daily thronged with crowds of purchasers, and that in self-protection many of them were closing their doors for a great part of the day.

> It is no uncommon spectacle to see queues of intending purchasers lined outside the shops waiting for the doors to reopen. In these circumstances it is evident that retail stocks will soon be sold out and replacement of them will cause prices to rise very much higher. Indeed, I understand that the unusual phenomenon exists of wholesale prices being now often considerably above retail prices, the difference in certain articles being nearly 100 per cent. Clearly, as long as such conditions prevail, there can be no limit to the rise in the cost of living as measured in marks, and settlements of wages' disputes are merely ephemeral.

Four days later Addison was repeating the same story from Berlin, even though the capital, being much further from the frontier, had suffered far less from incursions by foreigners anxious to benefit from the exchange rate.

> Many shops declare themselves to be sold out. Others close from one to four in the afternoon, and most of them refuse to sell more than one article of the same kind to each customer. The rush to buy is now practically over as prices on the whole have been raised to meet the new level of exchange. In almost every camera shop, however, the sight of a Japanese eagerly purchasing is still a common feature. But on the whole, as far as Berlin is concerned, it is the

Germans themselves who are doing most of the retail buying and laying in stores for fear of a further rise in prices or a total depletion of stocks.

Addison then had an interview with the Chancellor who said despondently that the continual, fast rise in prices was at last giving immediate concern for the maintenance of public order. Dr Wirth said that all reasonable demands would have to be granted, but that the situation was altering daily so rapidly for the worse, and the constantly recurring difficulties which demanded redress cost so much extra, with no funds available to meet them, that the burden was becoming too great for the head of the government to bear.

'The Chancellor is doing his best to keep things quiet,' was Addison's opinion,

but the impossibility for the working classes to obtain even obvious necessities except at exorbitant prices, coupled with severe winter setting in, might lead to serious trouble. He was about to preside over a Cabinet convened to deal with fresh demands for increased wages put forward by the municipal employees of Berlin, and we were sitting in a semi-darkness caused by a partial strike of electrical workers which was only settled the next day by a promise of increases all round, involving an extra expenditure of 400 million marks.

'Dr Wirth,' Addison wound up gloomily, 'is a man of quiet determination with a leaning towards optimism.'

Although Addison regarded it as an almost universal German defect to view all difficulties through a magnifying glass, he accepted that not only were the middle classes in severe straits but that the working classes had lowered their standards to the bearable minimum. Neither he nor any of his German contacts were in any doubt that the chief elements which lead to disturbances and revolutions were present in Germany once again at the end of 1921. In late November, when food riots were taking place in Berlin and having repercussions over much of the country, the mark dropped to just over 1,300 to the pound.

They had repercussions too, in Austria, where the fall of the krone was gathering speed, and food was even shorter. Hand in hand with the exasperation caused by the continual rise in prices went the feeling of intense resentment and hate against all who had made, or were thought to have made, money out of Austria's misfortunes – the *Schieber*, the speculators on the exchange market, and inevitably the Jews.

The Viennese rioted on December 2, consequent upon another severe fall in the krone. The amount of glass smashed in the city that day was enormous. The unarmed crowd of 30,000, many hooligans among them, wrecked and looted food shops, restaurants and cafés everywhere, and attacked the hotels in the main quarter. It was only in the case of the Bristol Hotel, however, where Sir William Goode, the former president of the Austrian section of the Reparations Commission, was staying, that the crowd penetrated as far as the second floor to invade and ransack his apartment. According to a report, after Sir William had 'kept the mob for an hour from entering a room where several English and American ladies had taken refuge', he was robbed of all his effects.

The demonstrators' demands from the government included the seizure of all foreign currency – the medium which most shops in self-defence were insisting upon for purchases – and the State control of the securities market. They wanted all gold to be taken into State hands, including that which belonged to the churches and monasteries. They called for a progressive property tax, an immediate system of child insurance and a systematic reduction of food subsidies. The Chancellor gave ground on all these matters except the food subsidies, whose abandonment would have raised the apparent cost of living still more.

It had been a day of warning. The British Commercial Attaché in Vienna was still able to write, as the krone moved relentlessly downwards: 'I fear these disturbances presage collapse.' Until stabilisation came, it was of course the one thing anyone could be sure of, financially though not politically. Indeed, the capacity of the Austrians for long-suffering had proved remarkable. Whereas almost any other people in Europe would have exploded time and again long before now, Austria's reception of a four-year concatenation of financial crises had so far been relatively tame. The middle class were by far the hardest hit, and had not taken any effective public action to better their position. In fact, the December riots seemed to relieve the feelings of most Viennese for the time being. With the krone at more than 2,000 to the pound, Austria quickly settled back into her usual state of lethargy. Vienna University closed down for the winter because of the cold. The Stock Exchange went on strike because of a tax on its members. Railway fares were raised 300 per cent. And while the night-life of the rich grew more and more phrenetic, retired barristers and ex-generals could have been found stone-breaking beside the Danube.

5: The Slide to Hyperinflation

Social unrest was one of the obvious symptoms of inflation. The disease, the Austrian and German financial world seemed to agree, was itself not containable without international goodwill and a significant relaxation of the obligations under the peace treaties. Germany's politicians therefore set about relieving the symptoms wherever possible. More measures were brought in so that the government might be seen publicly to be dealing with profiteering. The Prime Minister of Bavaria even submitted a Bill to the Reichsrat to make gluttony a penal offence.

For the purposes of the Bill, a glutton was defined as 'one who habitually devotes himself to the pleasures of the table to such a degree that he might arouse discontent in view of the distressful condition of the population.' It was proposed that such a one 'may be arrested on suspicion, and punished by imprisonment and/or a fine of up to 100,000 marks (about £75) for a first offence'. A second outbreak of gluttony was to entail for the offender penal servitude of up to five years, fines of up to 200,000 marks, and the deprivation of civil rights. Provision was also made for punishing caterers who abetted or connived at the crime, and a special section provided that foreigners, on conviction, would be liable to the extra punishment of expulsion from the Reich.*

The Bill – reminiscent of a recent Austrian move to tax anyone who gave a luncheon or a tea party – was of little enough importance as it was never enacted. It was indicative, none the less, not only of the

---

* The Foreign Office document containing this report bears Lord Curzon's scribbled comment 'Amusing', and a suggestion that it should be sent on to divert the King.

great offence caused both by German profiteers and by the foreigners swarming in to take advantage of the exchange rates, but of the desperate, not to say absurd, lengths to which respectable politicians were already being pushed.

In so far as the fall of the mark was due directly or indirectly to the reparation obligations which Germany could not possibly meet, it was universally presumed that even temporary alleviation of those obligations would send the mark briskly in the opposite direction. A third London conference was convened for December 18; and the announcement was taken to mean that the Allies had at last appreciated that the gold payments due in January and February 1922 were virtually unmeetable. This consideration sent a wave of confidence crashing dangerously back through the exchanges – confidence that at last the intolerable blight on the financial system would be removed. On December 1, 1921, the mark soared upwards, regaining a quarter of its November value. By the time it reached 751 to the pound (against its November average of 1,041) the paper-mark prices of many stocks and shares, although still well above the levels of December 1920, had declined by half or more,* while the Reichsbank was buying foreign currencies heavily.

Mr Seeds reported a similar panic in Munich, where some of the smaller banks and financial concerns had been very hardly hit. 'The press have said that the London financial negotiations are no ground for a sudden improvement in the rate, and are trying to discourage speculation,' he wrote.

> But in this respect conditions are hopelessly unhealthy, and the public will continue to be swayed by rumours and to speculate either in goods or in stocks and shares.
>
> As regards dealing in shares, all classes of the population have for months been speculating with a fine disregard for common-sense.

---

* e.g. Daimler: (Dec 1920) 295; (Nov 1921) 800; (Dec 22, 1921) 490. *Allgemeine Elektrizitatsges.* 319: 1,100: 657. Deutsche Bank: 327: 701: 475.

Shares have been freely bought in totally unknown concerns, in some cases with the object of exchanging valueless paper money for what was considered a good security, but generally in the hope of profiting by a rise in the stocks. Shares in respectable concerns which had paid a 20 per cent dividend, say, were pushed higher and higher till the final holders could not expect a return of even 1 per cent, with the result that the improvement of the mark has brought not satisfaction but the very reverse.

The previous fall in the mark had also produced unfortunate results by driving the population in shoals into the shops in a mania of purchasing. While abusing the foreigner for buying out Germany with his profitable rate of exchange, the native has been no whit behind in emptying the shops of their stocks ... Many thought that their money would soon have no value whatever and that it must be exchanged for goods while there was yet time: others realised that the purchasing mania would help the falling rate of exchange to raise prices, and they therefore bought on speculative grounds.

The press pointed out that a disastrous slump in trade could not but ensue when the purchasing power of the population was exhausted, and that meanwhile the poorer classes were suffering. All efforts, however, were in vain to drive sense into a panic-stricken people, and articles in the shops could be seen being marked up to a higher price day by day.

German currency is of course stigmatised as shoddy paper of no value. Still, it has always been a striking fact that the German of the more modest classes has always had sufficient thereof to spend on luxuries such as theatres, cinemas, skating rinks, excursions to the country and so forth. The amount spent during the craze for buying must have been very large. The explanation – usually given is that the money was provided out of capital and savings. Discussing the question with me the other day, the Minister of Commerce gave the same explanation and dwelt on what he considered the most serious part of this state of affairs, namely that the people's confidence in, and loyalty to, the State had been gravely undermined: those who had supported the government during the war by buying State bonds had lost heavily by the depreciation of the mark, and the whole population were now engaged in evading taxation and devoting their money to speculative purchases, either of carpets and the like or of so-called 'securities'.

That the German government was now confronted (in the words of a member of the Disarmament Control Commission) with the problem of a whole community of taxpayers making, wherever they could, false returns, was bad enough. The growing disillusionment – almost universal already, in all conscience – with the government itself, which the Bavarian Minister of Commerce had spoken of, made it worse.

'The reins are trailing on the ground,' complained the *Berliner Tageblatt* on December 6 in a leader.

> Nobody can say what will become of the whole batch of taxation proposals ... [because] the Finance Ministry is 'run' by the Food Minister as a sideshow ... More new banknotes were issued during the last week in November than ever before: 4.5 milliards of marks – practically double our entire note circulation before the war. If we do not make up our minds to put our finances in order we shall have compulsory administration forced on us by our creditors.

Lord D'Abernon had already reached much the same conclusion about the Chancellor. His diary entry for November 24, 1921 states, not without conscious humour:

> I am increasingly convinced that Wirth understands very little about figures and regards them mainly as pegs on which to hang rhetoric. Directly one discusses the details of the German budget with him, his attention flags and he seems quite unable to follow even my most lucid developments.

It may be that, with others, Dr Wirth at that stage regarded the balancing of the budget as a more academic than practical project while France was calling upon Germany, as he put it, 'to lay milliards of gold by the sack upon the table'. The *Berliner Tageblatt* faithfully reported him on December 16, saying that he regarded the economic system as something which was artificially swollen by the fall in the rate of exchange, which might lead to a very bitter disillusion in the course of a few months. 'This fictitious prosperity with which we are often reproached by our adversaries,' he said, 'is evident in quite another form in other countries. In England and America it takes the form of unemployment.'

Dr Wirth declared that it was impossible to restore the world, and especially the European, economic system when all Eastern Europe lay shattered, and when the incapacity of the peoples of Eastern Europe to purchase was spreading to Central European countries. The only cause for hope, he thought, was that the world, and 'English haute-finance' in particular, was at last heeding Germany's explanations of why she could not pay what was asked, that the London Ultimatum had rendered Germany uncreditworthy, and that the problem was minutely related to the world economic system.

The press received his speech coldly. An innately law-respecting country which was already undergoing outbreaks of plundering by its own population needed action rather than excuses to encourage it. Unfortunately, to put its reforms into effect the Socialist government supremely depended upon the most reactionary official classes, whose goodwill had dwindled with their savings and incomes. The result was that less and less was done, and that the government was losing the support of the workers who stopped even bothering to vote. For them, politics were becoming irrelevant: at Christmas 1921 the rising cost of living and how to cope with it had become their only concern.

In the eight years since 1913, the price of rye bread had risen by 13 times; of beef by 17. Those were the commodities which had fared best. Sugar, milk (at 4.40 marks a litre), pork and even potatoes (at 1.50 marks a lb.) had risen between 23 and 28 times; butter had gone up by 33 times. These were only the official prices – real prices were often a third higher – and all these prices were roughly half as much again as in October, only two months before.

The brief December recovery of the mark brought no relief. That event, which caused unemployment transiently to treble to 3 per cent, gave another warning of what would inevitably have to be suffered when, one day, the printing presses stopped printing banknotes to order. Before the war, when the mark was sound, there were normally about 9,500 bankruptcies a year. As wartime inflation increased, the number regularly dropped, from 7,739 in 1914, to 807 in 1918. The total number in 1921, during the first seven months of which the mark was fairly stable, was 2,975, more than double the 1920 figure and three times that of 1919.* The 1921 figures were the most indicative; for in comparing the number of bankruptcies during the various months of the year it could be shown that a falling mark was associated with a decline in bankruptcies, and vice-versa. The largest number, 845, was in the spring when the mark stood highest; but after it reached its lowest in November the number was 150. The *Frankfurter Zeitung* commented: 'It gives some inkling of the awful *débâcle* which may be expected if a rapid and permanent improvement of the mark actually takes place.'

The London conference between Mr Lloyd George and the French Prime Minister, M. Briand, came and went and solved nothing. The reparations question was postponed until after the New Year, when there was to be a further conference at Cannes. Its principal decision was to grant Germany a moratorium on the January and February instalments but to oblige her thereafter, pending a new readjustment, to pay 31 million gold marks every ten days. Diplomatically, however, the Cannes meeting went dismally. The German delegation headed by Dr Rathenau, the Minister of Reconstruction, was snubbed and

---

* The annual bankruptcy figures from 1912 were: 9,218, 9,725, 7,739, 4,594, 2,279, 1,240, 807, 1,015, 1,324, 2,975.

ignored by the French for the first four days. And when M. Briand was seen to be taking instruction on the golf links from Mr Lloyd George, he was accused by his French colleagues of being subservient to British policy. He was recalled to Paris by President Millerand the day before the conference concluded, and was replaced by M. Poincaré. Poincaré attained office on the simple programme of making Germany pay; or, as he put it himself, 'to uphold firmly all France's rights under the Treaty of Versailles'.

'The fees in the Courts of War,' wrote Lloyd George, with a fine touch for epigram, 'are all on the highest scale.' Germany had lost the action and had to pay the full costs. With Poincaré, however, the justice had to be not only preventive but retributive. Lloyd George had this to say about the French leader of 1922:

> He had no use for the Cannes conference. He knew how to get money out of Germany – by the lash! … Briand was a Breton. M. Poincaré was a Lorrainer born in a province repeatedly overrun by Teutonic hosts … he himself twice witnessed the occupation of his own cherished home by German troops … He is cold, reserved, rigid, with a mind of unimaginative and ungovernable legalism. He has neither humour nor good humour … He was not concerned about a just, and least of all, a magnanimous peace. He wanted to cripple Germany, and render her impotent for future aggression … The fall of M. Briand sent the world rolling towards the catastrophe which culminated in 1931.

It rolled, of course, via the collapse of the mark, the disillusion of Germany, the progressive raising of world tariffs, and the cessation of trade, to depression and slump, and on to something much worse. But Lloyd George was writing only in 1932,* when the ultimate disaster already seemed to have struck Europe, in no small part the

---

* The extract is from *The Truth about Reparations and War-debts*, by David Lloyd George, Heinemann.

consequence of France's refusal to allow Germany to recover from the war.

Germany's effort to meet the reparations burden by implementing the taxation proposals of July 1921, still showed no signs of producing the desired effect. What was wanted, wrote the British Commercial Secretary in Berlin, was not a further set of imposts which would not be collected and would still further confuse the already labouring fiscal apparatus, but rather a readjustment and ruthless application of existing taxes. He thought that strong pressure ought to be brought against the wealthy – especially the industrialists – to make them disclose their foreign holdings.

How effective such a method might have been was shown by the reaction when, earlier, the government proposed to annex a portion of dividends. Sooner than admit this direct participation of the State, and in order to avoid any future interference with actual property, the industrialists proposed to assist the State by placing a proportion of their foreign holdings and foreign credit at its disposal for the payment of the reparation instalments, in return for which a proportion of future taxation would be remitted. The manner in which this proposal was made to the government (in September 1921) was hardly that of subjects to their sovereign authority, nor of the taxed to the tax-gatherer: in fact the industrialists actually made their offer conditional upon the transfer of the railways from the State to themselves. The government rightly refused any such bargain.

With the Cannes conference over and the prospect of a new and harder French line on reparation payments, the mark started to drift downwards again, reaching 850 to the pound in the last week of January 1922. One whom Lord D'Abernon's diary described baldly as 'one of the most influential men in the country whose name must not be mentioned' compared the country to an automobile which could not be stopped in five yards. Everyone recognised, he said, that the deflation period was going to be disagreeable, with men out of work and factories closed, and that there would have to be a limit fixed to printing notes. But, he added, 'Do not pull us up too short. Give the car time to stop without skidding.'

With a government and a commercial world convinced that it would be unwise to do anything in the least precipitate, life ground on in a pother of financial worries for all classes. Seeking somebody with commercial experience to represent Germany in Washington, Dr Rathenau was heard to complain not only that very few business men had diplomatic experience, but that, of those who had, all preferred to restore their private fortunes than to enter government service. Very few now had considerable private fortunes left, and Herr Cuno, for instance, who was to become the leader of the Rightist government the following year and who might have done for Washington, in the meantime desired to make his financial position secure.

In Bavaria the principal winter apprehensions were that the coming tourist season would see the food supplies eaten up by other Germans and foreigners, specially those drawn to the area by the Oberammergau Passion play. Measures were being taken to assign the relatively expensive imported foodstuffs to the tourists, leaving the home produce for the local population. Berlin enjoyed an extensive strike early in February of public employees, which halted the railways as well as the usual services. This was something that Berliners were growing used to, and before the city's water was cut off consumption was three times the normal as everybody filled up baths and every other receptacle to meet the occasion. Moscow was generally blamed for backing the workers' agitation with money, and public opinion turned against the Communists.

It was natural that a people in the grip of raging inflation should look about for someone to blame. They picked upon other classes, other races, other political parties, other nations. In blaming the greed of tourists, or the peasants, or the wage demands of labour, or the selfishness of the industrialists and profiteers, or the sharpness of the Jews, or the speculators making fortunes in the money markets, they were in large measure still blaming not the disease but the symptoms.

It was significant enough that union demands were still for higher wages to meet rising prices rather than, before all else, stable prices and a stable currency. A few of the financially sophisticated could be heard blaming the government, and the Finance Minister in particular, but a typical view was that prices went up because the foreign exchange went up, that the exchange rate went up because of speculation on the Stock Exchange, and that this was obviously the fault of the Jews. Although the price of the dollar was a matter for almost universal discussion, it still appeared to most Germans that the dollar was going up, not that the mark was falling; that the price of food and clothing was being forcibly increased daily, not that the value of money was permanently sinking as the flood of paper marks diluted the purchasing power of the number already in circulation.

Strangely enough the vision of the Allied Reparations Commission was similarly obfuscated. When the rate of exchange fell between February and March, 1922, from 45 to 70 paper marks to the gold mark (or otherwise from 900 to 1,400 to the pound), the commission demanded that the German government raise another 60 milliards in new taxes. It did not occur to them to demand a restoration of the level of exchange: still less did they see that there was little chance that taxes increased to an impossible level could conceivably make good such a depreciation.

Dr Rathenau accounted for the absence of unemployed in Germany by pointing out that a million men were working to pay reparations, a million to produce goods to buy food abroad, and another million simply to make up the loss of output since the eight-hour day was introduced. He did his best to explain to the Reichstag what was happening to the mark by alluding lengthily to the vicious circle of an adverse trade balance, the consequent necessity to sell German currency abroad, and its resulting depreciation, followed by the fall in the exchange rate and inevitable rise of home prices, leading to increased costs of materials and labour and so to new rifts in the budget. Dr Rathenau expressly and publicly denied that the printing press had any role to play in that permanently spiralling sequence of events, and by ascribing the country's ills primarily to the unfavourable trade balance caused by reparation payments he totally failed to understand the reality that the country was living far beyond its means, printing money to pay for excesses which included over-employment, the inordinate subsidy of industry, the import and manufacture of luxuries for domestic consumption, and a grossly inefficient tax-collection system.

Most successful businessmen, however, stuck happily to the heresy that only by a continually falling exchange rate could Germany compete in neutral markets. After them, the deluge. Neither they, nor the politicians, nor the bankers – with distressingly few exceptions – perceived any direct connection between inflation and depreciation. And yet, as the printing presses churned out bank notes the exchange continued rapidly to fall. What impressed the ordinary politician was the danger of social unrest which would, in his opinion, inevitably arise if there were any scarcity of currency. He could not see, or intentionally ignored, the obvious danger which proceeded from continuous inflation. Social unrest appeared, just the same.

During the first three months of 1922 the economic situation became notably worse. The two-month moratorium on reparation payments did no more than postpone the January fall of the mark until, at the end of February, the first 'ten-day payment' became due. Throughout the whole of March the fall went on; and only in April did a rally come, when the European financial community, whose willingness to grasp at straws was still amazingly unaffected by frequency of disappointment, decided that the international conference billed to begin in Genoa that month might bring salvation. The meeting brought an extra-mural crisis which put an unpleasant complexion on the five weeks of deliberations – the Treaty of Rapallo signed, after secret negotiations, between Germany and Russia, who mutually feared that they were being shut out of any say in the future of Europe. The Genoa conference over, the prospect of thrice-monthly squeezing of Germany's real resources returned.

The second half of 1921 had already brought a 50 per cent increase in the official food prices. With that rise the real wages of a single workman had more or less kept pace. The married workman, on the other hand, was worse off because of the greater demands upon him for clothing and warmth whose costs were rising faster. In practice the prices of most articles depended on the luck or skill of the purchaser. According to Mr Seeds, the Consul-General in Munich, who required his German chauffeur to keep careful notes of his family expenditure, such goods as butter could only be bought at considerably above the nominal cost. Milk in Munich, at 4.50 marks a litre in December 1921, rose to 6 marks in March 1922 and to 7 in April. Butter at 42 marks a lb. in December (9 marks above the posted price) could only be had for 50 marks in April. Eggs had risen from 2.50 apiece to 3.60; beer from 3 marks a litre to 5.60; and the prices of sugar, meat and potatoes had all doubled.

For any whose incomes were failing to keep abreast of, or somewhere close to, increases such as these, the tempest was blowing. The Allied blockade was still taking its toll on the young generation, its effects now dangerously amplified by inflation-bred poverty. All children of every class, according to a study in Frankfort-on-the-Main in February 1922, were two years physically and mentally backward for their ages. It remained difficult for them to recover those lost years because milk was obtainable only for the sick during the winter, and the price of bread was rising. It was a not uncommon sight to see anxious mothers searching in the dustbins of private residences in the richer neighbourhoods in the hope of retrieving scraps of food from the garbage.

Those lucky enough to have the monopoly power of an organised trade union to protect them were still in the shelter. They faced their employers, the German manufacturers as well as the central and local governments, with theoretically crippling wage demands. The employers' choice was between granting them or being prepared for wholesale strikes and disorders such as had recently been undergone in Britain. In the nine weeks or so after the Rapallo Treaty was signed, although the exchange rate was comparatively static at around 1,300 to the pound, the cost of food soared upwards. The 50 per cent rise during the second six months of the previous year now became a desirable objective, and in Hamburg the price rises monitored for food alone in April, May and June were respectively 46 per cent, 51 per cent and 56 per cent.* For a brief time in May when the price of meat doubled in a matter of a month the rise in the cost of living was so abrupt and startling that the unions for a space were unable to decide what demands to put forward.

In view of the rocketing cost of labour, the eagerness of manufacturers to extend their works, renew their plant and embark on large improvement schemes was at first sight somewhat extraordinary. From a social point of view, too, so much commercial building was unfortunate in a country now short of over a million houses – in part the result of the rent restriction Acts which had throttled the private sector of the building industry. But German industrialists had been unable to build up liquid reserves which would keep their value, and such cash as they could not hold illegally abroad in a foreign currency was generally converted – as Sir Basil Blackett had remarked – into real or fixed assets. For that reason an appreciation of the mark was greatly feared, and even the few weeks of post-Genoa 'stability' invited stagnation in business. Industrial circles were faced with the danger that cash would become more valuable than goods, and of a crash when everyone attempted to convert their assets back into money again.

A further reason for their viewing any appreciation with dismay was noted in a report by a member of the Rhineland High Commission at the end of May. It would have rendered the payment of taxes not an academic hardship but a real one. A mark received as income in 1921 had an actual average value of, say, a penny. A year later when the tax was due on it, it was worth a fifth or sixth of that figure – and incomes

---

* Phillip Cagan defined hyper-inflation as beginning in the month in which price rises first exceed 50 per cent (equivalent to an annual rate of 600 per cent): cf. his essay in *Studies in the Quantity Theory of Money*, edited by Milton Friedman, University of Chicago Press 1956.)

had increased in the meantime, if not in the same proportion, at least very substantially. The longer payment could be postponed, the greater the gain could be.

'The big interests believe,' said the report, 'that as the mark is doomed as a currency beyond hope of recovery, all efforts to support it are costly, useless, and dangerous to their or, as they put it, the country's interests.'

The better German industrial concerns had particular reason for satisfaction with their lot. They might look weak financially, but many possessed enormous concealed reserves because their debenture shares and other prior-charge debts had been contracted on the basis of the gold mark, and gold-mark equivalents of goods and services had been received for them. The mighty Stinnes group, for one, was still working on gold capital. The fall in the value of the paper mark, however, had written off 98 per cent of the gold debt – to the companies' gain and to the shareholders' loss. New borrowings from the Reichsbank, furthermore, from whom commercial enterprises could obtain credit at very low discount rates even at the height of the crisis in 1923, were automatically written off in the same way: rapid depreciation caused the real value of repayments to be smaller than the original loans by whatever factor time and the rate of fall dictated.

Hugo Stinnes himself, the richest and most powerful industrialist in Germany, whose empire of over one-sixth of the country's industry had been largely built on the advantageous foundation of an inflationary economy, paraded a social conscience shamelessly. He justified inflation as the means of guaranteeing full employment, not as something desirable but simply as the only course open to a benevolent government. It was, he maintained, the only way whereby the life of the people could be sustained.

The President of the Reichsbank whose industrial interests were negligible did not in essence depart from this argument, and in a speech on German currency in May 1922 greatly vexed Lord D'Abernon because he had (in the ambassador's words) 'pressed into the shortest space the maximum number of fallacies and errors'. As though his powers to wreck the economy were not great enough already, at the behest of the Reparations Commission, and in the expectation that money supply would thereby be divorced from political expedience, the Reichsbank was that same month declared autonomous, with Dr Havenstein its uncrowned king. He quickly showed that he, too, considered the fall in the exchange to be quite unconnected with the gigantic increases in note issue, and went on 'merrily turn[ing] the handle of the printing press completely unconscious of its disastrous effect'. There was evidence, D'Abernon believed, that 90 bankers in Germany out of every 100 expressed and perhaps held the same views. At any event, the financial press reported them without dissent.

Ever-climbing wages and the high expenditure plans of the industrialists jaundiced and clouded many a foreign eye, notwithstanding the penury that had hit so many. *The Times* on April 18, 1922, printed a bitter report from 'a man of business' recently in the country:

> The greatest fraudulent conspiracy in the history of the world is now being enacted in Germany with the full concurrence and active support of its 60 or 70 millions of people. And this conspiracy is brazenly enacted under the very noses of the Allies. Germany is teeming with wealth. She is humming like a beehive. The comfort and prosperity of her people absolutely astound me. Poverty is practically non-existent. It is all the other way ... And yet this is the country that is determined she will not pay her debts ... They are a nation of actors ... If it wasn't for the fact that the German is guiltless of humour, one might imagine the whole nation was bent on perpetrating an elaborately laborious practical joke.

Of course prosperity existed for some, and was to be seen on the surface. Those eating well in restaurants were those who could afford to eat well in restaurants. As money saved diminished like a lump of ice on a summer's day, there was in any case every incentive to eat it, drink it or be merry on it. The Bavarian government's gluttony Bill of the previous autumn had drawn in its preamble the nice distinction between habitual gluttony and occasional overindulgence on festive occasions. The man of business must have overlooked not only the haunts and troubles of the poor, just as he would probably have overlooked them at home in Britain: the plight of the pensioners and of the *rentier* classes had escaped him altogether.

In Hamburg where the authorities were particularly concerned to stamp out the iniquities which aggravated social distress, the regulations formulated to check profiteering were having only moderate success. In the first three months of 1922, the 175 actions brought by the state resulted in fines totalling 347,000 marks – by then worth less than £1,500 – and prison sentences amounting to 1,635 days. Of these punishments, the highest fine imposed was one of 50,000 marks for profiteering in flour, and the longest jail sentence a year and nine months for profiteering in coal. By June the *Wucheramt*, the office for the suppression of profiteering, had stepped up its activities to deal with the 185 cases reported during the month and collected 1.4 million marks in fines – now only worth about £1,000 sterling.

Apart from the bigger sentences, these figures can have brought small comfort to the Hamburgers who in the same month received an average of 105 marks (enough to feed the statistical family of four at official prices for only one day) for each of the 200,000-odd articles pledged at the municipal pawning establishments; who since April had had to pay 20 times the registered fare for their horse cabs and 25 times for their taxis; and whose cost of living, like everyone else's, was now rising by not less than half every four weeks.

In the spring of 1922, Germany was evincing many signs of national despair. It was apparent to most that under the Imperial dispensation the nation had at least been confident as well as prosperous. What was disturbing at any rate to the older generations of the upper and middle classes was their realisation of the superficiality of Prussian culture. Younger people, some of whom later remembered those years not as a nightmare but as an adventure, were mainly confused and disillusioned. The self-confidence of the country ebbed away along with its prosperity, and as it did so the moral degeneration of the nation and its institutions set in. Pessimism and restlessness grew as sense of security, community spirit and patriotism dwindled. Neither the hatred of French militarism in the abstract and of France in general, nor a growing desire for revenge, were enough to hold together what had been the most law-abiding people in Europe when the very fabric of that nation was crumbling along with its ethical values, and when the moral, material and social ravages of inflation were undermining and immeasurably worsening the condition of both.

Among some, it was true, the rebirth of the German soul, battered by the war, hardship and humiliation, was becoming something of an obsession. Not just the militarists of *Frontkämpfertag* and the academics of Königsberg but many of all classes who were victims of inflation began to long for a great leader: not a ruler (thought one contemporary observer) of the type of the Kaiser or of Tirpitz, but one possessed of the attributes and Spartan values of the legendary figures of early Teutonic history. It was a longing which Hitler, with his attraction to Wagner, fully understood, and one which his National Socialist Workers' Party (NSDAP) was already exploiting in Munich. When a nation is falling apart, its old values challenged by new conditions, there are always elements who will seize on any means of cohesion.

'Inflation finished the process of moral decay which the war had started.' Erna von Pustau told Pearl Buck.

> It was a slow process over a decade or more; so slow that really it smelled of a slow death ... In between were times when the mark seemed to stop devaluating, and each time we people got a bit hopeful. People would say, 'The worst seems over now.' In such a time Mother sold her [tenanted] houses. It looked as though she had

made a good business deal, for she got twice as much cash as she had paid. But the furniture she bought … had gone up five times in price and … the worst was not over. Soon inflation started again with new vigour, and swallowed bit by bit the savings accounts of Mother and millions of others.

Frau von Pustau explained that one house was sold because the couple living there had had both sons killed in the war, had no one to care for them, had had their life savings devalued, and so had gassed themselves. 'Our times,' she went on, 'made us cynical. The pie was growing smaller and more people wanted to have pieces of the pie, and so there was nothing left from the "good Neighbour" atmosphere of former days. Everybody saw an enemy in everybody else.' Her father complained that 'we of the middle class are not organised against the wholesalers, while the workers are organised against us'. The middle classes, in other words, were being squeezed between the two big classes of big business and the workers.

In the summer of 1922 the small businessman saw his enemy in the big businessman, personified by Herr Stinnes, 'the greatest obstacle to currency reform', as Lord D'Abernon described him. The Right, now intriguing in Berlin for the return of the Hohen-zollerns and in Munich for the return of the Wittelsbachs, saw its enemy in the Republican government. More ominously, it saw treachery in the policy of fulfilment of the reparation debt personified by Dr Rathenau. Neither Rathenau nor Stinnes trusted the other, but perhaps they came nearest to mutual comprehension in the early morning of June 28 on the way home from a late evening of argument about coal deliveries to the Entente at the American Ambassador's house in Berlin. Rathenau, a Jew like Erzberger, had just undergone, like Erzberger, a vitriolic attack in the Reichstag from the Rightist leader Dr Helfferich.

A few hours later, as Rathenau was driven from his home to the Foreign Office, the path of his car was blocked deliberately by another, while two assassins in a third car which had been following riddled him with bullets at close range. A bomb, thrown into his car for good measure, nearly cut his body in two.

6: Summer of '22

The murder of the apostle of 'fulfilment', a statesman whose cosmopolitan approach transcended the narrowness of nationalism, burst the dam and sent the mark skidding off the plateau it had occupied since the beginning of April. The currency once more collapsed – a word which must serve again although it scarcely permits adequate description of what was to come – from 1,300 to 1,600 to the pound at once, and within a week to 2,200, nearly 500 to the dollar.

Not Rathenau's death alone, celebrated as it was by a general strike in Berlin as a warning to the Right, lay behind the latest fall. In Bavaria, for example, the state finances were already in a hopeless condition because of the incapacity of the revenue officials to deal with the overwhelming arrears of tax, and because the estimated deficit for 1922 had doubled. Although reduction of expenditure was as easy to preach and as difficult to carry out in Bavaria as anywhere else in the world, the continued steep decline in the purchasing power of the currency made things vastly more difficult. In June 1922, the authorities had not yet dealt with the Federal taxes for 1920 – an echo of the central government's own difficulties. (A measure of the Bavarian Landtag's grasp of the situation was its decision, notwithstanding these conditions, to double the annual subsidy for encouraging gymnastics.)

There were external factors, too. Negotiations (through the Morgan Committee) to arrange further international loans in Paris had failed, against expectations and hopes, and the ability of the financial authorities to ward off sudden movements in the money markets ceased. The *Frankfurter Zeitung* on July 7 noted that the fear of internal disturbance in Germany seemed to have caused a panic, the larger industrial companies starting it with heavy buying of foreign bills in order to safeguard future supplies of raw materials. For the first time since the Armistice, the newspaper remarked, appalled, foreign countries had refused Germany a loan which until then had been obtainable by selling paper marks abroad: 'The mark for the moment is unsaleable.'

A new development was the rapidity with which prices now moved after the exchange rate. Until the early summer there had been a considerable interval between the depreciation of the mark at home and abroad. Just before the post-Rathenau collapse an increasing number of industries were declaring that their costs of production were reaching world market levels, so that they could no longer compete abroad. This development, needless to say, puzzled those who observed that the cost of labour remained cheaper in Germany and that other industrial subsidies continued as before. Far from having unemployment, it was pointed out, there was actually a labour famine, for one reason because many German labourers were seeking higher wages in Belgium, Holland and even in the border areas of France.

In the spring of 1922 a growing divergence had been evident between the rate of increase in the floating debt and that of the volume of money in circulation. Behind this lay, first, the inability of private banks any longer to advance the loans needed to keep industry and commerce going; and, second, the corresponding liberality with which the Reichsbank conceived it its duty to fill the gap. From the summer onwards, commercial bills were dealt with as generously as Treasury bills, and the loans available to business were at far more indulgent rates than the private banks could possibly have offered. The discount rate for these commercial bills remained at 6 per cent throughout August while during the same month the mark fell by 250 per cent against the pound. Within six months commercial bills were approaching three-fifths of the Bank's holding of Treasury bills. The demand for extra credit which the Reichsbank's behaviour stimulated was scarcely less critical in promoting inflation than its profligate bounty towards the government itself.

The most notable thing about the puzzlement of the financial world, not least the writers of the *Frankfurter Zeitung,* was the complete failure to consider the continuing flood of new banknotes as one of the reasons for the mark's behaviour. Its latest fall was reckoned disastrous for the finances both of the Reich and of the regional governments: all efforts to restore order in the federal budget had been rendered void. It meant the further impoverishment of the classes on fixed incomes, state officials included, and (as another newspaper feared) further recruits for the radical circles of the Right from these 'social *déclassés*'.

'Grave feeling of disquiet here,' wrote D'Abernon in Berlin in his diary entry for July 10, 1922.

> The whole sky is overcast and gloomy. The fall of the mark continues – today it is 2,430, or about half the price of a month ago. Prices are rising and will soon be double the level of June 1, wages and salaries must be adjusted. Adjusted to what?

The financial position in Germany, he noted, was precisely that in Vienna a year ago, with the exchange between 2,000 and 2,500. 'Today exchange in Vienna is about 95,000. Will Berlin a year hence be at this level?'

Lord D'Abernon blamed the German authorities as much as anyone else for what was happening. He considered their recklessness with note issues the blindest folly – 'it requires handcuffs', he wrote 'to stay the hand which turns the crank of the printing press'. However, unpromising as things were, it was found that the activities of the Reparations Commission could usually be relied on in those days to eliminate the slenderest hope that confidence would return. Their very presence in Berlin produced panic. 'The moment they appear,' said Lord D'Abernon, 'the mark bolts.'

While the commission's Committee of Guarantees visited Berlin in September 1921, the mark had fallen from 350 to 650 to the pound. Now, during their extended midsummer visit it had plunged from

1,800 to 2,400, and the German government had been happy to remind them of that fact: six weeks of expenses, including that of their special railway carriage which waited in Berlin throughout that time, were paid in 20-mark notes, which required seven office-boys with huge waste-paper baskets to carry to the railway station. Meanwhile, the commission's insistence on making the Reichsbank independent of government control (implemented in May 1922) had turned out, in the British Ambassador's view, to have been like giving maniacs the control of the asylum. 'Last week,' stated his July 10 diary entry, 'when by the blessing of Providence, the printers struck and the printing of notes was perforce interrupted, Havenstein brought in strike-breakers to get the presses going again.'

There was more behind the printers' strike than D'Abernon's brief account. An extraordinary amount of paper money had been needed in June, causing the Reichsbank to issue 11,300 milliard marks in new notes. Owing to strikes, the usual inflow of these notes back into the bank had not happened, so that there were none in reserve. About six months before, according to a confidential memorandum given to the Chancellor, contracts were awarded for the supply of a special new paper which made practicable the quick printing of notes bearing a simple imprint which could not be imitated. The paper arrived at the printing offices unexpectedly on July 7. It should have been possible to print enough 500-mark notes by July 13, a Thursday, in time for delivery on pay day. In spite of the readiness of the trade unions to go ahead with the new paper, the printers themselves suddenly withdrew their consent.

'It was plain,' said the memorandum, 'that other forces were at work than a mere wage or sympathy strike. It seemed probable that hidden and illicit leaders were trying to seize the State by the throat.'

If on the half-monthly pay day for many of the great industrial works no money was forthcoming, the government would be faced with the danger of popular disturbances. Before making its decision to break the strike, the government was also faced with the danger of the Berlin strikers' destroying the machinery if volunteers were taken on.

The British Consul at Frankfort-on-the-Main reported in late July that there had been an instantaneous rise in the price of the necessaries of life. The workman's wage had naturally been raised in proportion, and a skilled workman was now demanding 100,000 marks a year – £5,000 a year in pre-war money, but by then barely enough for subsistence. A manual worker's wage was worked out on the same basis. 'Such rates,' said the consul, 'leave the professional man, the doctor, the teacher and the bank clerk far behind in their capacity as wage earners: a trained bank clerk, for instance, can only aspire to a maximum yearly salary of 12,000 marks' – or about £5 if changed in London.

In the four weeks of July the index for the wholesale prices of 98 varieties of food had risen from 9,000 points to 14,000, another monthly rise of well over 50 per cent. The *Frankfurter Zeitung* recorded that the wholesale price of 'goods' had gone up by 139 times since before the war; of leather and textiles by 219 times. Against these figures, the American index representing world prices, with a fall in cereal prices since before the war and an increase in metal, had remained steady. The Communist newspaper *Rote Fahne* (whose statistical material was also generally accurate) reckoned that at that date the 'minimum of existence for a four-person family', in Germany, had increased since 1914 by 86 times while the average wage had increased only 34 times. An egg which had once cost 4 pfennigs now cost 7.20 marks, a 180-fold increase. In the course of the first week of July alone, the four-person-family weekly minimum (a little more than £1 in London terms, or $5 in New York) rose from 2,300 to 2,800 marks. A bank clerk's annual salary would therefore keep his family alive for about a month.

The Austrian situation was thus being relentlessly reproduced in Germany, with the more educated classes, deprived in most cases of the right decently to live and bring up their families, becoming more and more hostile to the Republic and receptive to the forces of reaction. The consul in Frankfort reported a virulent growth of anti-Semitism.

It is no exaggeration to say that cultured German men and women of high social standing openly advocate the political murder of Jews as a legitimate weapon of defence. They admit, it is true, that the murder of Rathenau was of doubtful advantage … but they say there are others who must go so that Germany shall be saved. Even in Frankfort, with a prepondering Jewish population, the movement is so strong that Jews of social standing are being asked to resign their appointments on the boards of companies.

Erna von Pustau recalled the same trend in Hamburg, where 'stock exchange' and 'Jews' were ideas very much connected in the minds of the people, and where the circumstances of a situation which no one really understood made those who had lost their savings or their fortunes ready prey for anti-Semitic propaganda. Her father began to speak against the Jews more and more, asserting now that 'creative capital is the capital we Germans have: parasitical capital is the capital of the Jews.'

'You should have known my father as he used to be,' she told her friend.

The political education I had I got from him. He explained to me things against the Kaiser, and our Parliament. But now he has stopped thinking and reasoning, and this will do more damage to us than it will ever damage the Jews.

At what might otherwise have been the height of the immediate crisis at the end of July 1922, the Reparations Commission decided to take its summer holidays, effectively postponing any settlement of the exchange turmoil until mid-August; and M. Poincaré, bent as ever (it was believed) on Germany's destruction, sent a Note to Berlin accusing the government of wilful default on its debts, and threatening 'retortion'. The effect on the financial situation was calamitous. The rise in prices intensified the demand for currency, both by the State and by other employers. Private banks could not meet the demand at all, and had to ration the cashing of cheques, so that uncashed cheques remained frozen while their purchasing power drained away. It became impossible to persuade anyone to accept any description of cheque for that reason, and much business quickly came to a standstill. The panic spread to the working classes when they realised that their wages were simply not available.

Because the Reichsbank's printing presses and note-distribution arrangements were insufficient for the situation, a law was passed permitting, under licence and against the deposit of appropriate assets, the issue of emergency money tokens, or *Notgeld*, by state and local authorities and by industrial concerns when and where the Reichsbank could not satisfy employers' needs for wage-payment. The law's purpose was principally to regularise and regulate a practice which had gone on extensively for some years already, with the difference that authorised *Notgeld* would now have the Reichsbank's guarantee behind it. Before long, as that guarantee became increasingly less esteemed, the tide of emergency money that now entered local circulation, with or without the Bank's approval, contrived enormously to raise the level of the sea of paper by which the country was engulfed. As the ability to print money privately in a time of accelerating inflation made possible private profits only limited by people's willingness to accept it, the process merely banked up the inflationary fire to ensure a still bigger blaze later on.

Because of the excessive rise in the cost of living in these weeks, ever more pressing demands for higher wages flowed in from all classes with any leverage on their paymasters. Strikes accompanied those demands. A strike of shop employees in Frankfort on August 8 resulted two days later in a wage increase from 7,200 to 9,600 marks a month backdated to the beginning of July. It was followed at once by a compositors' strike, which closed down the newspapers for two weeks and then produced a settlement which promised a weekly wage increase of 500 marks effective until September 1, after which it would rise to

800 marks until September 16, at which point the results of further negotiations would apply. Government officials were awarded a 38 per cent increase from August 1, and government workers an additional 12 marks an hour – a further burden on the budget of 125 milliard paper marks. There were no plans to meet this burden beyond a 50 per cent increase in rail freight charges from September 1 and another increase in the postal rates (the face values of new postage stamp issues which in 1916 had ranged from the 2-pfennig grey to the 4-mark red and black, in late 1922 started at the 50-mark blue and went up to the 100,000-mark red).

Mr Seeds wrote from Munich to say that his chauffeur's weekly expenditure on food was now $5^{1}/_{2}$ times as great as it had been a year ago, in August 1921. On the other hand, his wages were nearly six times higher. Since these were fixed according to the average rate paid to his class of worker, he was not suffering unduly except in so far as wage rises, a monthly occurrence by this time, always lagged a little behind price rises which took place weekly, if not daily. This was the case for the vast mass of artisans and workmen, but of course, Seeds said, the middle class, including officials and journalists, were far from being in the same satisfactory position. It was from this latter group, he pointed out, that foreigners mostly derived their information, which was why the accounts of the incidence of inflation published abroad were almost unrelievedly gloomy.

The young Ernest Hemingway, however, working for the *Toronto Daily Star*, crossed the frontier from France at about that time and managed to be equally gloomy from the other side of the fence:

> There were no marks to be had in Strasbourg, the mounting exchange had cleaned the bankers out days ago, so we changed some French money in the railway station at Kehl. For 10 francs I received 670 marks. Ten francs amounted to about 90 cents in Canadian money. That 90 cents lasted Mrs Hemingway and me for a day of heavy spending and at the end of the day we had 120 marks left!

Our first purchase was from a fruit stand … We picked out five very good looking apples and gave the old woman a 50-mark note. She gave us back 38 marks in change. A very nice looking, white bearded old gentleman saw us buy the apples and raised his hat.

'Pardon me, sir,' he said, rather timidly, in German, 'how much were the apples?'

I counted the change and told him 12 marks.

He smiled and shook his head. 'I can't pay it. It is too much.'

He went up the street walking very much as white bearded old gentlemen of the old regime walk in all countries, but he had looked very longingly at the apples. I wish I had offered him some. Twelve marks, on that day, amounted to a little under 2 cents. The old man, whose life savings were probably, as most of the non-profiteer classes are, invested in German pre-war and war bonds, could not afford a 12 mark expenditure. He is the type of the people whose incomes do not increase with the falling purchasing value of the mark and the krone.

Hemingway recorded that with the mark at 800 to the dollar, or 8 to the cent, a pound of coffee could be had for 34 marks. Beer was 10 marks a stein, or one cent and a quarter. Kehl's best hotel served a five-course meal for 150 marks, or 15 cents.

The French cannot come over to buy up all the cheap goods they would like to. But they can come over and eat … This miracle of exchange makes a swinish spectacle where the youth of the town of Strasbourg crowd into the German pastry shop to eat themselves sick, and gorge on fluffy, cream-filled slices of German cake at 5 marks the slice. The contents of a pastry shop are swept clear in half an hour …

The proprietor and his helper were surly and didn't seem particularly happy when all the cakes were sold. The mark was falling faster than they could bake.

Meanwhile out in the street a funny little train jolted by, carrying the workmen with their dinner-pails home to the outskirts of the town, profiteers' motorcars tore by raising a cloud of dust that settled over the trees and the fronts of all the buildings, and inside the pastry shop young French hoodlums swallowed their last sticky cakes and French mothers wiped the sticky mouths of their children. It gave you a new aspect on exchange.

As the last of the afternoon tea-ers and pastry eaters went Strasbourg-wards across the bridge the first of the exchange pirates coming over to raid Kehl for cheap dinners began to arrive.

The mark plummeted downwards. Dr Wirth, dining with Lord D'Abernon on August 16 said that that day, when the mark had fallen to below 1,000 to the dollar compared to its par price of about 5, had been one of the worst in the history of Germany and also one of the worst in his experience. He had been inundated with visitors, many of them in a state of semi-panic about the financial crisis and with all kinds of unworkable or impracticable solutions to the country's difficulties.

The Chancellor would accept no connection between printing money and its depreciation. Indeed, it remained largely unrecognised in Cabinet, bank, parliament or press. The *Vossische Zeitung* of August 16 declared that

the opinion that the flood of paper is the real origin of the depreciation is not only wrong but dangerously wrong ... Both private and public statistics have long shown that for the last two years the interior depreciation of the mark is due to the depreciation of the rate of exchange ... It should be remembered today that our paper circulation, although it shows on paper a terrifying array of milliards, is really not excessively high ... We have no 'dangerous flood of paper' but, on the contrary, our total circulation is at least three or four times as small as in peace time.

Lord D'Abernon described these remarkable views as 'far from exceptionally retrograde', and in fact typical of enlightened Berlin opinion. The *Berliner Börsen* Courier a couple of days later showed greater concern for the social consequences but no more awareness about the reasons. It regretted that the German mark at one-three-hundredth of its par value was now in the same class as the Hungarian korona. The proletariate was becoming restless, said the newspaper, and the State whose taxation estimates were based on an average exchange rate of 500 to the dollar was helpless.

> But the real tragedy of the depreciation may be described as 'the moral effect'. An apparently endless fall in the value of the mark predicted abroad will cause at home an unbearable increase of uncertainty. No economic discussions will pacify the masses, or hide from them the price of bread.
>
> It has long been realised that the printing of notes is the result and not the cause of depreciation, and that the amount of currency, as it increases in bulk, is really decreasing in value. A point has now been reached where the lack of money has a worse effect than the depreciation itself ... Even should the quantity of paper money be three times its present size, it would constitute no real obstacle to stabilisation.
>
> Until such a time, therefore, let us print notes!

It was clear to this leading financial daily what was happening: that as the total of paper marks in circulation had risen from 35 milliards in December 1919 to 200 milliards in July 1922, the equivalent sterling value had fallen from £193 million to £83 million. Before the war the currency circulation of 6 milliard marks had been worth about £300 million. The cause, however, was still a matter for firmly asserted conjecture.

Dr Hummel, the young but influential State President of Baden, stated that he, for one, would not like to take responsibility for halting the presses. He attributed the fall in the mark variously to moral and psychological causes, the posturing of Poincaré, and the burden of reparations as well as to the note-printing. Doubtless they were all contributory factors; and D'Abernon himself likened Poincaré's attitude to a teacher constantly rapping a pupil on the knuckles without realising that he was moribund. Yet the catastrophe of Austria was an object lesson for all to see. 'A continued panic in the mark is probable,' the ambassador wrote, 'unless the immediate cause of its fall – i.e. the continuous outpouring of notes from the printing press – is stopped. It will require a surgical operation to get this into the heads of authorities here: nothing short of trepanning will do it.'

On August 24, more strained than ever, Dr Wirth was telling the ambassador about his fears that Germany would be unable to find enough food to feed people during the coming winter, least of all while reparation payments went on. As they were talking, D'Abernon recorded, 'a card was brought in giving the dollar exchange at 1,837 – an enormous fall since yesterday'.

The confusion of the people and the government in the face of such total lack of certainty in financial matters was echoed at diplomatic levels. A fine instance found its way into D'Abernon's diary on August 26:

Met the American Ambassador this afternoon, who said, 'I know a great many things; how much do you know?' But I could not get out of him what the deuce it was. He said, 'We are almost at war'; but whether he meant America and England, or France and Germany, or some other complication, I have no idea.

7: The Hapsburg Inheritance

Unquestionably the post-war years had brought about a remarkable redistribution of wealth and income in Austria. The main problem it gave rise to was that an excessive proportion – that received by the working classes – now escaped taxation. It was beyond the wit of the government to find a means of taxing wages which the workers would not be able at once to pass on to the employers (especially when the employer was the State or the Vienna municipality), which the employers would not pass on to the consumer, and which would not then be passed round again to the printing press in consequence of the increases in wages and prices which mechanically followed. An alarming picture both of national selfishness bred by inflation and political ineptitude bred by economic uncertainty was painted by Mr O.S. Phillpotts,[*] the Commercial Secretary at the British Legation in Vienna:

> The Austrians are like men on a ship who cannot manage it, and are continually signalling for help. While waiting, however, most of them begin to cut rafts, each for himself, out of the sides and decks. The ship has not yet sunk despite the leaks so caused, and those who have acquired stores of wood in this way may use them to cook their food, while the more seamanlike look on cold and hungry. The population lack courage and energy as well as patriotism. During the recent railway strike the authorities applied to an automobile club for volunteers, but none came forward; and to a local firm for

---

[*] Owen Phillpotts was a man with long experience of the country, having been Vice-Consul, then Consul, in Vienna from 1906 to 1914.

the loan of lorries, but these were refused unless the government would buy them.

For all Lord D'Abernon's concern that the mark would soon be at Austrian levels of exchange, therefore, the collapse of the krone was still magnificently outperforming it. May 1921 had seen the krone reach 2,000 to the pound. May 1922 found it at 35,000. The root causes were much the same as they had always been, supported by international doubts and led by a public domestic pessimism which drove the Austrians to purchase all they could with all the cash they had, and their determination, despite the harsher penalties recently imposed, to hoard all the food obtainable. Shopkeepers had recently been obliged by a new edict to accept the State's banknotes; but since it also permitted the continued use of foreign currency for all purchases, tradesmen generally found excuses for accepting little else. The move led to considerable aggravation as every shop in Vienna was crowded, the peasants trooping in thousands to the old imperial capital to rid themselves of their money.

'Women bought in stocks of sugar, coffee, and other goods against a rise in prices, or spent their money on clothes and furniture,' wrote V.W. Germains.*

> Others squandered money recklessly; wine would be dearer tomorrow! On days when the dollar rose there would be a run on the shops. Prices would rise from hour to hour; the public was seized with a mania for buying. Stories are told of an old bachelor who bought swaddling clothes because the local shop had nothing else to sell ... Shopkeepers countered by closing their shops on various pretexts, on account of illness, family affairs, stocktaking.

There were those, too, from the towns especially, with no spare money to squander.

---

* Author of *Austria of Today*, Macmillan 1932.

In the middle of May 1922 Dr Schober's gallant, almost single-handed efforts as Chancellor to bring order to Austria's economy and moderation and common-sense to her politics came to an end. His administration was defeated in parliament a bare four weeks after he had persuaded the Allies at Genoa to relinquish their prior mortgage rights on all Austrian State property held to meet occupation and reparation costs – an agreement which cleared the way for raising an Austrian loan. The politicians may have felt that Schober had served his turn, but the dismissal of the country's strongest statesman immediately sprinkled question-marks over the country's creditworthiness so long as she controlled her own finances. With the news of the ex-police chief's resignation the British credit promised by Lloyd George ran out, that from France and Italy never materialised, and the krone began to slip away again. Austria's condition stayed particularly critical, in contrast to that of Hungary or Germany, because of her heavy dependence upon foreign imports.

After June 1 the graph of the krone's fall became vertiginous. The June 5 figure of 52,000 to the pound, well over 10,000 to the dollar, produced something of a panic which contributed during the next two days to a further fall of 40 per cent. On June 9 the pound was at 70,000 kronen, the dollar at more than 15,000. Within a month of Rathenau's assassination in Germany at the end of June, the krone dived in sympathy with the mark from 100,000 to 125,000. In parallel with the fall came huge price increases, the index whose base had been 100 in July 1921 reaching 2,645.

The Viennese politicians' competence to deal with such a situation had become merely a bad joke in the capital, while outside it contempt for and dislike of the central government increased still further. In Styria and the Tyrol union with Italy was widely canvassed as the better alternative. In Vienna talk of *Anschluss* with Germany continued, encouraged by the Pan-Germans, forbidden as it was by the peace treaties and disparaged as it now was by Berlin – 'Who would want to join us,' Dr Wirth asked, 'with the mark in the condition it is?'

The League of Nations Council refused the necessary permission, and Communist subversion of the country increased, with more finance from Moscow.

In fact the Austrian Communist Party itself was as completely and hopelessly bankrupt as the country, but Moscow thought it worthwhile supporting because of its relations with Germany's more significant movement. It was well organised and, apart from protests against rising prices and routine appeals to confiscate the wealth of the rich, interested itself successfully in either provoking or extending strikes. A notable development was that, far from being the covert organisation of heretofore, individual Communists had begun to show their allegiance and their hands quite openly.

In August 1922 a new, despairing plea was sent by Dr Ignaz Seipel, Schober's successor as Chancellor, requesting from the Entente a loan of £15 million. In the name of the Supreme Council Lloyd George refused it, regretting that Austria since the war had 'already received so much from them with such disappointing results'. Austria was cuttingly referred to the League of Nations, and by the end of the month the krone had fallen to 350,000 to the pound, exactly one-tenth of its value in May. Despair was complete. The Austrians waited for the sky to fall as though it had not already done so a dozen times. The chief of police publicly announced that he had 20,000 men he could count upon to disarm the dangerously Left-wing Austrian army. The American minister in Vienna warned visitors not on business to stay away. Frequent as were strikes and demonstrations, greater disorders were prophesied, and 'timid Jewish businessmen' were reported by the British Legation to be hastening to get their passports in order. The risk of plundering by hungry, workless mobs daily grew, for since July the cost of living index had increased by 124 per cent. In July alone the State could only meet its liabilities to its employees of 150 milliard kronen by paying in instalments. The August increase raised the obligation to 344 milliards, and the national wage figure for the month was about 700 milliards – in any case, far more than the existing circulation. The collapse of all governmental authority was imminent.

The situation of course reflected Austria's basic financial problem of her excessive expenditure on superfluous official salaries and wages (the number of whose recipients had greatly inflated during the war years) which, as they rose automatically on the index, could only be met by printing more money. The trade unions by the end of July were protesting that the index, adjusted monthly on the basis of the rise in the cost of living for the previous month, no longer sufficed to keep pace with prices; so that the pressures to print more were constantly growing. In August alone, the extra issue of uncovered banknotes was 560 milliards – a sum which helped to make nonsense of the Act passed in July to set up a new bank of issue with a capital of 800 milliards supplied half by a forced loan and half by new taxation. Though encouraged by the Reparations Commission, the scheme was stillborn simply because the scale of the depreciation made it out of date.

With July's crash of the krone a substitute Bourse, the *Devisen-zentrale*, was set in motion in Vienna, a means of regulating transactions and movements in foreign currency which Germany and Hungary both emulated within a couple of months. Not only did it fail to stay the rout: it could not bring back that critical £18 million worth of Austrian gold now reckoned to be lodged in Switzerland. It did not alleviate the harassing conditions of the Austrian middle classes, nor the terrible life of the lower. Neither, for that matter, did it have any noticeable effect on the operations of the speculators, the deprivations of the profiteers, or on the process of the devaluation of the currency. As the krone became unacceptable and unaccepted, those with foreign banknotes, the main medium of exchange, began to refuse to part with them at all. The Austrians were back where the war had left them, a few million bankrupt, hungry people floundering about on a map they did not recognise.

Austria, however, barely afloat as a nation on the tumultuous European seas of 1922 (nautical metaphors suited her condition very well), was suddenly to find ground beneath her feet. Refusing to await supinely the approach of ruin, Dr Seipel at last resolved to trade part of his country's independence in return for its survival at all. 'Now was seen,' said one commentator, 'the hitherto unparalleled spectacle of an Austrian Chancellor touring Europe offering his country to the highest bidder.'

Seipel's tour embraced each of Austria's neighbours in turn, and was a subtle diplomatic prelude to his moving appeal made to the League of Nations in Geneva in early September. To this body he demonstrated conclusively that without financial help the Austria established by the Treaty of St Germain would fall to bits; and he announced that Vienna was prepared to accept whatever degree of discipline the League might require in putting her house in order. The pistol at the League's head was less the horror of Austrian disintegration than the threat of an Austrian customs union, not to mention some politically stronger entity, with one or other of her neighbours – Germany, Bavaria, Italy, or the Danube States – which was speedily becoming the only other viable solution of any kind. That Austria might become an Italian protectorate, part of a Greater Italy, gave France particular cause to think twice.

The entire position changed miraculously as negotiations with the League began. The krone which reached its nadir on August 25 rose a little, from 350,000 to 335,000 to the pound, in the first week of September – and there, helped by the confidence which the talks engendered, the government managed to hold it. The Geneva Protocols were prepared within a month. One guaranteed Austria's political and territorial integrity; a second provided for Britain, France, Italy and Czechoslovakia to underwrite an Austrian loan of 650 million gold kronen; and a third pledged Austria to put her finances straight, to cease discounting Treasury bills, and to set up a new bank of issue. The whole was to be guaranteed by investing absolute financial power in a Commissioner-General appointed by the League.

After Austria's price index reached its maximum on September

15, 1922, prices fell continuously until the end of the year, losing 20 per cent in that time. More remarkably, after September 2 the value of the krone against the dollar never fluctuated again, despite the fact that the inflation of the money supply continued for another two-and-a-half months and the note circulation more than trebled. Until mid-November when the new Austrian National Bank was set up and the proceeds came through from a short-term internal loan loyally subscribed by Austria's bankers, the deficit on State expenditure was covered by the printing press. Living on credit inspired by the hopes aroused in Geneva, the government was walking the thinnest of tightropes.

The post-stabilisation inflation, an oxymoronic situation noted with interest by economists of the period, sprang from the need to replace with krone-notes the large number of foreign banknotes in circulation. There was also a genuine shortage of cash which the printing press had physically been unable to make good: in August 1922 the amount circulating represented a little more than 80 million gold crowns, compared with the 500 million which had circulated before the war (albeit under somewhat different circumstances) in the same area. Two factors contributed to the lowering of prices: that they no longer had to be exorbitant to ensure profitability; and that since the market for goods had been saturated during an extended spending spree prices naturally fell with demand.

After the middle of November, when the success of the operation was becoming evident to all at home and abroad, the government's policy was primarily to prevent any *improvement* in the value of the krone. Vienna had already witnessed the distressing effect on Czechoslovakia when her finances had been rudely deranged by speculative buying of the Czech crown in Germany. Austria by 1922 'had become so geared to continuous depreciation that stabilisation alone was enough to create an acute economic crisis. The government's need was for kronen; and these were issued against the foreign currency received from either domestic or foreign sources, the foreign currency going to swell the bank's reserves. The bank was in fact obliged to buy more foreign notes than it needed.

The speed with which confidence and stability, although no degree of prosperity, were restored in Vienna indicated the extent to which Austria's particular problem had been mainly psychological and administrative. The population of Austria from the beginning had always shown a profound distrust in themselves and in their government, and an equally childlike reliance on foreign help and control. In large measure this was perhaps because the void of traditional authority which the revolution had swept away, creating simultaneous disenchantment among the impoverished official and ruling classes, remained lamentably unfilled.

Dr Seipel, needless to say, came under the strongest attack from his political opponents for having bartered for gold the sovereignty of the new Republic; but the Socialists were finally silenced in mid-October by Mussolini's *coup* in Italy, which raised for them the bogey of a fascist Austria if the League loan did not go through: *fascismo* was currently a popular cause among many Austrians. The League finance committee, however, understood at once that no Austrian government would be strong enough in parliament to effect the kind of economies necessary or to extricate the country unassisted from difficulties which ranged from the promise of anarchy to the threat of famine. The short-term internal loan which established the new bank was followed at once by a short-term international loan which more and more countries hurried to guarantee; and Austria settled down to wait for the long-term international credits which were still under discussion. Dr Zimmermann,* the League's Commissioner-General, arrived in Vienna in the middle of December 1922, and began at once to create and maintain the economic conditions which the Geneva Protocols demanded, recognising how much Austria by herself had already done in stabilising the currency to make that task easier.

The priority was to set in reverse a system which, based on a mixture

---

* Dr A.R. Zimmermann, formerly the Burgomaster of Rotterdam.

of political expedience and Socialist benevolence, was the negation of economics. Vienna was found to contain more State employees as a capital of a Republic of six-and-a-half million persons than as the capital of a monarchy of 50 million. Tax collection was entirely ineffective, and all State enterprises ran at a huge loss. The railway deficit of £6 million a year, one third of the national shortfall, arose not only from overmanning but from undercharging. Each mile of railway had three men to operate it against two in Switzerland; and while railway employees' wages had risen with the cost of living index, rail tariffs were at one-fifth of what they should have been to supply the corresponding revenue. Ministries, railways, the post office – all needed drastic pruning and reformation. The subsidies paid out were of startling munificence. Less than half of the users of the railways paid the full fare. This bankrupt country was even supplying cigars to the population at far below the cost of production.

However, alone of the former Central Powers, Austria's finances were now plainly on the mend. As public confidence returned despite the soaring unemployment, some of the great quantity of hoarded foreign currency flowed back into the market. Here at last was a base on which the country could build; or rather, as the independence on outside assistance had to be so vast, on which a country could be built.

By the spring of 1922 in the scale of financial and commercial disorder, Hungary, the other rump of the Dual Monarchy of the Hapsburgs,* was midway between Germany and Austria. As an agrarian country, her problems were different from either, for she possessed in theory enough to live on and something to spare. Considering her fundamentally promising physical condition, it was remarkable how faithfully Hungary followed the same path as her former allies towards financial disaster.

Between 1913 and the end of 1921, the currency in circulation

---

* Hungary had lost all her best territory under the Treaty of Trianon, keeping only 14 comitats out of 64. In the British Foreign Office itself it was admitted squarely although not publicly that 'reparations on top of that are a bit much'.

increased by 64 times. An average number of domestic articles purchased in 1914 for 100 korona now cost 8,260. Before the war, in the area which constituted the new Hungary, State revenue had been about one-tenth greater than expenditure: three years after the Armistice, expenditure was one-third higher than revenue. By 1921 the dislocation of normal monetary standards resulting from war, revolution, counter-revolution, Red Terror then White Terror, and at last Admiral Horthy's regency had brought about so great a feeling of despondency that the usual thought of anyone with money was to convert it into more stable assets – foreign currency, industrial stock, antiques or jewellery. As in Germany and Austria, speculation on the Stock Exchange was rife in every class, with all categories of share bought and sold, and the rate of various currencies eagerly watched from day to day.

The Finance Minister, Dr Hegedüs, openly regarded it as his first task in 1921 to stop the flight from the korona. Although it was at 2,100 to the pound in January, he would, he claimed, stabilise it at 400. As a matter of fact, six weeks after the Emperor Karl's first attempt to regain the throne of Hungary in April 1921, the rate against the pound was brought as low as 800. The Hegedüs reforms, however, might have been better spread over a decade than over nine months, and were so draconian as eventually to lead to his resignation in September. The 29 finance Bills passed by the National Assembly during his regime included a 20 per cent levy on capital and fierce fiscal attacks on 'war fortunes', shares, luxuries of all sorts, and property – Bills which were greeted with consternation or joy according to who was affected by them. A grave psychological mistake was committed by the embargo on the removing of 20 per cent of bank deposits, because the public, especially the peasants, thereafter became averse to confiding their savings to any financial institutions and hoarded them at home to the consequent dearth of currency.

Dr Hegedüs ascribed his failure to the fall of the German mark, to the poor harvest, and to the uncertainty about reparations. But his last act was to secure a vote of 960 million krone (£600,000) to increase the salaries of civil servants which had fallen far behind ordinary labourers' wages; and this measure became the official reason for the new inflation and the new depreciation as the printing presses started up again in earnest for the first time since March.

Dr Hegedüs's financial policy had affected Hungarian trade in a textbook manner. As the korona appreciated in the spring of 1921, unemployment, till then negligible, grew markedly because the goods and raw materials purchased when the overseas rate of the korona was at 2,000 to the pound could not be disposed of except at great loss when it improved to 800. As the korona improved, in other words, the position of merchants and manufacturers worsened; and when Hegedüs resigned and the korona fell a sigh of relief rose from the commercial world and work was restored to the industrial workless. On the other hand, the temporary rise had been profoundly welcomed by the official classes and others on fixed incomes. By contrast, the peasantry (two-thirds of the population) on the whole viewed it all with indifference as they were always able to sell their produce at something close to the world market price: possibly they were better off than any similar body in Europe.

In the last months of 1921 the government had to face again the survival problems of the official classes. Supplying them with food and other necessities at less than the cost price produced only slight alleviation. A high official such as an under-secretary of State, for example, still received his pre-war salary of 2,000 korona a month, sufficient in pre-war terms for a life of moderate luxury and enough to let him bring up and educate his family. Although aided now with subsidies worth 3,000 korona a month, he could not even exist on less than 20,000. This last sum, bringing in the equivalent of £120 a year in September 1921 (just before Karl's second attempt on Budapest), was worth less than £70 a year by Christmas. Clerical work, also remunerated at a fraction of pre-war rates, left its practitioners correspondingly miserable.

Mr Hohler,* the British High Commissioner in Budapest, reported:

> Under such circumstances one could scarcely be surprised were
> bribery rampant: and it says much for the Hungarian civil servants
> that cases of officials being corrupted are comparatively speaking
> rare. The official and cultured classes are by far the worst off.
> Reticence prevents ascertaining what proportion is actually in need.
> The sale rooms, however, indicate the straits to which so many are
> reduced.

Even so, many of the 'official' class, especially its younger members,
were finding outlets for their feelings in the mischievous activities of the
secret societies, most of which were violently anti-Semitic. These societies
attracted support, too, from the younger Army officers who also needed
a cause to work for and someone to blame for their poverty.

In June 1922 the days had passed when a Finance Minister might
have brought order to the Hungarian budget. Since January the note
issue had increased by 28 per cent, the price index by 36 per cent,
and the external depreciation of the korona by between 52 and 75 per
cent – the spread representing the disparity within a single June week.
In mid-June a pound would buy 4,500 korona, a reflection, stated the
new Finance Minister, Dr Kallay, of the financial state of Germany and
Austria. As in Germany, it was not supposed that the printing press
had much to do with the rate of depreciation, the orthodox financial
circles blaming the 'lack of confidence in Zurich' and asserting that
as the depreciation was so much greater than the increase in the note
issue, the latter could at most be a contributory factor to the former.
Again, the fact that for many months depreciation abroad consistently
preceded rather than followed fresh issues of currency led Hungary's
financial authorities to overlook the effect on Zurich of the knowledge
that the budgetary deficit would always be made good with paper, and

* Later Sir Thomas Hohler, born 1871, died 1946.

that notes would always be issued to satisfy the demand for currency which followed every increase in prices. In any event, no more than the German did the Hungarian government suppose that stabilisation was possible while the reparations debt remained unknown. The circulation had doubled in the year since the Treaty of Trianon was at long last ratified.

At the end of June 1922 appreciable unrest was brewing and the number of cost-of-living protests growing. Strikes by Budapest's 'municipal scavengers' and sewage-pumpers were bought off in the general round of wage increases granted at rates between 12 and 75 per cent. Dr Kallay professed himself irresistibly driven towards increasing the issues of paper money, whatever its dangers, so long as no break was in prospect in the spiral of rising prices and increased wages. Accordingly the korona which reached 6,000 to the pound on July 17 went to 7,000 a week later (it had already fallen substantially in sympathy with the mark after Rathenau's death), and the price of food moved up in step. New wage demands arrived at once.

The greater part of the nation's wealth, in the meantime, was being produced by the farming community whose taxes, despite the efforts of Dr Hegedüs, were the same in money terms as before the war, which was to say less than one-two-hundredth in real terms. This fiscal inequity would alone have been enough to intensify the enmity between urban, industrial and commercial circles on the one hand and the farmers and property owners on the other. However, the going financial opportunities encouraged the farmer to hold back his crops for as long as possible in order to create an unsatisfiable demand for them and a further increase in the average price. Hungary's doom was largely self-created.

The devaluation of the korona continued with alarming rapidity. September, when the note circulation rose by 25 per cent over the August figure and the korona dropped to 11,000 to the pound, found the Finance Ministry explaining that the latest banknote increases should not cause any depreciation because they merely reflected the increase in the country's assets with the gathering of the harvest; and that the currency newly issued would itself be gathered in as soon as the annual crop was distributed. Whether it sprang from cant or wishful thinking, the hope was vain, for it was not possible to move the harvest at the price.

In some panic the government set up an office for the control of foreign exchange – a *Devisenzentrale* on the Austrian model – in order to ward off financial disaster. While what were called its '*Kinderkrankheiten*', its teething troubles, persisted it made the situation greatly worse. Having fixed a rate of exchange for the korona below its market value and being thus unable to induce the holders of foreign currency to part with it, the office found itself without the means to help merchants to pay their foreign creditors. Previously traders had sold overseas on the basis of the exchange rate for the day, covering immediately in their creditors' currency. Under the new regulations each application for foreign money came before a badly organised office, and was delayed as much as two weeks – after which because of the shortage only a proportion of the application could be granted. Foreign trade therefore quickly slowed down, and this led to more unemployment.

By November, on the other hand, with the korona held artificially steady at 12,000 to the pound, Hungary's *Devisenzentrale* was working smoothly enough, and speculators were reported to be disgusted with it since the opportunity had gone of rigging the korona's price abroad. Exchange speculation had immediately given way to Stock Exchange speculation and a wild stampede to buy industrial shares. Shares quoted at 8,000 korona in the spring soared to 100,000 and more; and companies seeing their chance began to increase their capital and water their stock. The public went on spending; and it was remarked that even conservative investors had no idea of retaining their new holdings (whose dividends were ridiculously small in relation to the outlay) but rather of making a profit and selling out at the expense of their less astute compatriots. However, two months of an almost steady currency, combined with the preventive laws against exchange speculation, thereafter forced speculators to realise their share holdings. Quotations began to fall again, and many were badly bitten.

The watching public, too poor to gamble, can have had little heart to rejoice at that spectacle. Although the korona was firm, prices went on rising, adding 60 per cent in the two months before November 1. On November 13 the government raised rail fares and freight charges substantially, a move which had direct and fierce consequences for prices in general. 'All classes,' wrote Hohler, 'have completely lost any sense of proportion so far as costs are concerned. A Hungarian who merely shrugs his shoulders and murmurs something about the Treaty of Trianon when charged 5,000 kronen for a bottle of *vin mousseux* is exasperated by a rise of 5 kronen in the price of tram tickets.'

Hohler provided the Foreign Office with a detailed break-down of how the Hungarians were reacting to their new financial burdens. State officials, he said, had been extremely hard hit, unable to strike, and kept alive only because their still meagre salaries were supplemented by certain privileges such as nominal rail fares and the right to buy some of their needs cheaply. Even so, it was 'difficult to understand how those of them unable illicitly to *profiter de l'occasion* manage to exist'. Army officers were scarcely better off. A major, for example, who was paid 575 korona a week before the war now received 17,000 a week (or about £1 10s), whereas he would need 184,000 a week to regain his former spending power. In real terms a lieutenant was obliged to make do with one pound a week and a corps commander with about £2 5s. Married officers received a wife and child allowance of 3,500 korona a month (6s) per head.

Except for the lucky few who had capital in neutral countries, the rentier classes presented 'a most distressing picture'. The younger and the active had found work, but the older were destitute. The professional classes, the doctors and the lawyers, as in Germany and Austria were suffering from a shortage of patients and clients, but could adjust their charges to some extent – although the medical profession was not helped by all hospitals' having been denuded of the most elementary and necessary appointments from beds to bedpans. Professional men on fixed salaries had been 'reduced to absolute penury'. Clerks, who formed a highly important class in the capital, had entirely inadequate salaries ranging from 12,000 to 20,000 a month (a rate between £12 and £19 a year), shrinking all the time; but most could still get their luncheons for a nominal figure, supplied by their offices, so that body and soul could just be kept together. However, for those with families to feed 'the 60 per cent rise in prices for this class does not bear dwelling upon'.

Workers with trade unions to support them were, as usual, not so badly off, their pay being revised from time to time. Nevertheless they were not exactly fortunate. Whereas in 1914 it required 80 hours of work to buy a suit of clothes and in 1919 141 hours, by July 1922 381 hours were needed. Similarly, the hours required to buy a dozen eggs had moved from one to three, and for a kilo of bread from half to two.

In the countryside the landowners and farmers were less affected than anyone, producing most of their own essentials and putting up commodity prices as regularly as the shopkeepers. Landless peasants were not doing so well, and the large number of casual labourers whose wanderings had been limited by the new confines of Hungary formed a particularly destitute class. Hohler's account concluded with the comment that many were thriving in the economic crisis and were responsible for the superficial atmosphere of prosperity which Budapest presented – notably, he thought, the Jews who made up much of the capital's population.

It was clear as Christmas 1922 approached and as prices rose beyond the power of most of the urban classes to cope that the crisis could not be long delayed, nor support for the korona usefully continued. With the secret organisations growing in power, extreme nationalism burgeoning, and anti-Semitism in evidence even in official circles, Hungary was near the brink.

8: Autumn Paper-chase

Only the country people were surviving in Germany in any comfort: anyone who lived off the land had the readiest access to real values. It was not surprising that even when they ensured that the money receipts for their goods were no more than equivalent in purchasing power to what they were used to, they were accused of extortion – the more so if they delayed the sales of produce in the full knowledge that prices would be higher the longer they waited.

Erna von Pustau went to stay in the country and asked her hosts bluntly what they were doing with all the money they were squeezing out of the townspeople. They replied candidly that they were paying off their mortgages. The principle of *Mark gleich Mark* had helped agriculture enormously: for the country people, landowners, farmers or peasants, life had started again. At the end of August 1922 when the mark passed 2,000 to the dollar – 9,000 to the pound – a mortgage of seven or eight years' standing had been 399/400ths paid off. When Frau von Pustau returned home

> the talk in the family was about prices going up, about the credits which had to be reduced, about the middle-class party, about big business and the workers who always asked for more … The contrast between country and city was so enormous that it cannot be understood by people who have not lived through it.

Herr Hans-Georg von der Osten, who had formerly flown with Baron von Richthofen's Flying Circus and was later for a short time Goering's Aide-de-Camp (ADC) until he shot the Reichsmarschall's favourite stag, recollects that in February 1922, with a loan from a friendly banker, he bought an estate neighbouring his own property in Pomerania for 4 million marks (then equivalent to about £4,500). He paid the debt in the autumn with the sale of less than half the crop of one of his potato fields. In June of the same year, when prices were shooting up ahead of the mark, he bought 100 tons of maize from a dealer for 8 million marks (then about £5,000). A week later, before it was even delivered, he sold the whole load back to the same dealer for double the amount, making 8 million marks without raising a finger. 'With this sum,' he said, 'I furnished the mansion house of my new estate with antique furniture, bought three guns, six suits, and three of the most expensive pairs of shoes in Berlin – and then spent eight days there on the town.'

This was simple commerce: the only thing to do with cash by that time was to turn it into something else as quickly as possible. To save was folly. Undoubtedly, however, as in Austria, there were many farmers who behaved outrageously. Dr Schacht's account of the inflationary years recalled that farmers 'used their paper marks to purchase as quickly as possible all kinds of useful machinery and furniture – and many useless things as well. That was the period in which grand and upright pianos were to be found in the most unmusical households.' Anyone who was alive to the realities of inflation, he said, could safeguard himself against losses in paper currency by buying assets which would maintain their value: houses, real estate, manufactured goods, raw materials and so forth.

> Wholesale recourse to real values enabled not only the well-to-do but also, and especially, the unscrupulous to preserve and even possibly to increase their assets ... As a result of this struggle for self-enrichment and financial self-preservation, based on exploitation of the ignorance of the masses, every aspect of business life was vitiated.

To condemn the individual's struggle for survival in such chaotic circumstances as either selfish, or unnatural, or wrong, was in many ways unjust. When people do not understand what is happening, or why it is happening, and have no idea about what to do about it, and are not told, panic must follow. Even so, that the countrypeople were behaving naturally brought no comfort to townspeople who had no goods to barter, and whose incomes remained static.

A Hesse professor lamented as September came that professors, teachers and men of science were no longer given the right to live, and many would probably die in the coming winter for lack of food and warmth. He feared that their sons, instead of following their fathers' careers, as they had done for generations past, would by force of circumstances turn to manual labour to earn their bread.

It was obviously possible to be over-pessimistic: earning bread by manual labour over a critical period need not bind one permanently to that activity. Yet the professor's complaints showed the despondency to which the academic world had been reduced:

> Labour, wholly or partially educated labour, has already begun to rule in Germany, and there is no demand for brains: that is to say, brains have no longer a marketable value. The result can only be a catastrophe for Germany and the downfall of civilisation in central Europe if not, indeed, the whole world.

Already, however, a new element had joined the economic crisis. For the first time the wages paid for labour began to lag behind the rise in prices, noticeably and seriously, in spite of everything the monopoly of the unions could do about it. President Ebert, pleading with Curzon to engineer a further moratorium on reparations, pointed out that the conditions of existence for the working population had become 'completely impossible', and that the downfall of Germany's economic life was imminent.

A litre of milk, which had cost 7 marks in April 1922 and 16 in August, by mid-September cost 26 marks. Beer had climbed from 5.60 marks a litre to 18, to 30. A single egg, 3.60 in April, now cost 9 marks. In only nine months, Mr Seeds's chauffeur's weekly bill for an identical food basket had risen from 370 marks to 2,615.

> The rise of nearly 100 per cent within the last four weeks [reported the consul] has proceeded by such sudden leaps and bounds that no scheme for a simultaneous increase in wages can well be devised to cope with it: an increase of wages granted at the end of one week would not meet the rise in prices by the following Tuesday, for instance, and the working and salaried classes have suffered severely despite their continually increasing remuneration ... The wage situation is hopelessly dislocated at present.

On September 9 the financial authorities announced that in the previous ten days 23 milliard marks had been printed and distributed, representing 10 per cent of the total circulation of paper in the country. 'The daily production of the Federal printing press,' the newspapers dutifully recorded, 'has now risen to 2.6 milliards of paper marks. In the course of this month it will be increased to almost 4 milliards of paper marks, at which figure it is hoped the shortage of money will be definitely overcome.'

Shortage of liquid cash, indeed, was acute, and the July emergency money law was coming into its own. Large industrial concerns began to pay their workmen partly in notes and partly in coupons of their own, which were accepted by local tradesmen on the understanding that they would be redeemed within a very short time. Municipalities, too, started to issue their own currencies, aware that any delay in receiving their pay packets would dangerously aggravate workers whose main concern was to spend them before they depreciated. The cities and towns developed a parallel fear of unemployment which on a large scale might lead to outbreaks of Communist-inspired disorder, and so began artificially to create employment for their staff. The citizens of Frankfort noted with alarm that large tracts of quite serviceable road were being repaired outside the town and that the overhead system of telephone wires was being converted into an underground one.

The Reichsbank's September plans were duly fulfilled, but as by the second week in October the mark seemed to be entering a state of free fall, having moved from 9,000 to 13,000 to the pound in six weeks, the hopes that the demand for ready money would be met were as speedily dashed. Professor Keynes's prediction 15 months earlier that the mark would fall by a point a day until it reached 1,000 to the pound had been out by a factor of 13 in less than two-thirds of the time. He now wrote in the *Manchester Guardian* of September 29 that 2 milliard gold marks a year (£100 million) was the maximum that Germany could be expected to pay in reparations, that beyond that sum was to be 'in the realm of phantasy', and that there could be no certainty that even that amount could be paid. He described France's demand of over 3 milliards a year as based on the 'fallacy, which deceives many Frenchmen, that the extremity of France's need enlarges Germany's capacity'. In the meantime, however, Keynes, who was promptly invited with other independent experts to Germany to advise on measures to arrest the mark's fall, considered a 'breathing space' was essential before payments were resumed in even a modest way.

Albert Einstein, too, had views on the reparation problem as the fundamental cause of the mark's illness, and forwarded to Lord Haldane an article from the *Berliner Tageblatt* suggesting that Britain and France participate in German industry to the extent of 30 per cent of the share capital. Einstein, who desired Haldane to arrange 'so that my name shall not be given publicity in connection with this matter', considered it a happy solution.

Alas for everyone's hopes. Einstein's recommendation bore no fruit; and when in November the experts' report was published, suggesting a sensible programme of monetary stabilisation (at about 14,000 to the pound), budgetary equilibrium, foreign loans, and temporary relief from reparation charges, it too was totally ignored by debtor and creditor alike. There was, it is true, a good deal else to preoccupy them. In Britain that October Lloyd George's coalition government was displaced by a Conservative administration under Bonar Law. In Italy, Mussolini staged his *coup*.

At home in Germany, where people were resorting to trade by barter and progressively turning to foreign currencies as the only reliable medium of exchange, new Orders were brought in relating to the purchase of foreign bills and the use of foreign exchange to settle inland payments. In addition to imprisonment, fines could now be imposed of up to ten times the amount of an illegal deal. Further to prevent the flight of capital, its transfer from then on had to be authorised – not just notified – and the transactions of importers were to be closely regulated. These moves, unfortunately, apart from making legitimate trade more difficult, took no account of the fact that speculation could still be pursued in foreign stock exchanges, and were thus unlikely to prevent the mark's downward course.

In Oldenburg in an attempt to offer a safe investment to the public as an alternative to foreign currency 'rye bills' (*Roggenmarks*) were issued by the state bank, due for repayment in 1927. The issue price was the current value of 125 kilograms of rye, and repayment was to be in line with the average price of 150 kilograms of rye in the first quarter of the later year, the extra 25 kilograms representing four years' interest. The bills were bearer bonds, complete with stock exchange quotations and secured by the bank's total funds.

In the meantime, September's 26-mark litre of milk became October's 50-mark litre. Butter at 50 marks a pound in April could be had for 480. In two months the price of an egg had doubled to 14 marks. A pocket comb cost 2,000 marks; a pot of honey 8,000; a pair of child's trousers 5,000; a dozen kitchen plates 7,500; a pair of silk stockings 16,500; a roll of lavatory paper 2,000; a pair of children's shoes 2,800. Three masses for a relation, however, were still available at the old price of 150.

The deputies in the Bavarian Landtag vied with one another, irrespective of their political colour, in urging the central government to send relief for the state's poor, hundreds of thousands of whom, it seemed, were threatened with starvation. Their plight was made the more poignant with the arrival of the *Oktoberfest*, Munich's great annual three-week fair at which gargantuan quantities of beer and pork are consumed – and are sold at very high prices at the best of times. As the mark dropped away from 9,000 to 12,000 to 18,000 to the pound, as beer rose from 30 marks a litre to 78, merrymakers from the countryside, celebrating their harvest, became the objects of political denunciation in place of the tourists who had mostly gone home. Mr Seeds commented in the Munich consulate:

> The deputies are thoroughly justified in speaking of the excesses of the fair with bitter condemnation, but a foreign observer who noticed that the thousands and thousands of revellers were composed solely of the working and lower middle classes, would be justified in doubting the existence of the much advertised starving population. Except where certain sections of the middle classes are concerned, it is difficult to resist the feeling that the food subsidies are merely a means of passing on to the taxpayer a portion of the wages which should be paid by the industrialists.

Stinnes himself, that eponym of capitalist ruthlessness, at a meeting with British businessmen in Cologne in November 1922 was asked how long Germany's industrialists were prepared to see this state of affairs go on. He replied that they would try to carry on as long as they could – 'if necessary until the day after the French government makes up its mind to pursue a policy of understanding'. Stinnes was apt to seize any opportunity to drive a wedge between France and Britain, but probably genuinely regarded as secondary importance to the risk of unemployment the actual point to which the mark might sink. 'With a central government without power or authority, with acute economic distress, and with revengeful neighbours ready to fish in troubled waters,' he asserted, 'we will do everything in our power to keep our workmen employed.'

Sure enough, in the Ruhr, numerous factories were using various devices to avoid having to put men out on the streets. Bochumer Verein, in Essen, for example, engaged 1,500 men making stock articles for railways although there was no immediate requirement for them. Such measures, however, were only possible for firms with big financial reserves, and small firms were already dismissing workers in small numbers. With the November price increases – butter at 800 marks a lb., eggs at 22 marks each – shops were also cutting down on assistants because sales were dropping off.

The disparity between the rise in the cost of living and the rise in wages had now become very marked. Whereas since the war the former had gone up by about 1,500 times, the wages of the miner – in November 1922 the best paid worker – had gone up by barely 200 times. With the mark in mid-November at 27,000 to the pound and 6,400 to the dollar, and with prices following the course of both with unfailing regularity, not only were wages in general failing to keep pace but the workers were not even being paid what was their due. Owing to the shortage of paper money of all kinds, federal currency or *Notgeld*, they were finding that by the time the balance was paid it had lost 50 per cent of its value. The best-paid workers were unable to purchase the barest necessities of life. The others and – as ever – those on fixed incomes or dependent on savings suffered accordingly.

That suffering was acute and, although worse was to come, was only the culmination of many months of increasing misery. Conditions in Berlin may not have been typical of every urban community in the country, but were at least indicative of the general distress. The figures issued by the chief burgomaster of Pankow for 1922 showed that nearly 25 per cent of the children leaving school were below the normal spread of weights and heights, and 30 per cent were unfit to work for reasons of health. In Schöneberg, where in 1913 8 per cent of school leavers had been tubercular, the figure was 15 per cent. 'Want,' said the burgomaster's report, 'is gradually strangling every feeling for neatness, cleanness, and decency, leaving room only for thoughts of the fight with hunger and cold.'

The failure of wages to keep pace with prices, and the consequent impoverishment of even the most fortunate workers, had a direct effect upon the trade unions. Owing to the tumbling value of union funds and the impossibility in such hard times of raising subscription, ordinary strikes became less and less practicable. Union leaders, by the same token, became less able to extract and deliver the higher wages which the workers and their situation demanded, and so lost first their influence and then – although they would not admit it – their control. In an increasingly nervous state, they were finding it necessary to make repeated appeals to their members to maintain discipline and abide by union decisions.

The workers, on the other hand, became easily roused by extremist factions, and were liable to get out of hand and start rioting, especially when they believed that the greatest achievement of the Revolution, the eight-hour day, was under attack from the big industrials. Since there were many local authorities who would not have hesitated to fire on a rioting mob, the mixture was unusually volatile. In the third week of November, there were serious collisions between the police and a crowd of angry workers after the employees at the Mannesmann works demanded a 100 per cent wage increase and tried unsuccessfully – though with Communist encouragement – to declare a general strike in the city. A similar manifestation occurred in Cologne. In Dresden there was a fierce outbreak against the cost of living, with provision shops looted and damage estimated at 100 million marks; and a noisy display of xenophobia before the principal hotels which habitually housed the foreigners whose presence in the country was popularly supposed to be the cause of the rise in prices. In Braunschweig there were food riots and shop-plundering, and more food riots in Berlin. Most of these were controllable, but all were symptomatic of general distress and unrest.

The gold value of the money in circulation, equivalent to nearly £300 million before the war, and to £83 million in July 1922, had by November fallen to £20 million. The more notes were printed, the lower the value fell – illustrating the Copernican thesis expounded by King Sigismund of Poland in 1526 that 'money loses its value when it has become too much multiplied'. How the business of the country could be carried on with so small an amount of real currency mystified many observers, and accounted for the ever-mounting pressures on the bank to go on printing. That trade continued notwithstanding was usually explained by reference to the accelerating velocity with which money circulated. Notes were held for as short a time as possible. Private-account cheques were hardly accepted. Anyone receiving money for goods quickly converted it back into other goods, and the money never stopped moving, doing the work of ten times the amount moving a tenth as fast.

Chancellor Wirth's government broke down under the strain in mid-November, and as that month passed away the mark fell to 30,000, 32,000, 34,000 to the pound – 8,000 to the dollar. The Reichsbank had proclaimed, and was now carrying out, a programme of unlimited printing of notes. More and more printing presses were employed for the work, and by December the amount issued was limited only by the capacity of the presses and the physical fatigue of the printers. Lord D'Abernon reported to London: 'The exchange market and the Reichsbank are like a runaway horse with an incompetent rider – each aggravates the folly of the other'; or, as he described it in another happy burst of metaphor: 'In the whole course of history, no dog has ever run after its own tail with the speed of the Reichsbank. The discredit the Germans throw on their own notes increases even faster than the volume of notes in circulation. The effect is greater than the cause. The tail goes faster than the dog.'

Scarcity of money was one of the reasons for the precipitous drop in real terms – though not, of course, in money terms – of industrial shares. Towards the end of the summer, in terms of gold, they had fallen to about one-tenth of their pre-war value, a substantial loss for consistent holders of these securities, although nothing like that suffered by those who held War Loan and other fixed interest stock whose values were wiped out. In August the *Berliner Tageblatt* assessed the total value of all German companies at not more than 4 milliard gold marks (about £200 million), and said, while pointing to the danger that their shares might systematically be bought up by foreigners, that 'the picture of German industrial prosperity is widely different from that current in certain organs of the London and Paris press'.

In nominal terms, a basket of shares of companies which had not inflated or otherwise altered their peace-time capital had risen between July 1914 and July 1922 by 13.4 times. They included mining shares (Gelsenkirchen, up from 181 to 1,374; Muhlheimer, up from 155 to 1,990), and a broad spectrum of industry (Schwelmer Eisenwerk, from 135 to 2,800; Deutsche Waffen- und Munitions-fabriken, from 331 to 1,605; Kammgarnspinnerei Düsseldorf, from 131 to 2,550; Hotelbetriebs Berlin, from 136 to 2,100; Anglo-Continentale Guanowerke, from 119 to 1,776). But that rise compared with a 143-fold rise in the value of the gold mark against the paper one. At the end of the war the share price index had fallen in real terms to about one-third of its 1913 level. The year 1921 saw it at one-fifth. In October 1922 it dropped to three-hundredths, at which point it was a popular felicity that the Daimler Motor Company, factories, lands, reserves, capital and organisation, could have been swapped for the price of 327 of its cars. Demand for shares was small, too, because the average dividend yield on equities was only a quarter per cent – for the biggest shareholders preferred it so – and there were many less unsatisfactory ways of getting a return on capital when that was wanted.

The Report of the Deutsche Bank for 1921 showed clearly how greatly inflation had reduced the gold value of dividends, in contrast to the illusion of prosperity which high paper dividends caused. The bank's paper turnover of 2,125 milliards in 1921 had a real value of 85 milliard gold marks. In 1913, when the bank's ramifications were less extensive, the turnover had been 129 milliards. The 1922 dividend on a capital of 400 million was equivalent to 1.5 million gold marks, against the 25 million dividend distributed in 1913 at 12^1/$_2$ per cent on a capital of 200 million.

October 1922, however, was the nadir for shareholders. From then on not only did money find its way back into shares, but people who could obtain cheap credit, or were unable to send their money abroad, began to realise the advantages of buying up their own country's industrial and other assets at a fraction of their true value. Although in real terms the stock market began to go up, the mark's purchasing power continued to go down.

'By the end of the year,' said Erna von Pustau,

> my allowance and all the money I earned were not worth one cup of coffee. You could go to the baker in the morning and buy two rolls for 20 marks; but go there in the afternoon and the same two rolls were 25 marks. The baker didn't know how it happened ... His customers didn't know ... It had somehow to do with the dollar, somehow to do with the stock exchange – and somehow, maybe, to do with the Jews.'

Mr Seeds's chauffeur can have been no less confused. He and millions like him still instinctively regarded the mark as being as good as gold, failing to realise how desperately sick it had become. Milk which had cost him an unbelievable 78 marks a litre in the first week of November cost him 202 marks a month later. Butter had risen from 800 to 2,000 marks a lb.; sugar from 90 a lb. to 220; eggs from 22 each to 30. Although potatoes were still available for 8 marks a lb., an increase of only 1 mark, he had to pay 1,400 marks for 1 lb. of eatable sausages to go with them.

Issues of authorised *Notgeld* were now as common as Reichsbank paper over most of the country. These emergency notes could be printed in any denomination up to 500 marks, and in some cases up to 1,000 marks – the limits had to be regularly raised – and were redeemable in Reichsbank notes after two or three months. By the middle of November there were 40 issuing bodies in the occupied territories alone. They included industries as diverse as Anilin and Sodafabrik of Ludwigshafen, the Düsseldorf Landesbank, Stahlwerk Becker-Willich, and Linoleumfabrik-Maximiliansau – chemicals, banking, steel and flooring. The towns who were paying their employees with their own currency included Krefeld, Coblenz, Düsseldorf, Duisburg, Worms, Treves, Mayence, Bonn, and Cologne where the bills were signed by Konrad Adenauer.

It was against this background of exploding prices and a multiplying issue of national and local currency that the fourth London conference provided the curtain raiser to 1923, the year of the wheelbarrow. That meeting, itself a preliminary to another in Paris, met in December to consider whether a moratorium on reparations ought to be granted. It was remarkable not merely for the presence of Signor Mussolini representing Italy, but for M. Poincaré's firm announcement to Mr Bonar Law that, 'Whatever happens, I shall advance into the Ruhr on January 15.' It was France, not Britain who, in Sir Eric Geddes's famous phrase of 1918, was intent on getting 'everything out of Germany that you can get out of a lemon and a bit more', determined to 'squeeze her until you can hear the pips squeak'.

Lloyd George's opinion of Poincaré's proposals made in London four months earlier had been that they 'showed either a total inability to grasp even the alphabet of economic conditions governing payments from one country to another, or a sinister resolve to engineer a German default under the treaty which would justify an invasion of the Westphalian minefields with ulterior possibilities of detaching them from the German fatherland'.

Bonar Law, who fully appreciated that the stabilisation of the mark meant, for Germany, unemployment, an industrial crisis and enormous financial strain, whereas failure to stabilise meant catastrophe, was now equally unable to convince the French Prime Minister of the futility of amassing vast quantities of German paper marks by means of retortionary or extortionary measures. Already 1,500 milliards of them had been collected by the German customs on the Allied reparations account, which the Reparations Commission dared not cash because it would hardly get anything for them. Poincaré was obstinately sure, wrote Lloyd George, that the exploitation of the German forests could easily be carried out under the supervision of the Allied military authorities, and that it would be practical for them to control the Reichsbank and force up the value of the mark. The invasion of the Ruhr was to prove him tragically wrong. Whether it was intended to wreck Germany for ever or not, it was a policy that in time reduced the French franc to one-fifth of its pre-war value.

On December 10 the London conference received a Note from Germany's new Chancellor, Dr Wilhelm Cuno, suggesting various measures for stabilising the mark, including a two-year moratorium on reparation payments. The Note was rejected. Poincaré, insisting on 'productive pledges' from Berlin, was further angered just before Christmas by Germany's proposing a 30-year peace pact, which he regarded as no more than a manoeuvre.

Events moved inexorably on to the Paris conference and beyond. France and Great Britain parted brass rags on January 4. The French, Belgian and Italian members of the Reparation Commission with Britain dissenting decided on January 9, 1923, that Germany had been in voluntary default on her coal and timber deliveries under the peace treaty. There was then no legal way of preventing Poincaré from carrying out his threats, and the hope of America's interceding was vain. On January 10, indeed, the United States' occupying forces were withdrawn. On January 11 Poincaré despatched a control commission of engineers to the Ruhr 'for the purpose of securing deliveries', accompanied by troops 'for the protection of this commission and to ensure the execution of its mission'. For good measure, the French Prime Minister warned that, if necessary, sanctions and coercive measures would be used.

Ostensibly the purpose of the invasion of the Ruhr was, in the popular phrase, 'to bring Germany to her senses' and to compel her to pay up. How the temporary severance of her principal industrial region was to make it easier for her to do so remained unexplained. Lloyd George's opinion, strongly to be supported by the events of the summer, was that its true motive was to set up a Rhineland confederation friendly to France. He called it 'an act of military aggression against an unarmed nation that was as unjustified as it was to prove unprofitable'. It had one result fraught with long-term consequences – that of persuading many Germans that rearmament should be pursued at the earliest opportunity. Immediately, however, its effects on Germany were simultaneously dynamic and – in the dramatic sense – catastrophic. The country was scandalised. Lacking an army big enough to take counter-measures, she riposted in the only way that came to mind: the policy of passive resistance in the newly occupied areas.

The *Ruhrkampf*, as it was known, thus presented a tragically instructive economic picture. The industrial heart of Germany practically stopped beating. Hardly anyone worked: hardly anything ran. Coal mining never entirely stopped, some mine-owners pleading that reserves (which were always seized by the French) should be maintained. The population of the Ruhr area – 2 million workers, 6 million souls – had to be supported by the rest of the country. The German economy, however, called upon to subsidise an open-ended general strike, was not only denied its most important domestic products and raw materials – coal, coke, iron and steel in particular – but was robbed of its former enormous foreign earnings from Rhine-Ruhr exports. The Exchequer was itself deprived of all the normal tax revenue from a huge proportion of the nation's industry, as well as the coal tax and the income from the Ruhr railways. Furthermore, because of the Ruhr's international mineral importance, the world price of coal and steel, which Germany now had to import, proceeded to rise, increasing the difficulties still more.

Almost certainly the policy of passive resistance forced the invaders to act on a wider scale than they had contemplated. The French franc from then on moved sharply downwards and France's war indemnities drifted further off than ever. Yet France could not allow herself to lose the battle, any more than the German government could have capitulated before *force majeure*: the German nation would not have stood for it, least of all in the first months when the unity of purpose of all classes in the Ruhr so astonished everybody. Both sides were therefore totally committed in a holy war – and the German government knew of only one weapon. The Ruhr struggle was between French pressure and subversion on the one hand – it took many forms, economic, diplomatic, military, political – and the German printing press on the other. So long as paper banknotes were exchangeable for food, the fight would go on. When they were not, it did not.

Until the Ruhr invasion the reasons for the German inflation could have been put down, first, to the uncertainty of the aftermath of the war, and secondly, to the inexperience and weak acquiescence of the new men in power. Industry wanted neither heavy taxation nor to be hampered in its expansion at home or abroad: so the government gave way and replaced the missing revenue by printing it. Neither the industrialists nor the general public were prepared to pay the true costs of the railways, or of the post office, or even of bread: so the government understood, and printed the money to pay for them. Did Germany's nationals have claims arising out of the war, or, better, out of the peace treaty? Did one of the federal states, or the meanest district, look to Berlin to meet its financial requirements? The government printed notes to satisfy everyone, telling itself that as the granting of credit through cheques had so greatly decreased the actual currency in circulation had to be so much greater. The rich and the strong came off best.

One of the results of unlimited inflation had been the destruction of State credit abroad. At the end of 1922 other results were beginning to show. In consequence of Germany's strong competitive position, German goods again were available all over the world, although still in only a third of pre-war quantities: owing to everyone's spending most income as quickly as possible, Germany's home market had absorbed incredible amounts of the national product, to the greater short-term benefit of industry.

Since the middle of 1922, the problems of private payments and private credit, both in and outside the country, had become much more difficult; but the exporter was generally well placed in regard to restocking with raw materials, as he could use the proceeds of foreign sales. Comparison of various German exports, as for instance chemicals, earthenware or metalware, with those from other countries showed that German export prices were often ridiculously low; although part of the reason was that exporters were careful that their profits should not be made at the time of leaving Germany but on the subsequent resale, so evading the regulation by which foreign earnings had to be repatriated. Many export profits were thus immune from everything from capital levy to financial crash. On the other hand, those importing raw materials for selling on the home market were in a bad way. Exorbitant interest rates, at 25 per cent a month, and the universal shortage of money meant that normal commercial life was seriously hampered. It was enough that employers and employees were already in continual session fixing wage tariffs which were usually out of date as soon as they came into force, and that all internal values had become so distorted that confusion was complete at all levels of commerce.

Conditions in the motor trade reflected the difficulties of a manufacturing industry generally under the uncertainties of inflationary finance. The number of cars in the country in 1922, at one for every 360 people, was not great compared, say, to France (one for every 176), Britain (one for every 91), or the United States (one for every 10). But the scope for sales was correspondingly greater, and demand was very high. Foreigners, *nouveau riche* businessmen and, because it was found that cars were cheaper to maintain than horses, landed proprietors were usually the buyers: since the war, the gentleman owner who kept a car for the fun of it had practically disappeared. The cost of petrol, at 17 marks a litre (¹/₂d) in January 1922 was at 686 at the end of the year.

High demand availed the dealer little. The ten-horse-power car, for example, which (with lighting and starting sets, but no tyres, because they were generally purveyed separately) in January 1922 cost 220,000 marks (about £270), and in August cost 1.25 million, by January 1923 cost 11.4 million marks, or half, or twice as much depending upon which end of that frenzied month one bought it, the sterling price remaining much the same. Similarly, a four-ton motor lorry (without tyres, but with body, and with acetylene lighting) had risen in price between January 1922 and January 1923 from 265,000 marks (£320) to 12.9 million. Pneumatic tyres (one non-skid cover and one inner tube) had risen from 4,920 (£6) to 161,000 marks, and solid tyres even more, from 3,691 (£4 10s) to 202,095 marks apiece.

It was quite impossible to quote prices in advance, and customers themselves would not take the risk of committing themselves to the so-called 'gliding clause' in a contract: for otherwise, after payment of a non-returnable deposit, the final bill could be almost limitless, depending on the delivery date. As a result, dealers whose financial resources were already under enormous strain were constantly engaged in unpleasant correspondence with both clients and suppliers. Moreover, it took a long time for the trade to iron out the quarrel between dealer and manufacturer over the deposit paid by the one when ordering from the other: normally a third of the current price would have to be put down, but by the time of delivery, which was very slow, that deposit had become a minute proportion of the final price – and the manufacturers unfairly insisted that the full nominal balance should be met. In any case, throughout the trade it was being found that the sums realised from sales would not replace stocks.

The unsatisfactory conditions of internal commerce had their effect in persuading the Exchequer that an unbalanced budget had to be accepted. Revenue from taxation, export duties and customs dues in the last nine months of 1922 amounted to 324 milliard marks, or about £10 million at the current rate of exchange. Government expenditure over the same period, on the other hand, had come to 1,173 milliard marks, or about £40 million. The deficit had been made up by increasing the floating debt with note issues amounting to nearly 850 milliards. The very low levels in real terms of both expenditure and revenue showed how much the finances of a highly-industrialised nation of more than 60 million people had gone to pieces. Inside the country at Christmas time the mark was worth one-1,723rd of its pre-war value: outside the country it was worth only one-1,923rd.

In that unhealthy picture the government can have seen only two relatively bright patches. One was that the country's internal debt, to the distress of the stockholders, had dwindled to nothing. The other was the almost total absence of unemployment; but worklessness, of course, had been the Socialist government's greatest fear ever since the Army had started to disband, and that fear had been in large measure behind the inflationary policy.

Even in Bavaria, however, the close of 1922 for most people meant a return to wartime conditions. People were once more issued with bread and sugar cards, and supplies were doubly affected by the extreme shortage of fuel. For these privations the fall of the mark was the official excuse – but it was seldom believed, for prices were seen to rise equally steeply during periods of temporary currency stability. The coal shortage was attributed squarely by everyone to the Allies' demands in kind made under the peace treaty.

Apart from widows, pensioners, and the like, observed Mr Seeds, the population of Bavaria was not on the verge of starvation: the poorer quarters of English towns could have shown as many glaring cases of poverty. He thought the middle classes were still hard up rather than poverty-stricken – and out of a population of 7 million, a mere 16,000 were out of work. Bavaria, however, had become more than ever a forcing house for the reactionary movements, and the progress during the previous twelve months of the National Socialist Party had been one of the year's most remarkable features. Hitler's Storm Troops, the SA, founded in November 1921, numbered 6,000 within a year, and were permitted to train and manoeuvre alongside the Reichswehr.

'Formerly,' Mr Seeds reported to the Berlin Embassy,

> the NSDAP's existence was only known through enormous red placards, advertising public speeches to be delivered by Herr Hitler, which always closed with the notice 'No admission to Jews!' Anti-Semitism seemed the chief plank in his platform, but in general he was anti-everything: the Entente, the Reich government, the capitalists, the Bavarian government at times, the Socialists and the Communists – all were depicted in eloquent language as betrayers of the people. The public attitude was, at first, one of amusement; but as time went on and both political and economic conditions grew from bad to worse, the tendency arose to consider Hitler as the man who was always in the right.

Bit by bit, Seeds explained, the star of Hitler began to outshine the medals of Ludendorff. Economic salvation had become for most people the more pressing need. They were being turned from politics by the cost of living, poor wages and low salaries. Hitler alone was capable of trimming his ship to every wind; and, in a word, the middle class was going Nazi.

All this, and the Ruhr invasion too. As a result of the war Germany had lost nine-tenths of her merchant fleet and all her colonies. She had lost the coal and zinc of Upper Silesia, the potash of Alsace and the iron ore of Lorraine. She had lost to France the control of the Saar mines. She had lost more than 14 per cent of her cultivated land – 15 per cent of her former wheat crops and 18 per cent of her potatoes. All German capital held abroad had been confiscated.

Looking at it in its worst light – as Dr Stresemann was happy to do as Chancellor later that year when appealing for overseas aid – Germany was already an amputated corpse (he said) racked with bitterness, working only an eight-hour day, when the French and Belgian armies under General Degoutte moved in to claim their missing telegraph poles on January 11. The Ruhr basin in 1923 provided nearly 85 per cent of Germany's remaining coal resources, and 80 per cent of her steel and pig-iron production; accounted for 70 per cent of her traffic in goods and minerals; and contained 10 per cent of her population. The loss of the Ruhr's production, and all it implied, was therefore a bale of last straws. At 35,000 to the pound at Christmas 1922, the mark fell to 48,000 on the day after the invasion, and at the end of January 1923 touched 227,500, well over 50,000 to the dollar.

That was the moment when the Reichsbank circulated its first 100,000-mark note. Its purchasing power equalled a little more than two dollars, or ten shillings sterling: perhaps a tenth or a fifteenth of what its face-value must have been when it was on the drawing-board. It did not matter: a million-mark note was on the stocks and would be issued within another three weeks.

9: *Ruhrkampf*

It is a phenomenon of any national group that, almost however much it is riven with dissent, an external threat will unite it. By all accounts the entry of the French and Belgian armies into the Ruhr had a galvanising effect on a disintegrating German nation. As Tirpitz felt called upon to say in an unwelcome eulogy of the Anglo-Saxons, fate seemed to have assigned to France 'the historic role of welding the divergent forces of our people into unity again and again'. Not only did all Germany rally at once to the notion of supporting their brothers on the Rhine: the socio-political fever in the industrial areas itself subsided in a torrent of national passion directed against the common enemies.

A sudden absence of class hatred was a remarkable feature, helped by the willingness of some of the industrialists – notably some mine-owners and directors – to be arrested and imprisoned for non-cooperation along with their employees. They became national heroes. In Berlin, even the Left-wing Independent Socialist Party was happy to give its temporary support to the government of Cuno. Indeed, what was termed 'the revival of the national spirit' was a matter for universal comment. Only Ludendorff failed to cash in on the new awakening by taking the appeal for unity all the way to Vienna where, though still in desperate poverty despite the health of the krone, people remembered on which side their bread was buttered: he was greeted with shouts of 'To the gallows!' and 'Down with the murderer of millions!' and had to be smuggled back to his own country.

'All the old patriotic songs were sung,' said Erna von Pustau. 'Even Father gave money to help the Ruhr. Clothes were collected. The coal shortage began. We had cold houses again, but we were willing to suffer cold for our fatherland.'

With the absence – in prison or the unoccupied part of the country – of the managerial staff of the mines and forests, what had begun (ostensibly at least) as an administrative operation quickly escalated into a stark and often brutal military occupation. The Ruhr basin's Coal Syndicate was replaced with Franco-Belgian officials. The administration of forests, customs and export licences throughout the newly occupied area was taken over. A customs cordon was set up between the Rhine-Ruhr and unoccupied Germany, through which all coal exports were prohibited. The rail link between unoccupied Germany and Switzerland was cut, and French and Belgian personnel were introduced to the Ruhr state railways. With these alien operatives the German workers would have little to do, and their former management and officials suffered accordingly.

Within a fortnight of January 11, mayors, lord mayors, customs officers at all levels, police directors and commissioners, local councillors and revenue officers were being hounded out of their jobs and homes. The Chief Commissioner of Forests was dismissed, along with his assistant commissioners at Cleve, Speyer, Mainz and Treves. The director of the Wiesbaden chief customs house was replaced. In protest at the arrest of the Mayor of Essen, all shops and restaurants in the town were closed in the middle of the day – until the French forces started reprisals.

These examples give an idea of the petty official level at which the Ruhr operation was directed. Its scale, however, was far from petty. During the occupation 147,000 Germans were actually expelled from the Ruhr by General Degoutte, including 5,764 railway workers and 17,237 of their dependants. More than 2,000 people were wounded and 376 killed. Every town in Germany as far east as Breslau was burdened with Ruhr refugees. Apart from the economic damage it did, the Ruhr struggle added incalculably to an already horrific sum of human misery.

The passive resistance was not so passive as the government quite genuinely intended it to be. Sabotage of the railways became a popular pastime, and bridges, points and junctions were dynamited at regular intervals. Signals were jammed, and the railway officials made a point of losing or destroying freight waybills, particularly any relating to perishable goods which were subsequently pillaged. French military trains were derailed and ships sunk in the canals; and no coal flowed westwards except at sporadic intervals.

With the wave of nationalism that swept through Germany after the French invasion, the reactionary movements hurried out into the open with the tacit support of the German Army and financial encouragement from the industrialists. The National Socialists, the Deutsche National Volkische Partei and the Fascisti organisations made huge capital out of 'Ruhr patriotism' – Hitler appeared personally in the Ruhr on a recruiting drive – and played as large a part as any in arranging the disruption of the area. Most of these movements, notably the 'Orgesch' (which was known to be supported by Stinnes), had strong military and student backing, and were based in Bavaria. However, the disaffected and out-of-work in the Ruhr did their share of discouraging the forces of occupation; and there were even instances of well-paid workers from the rest of the country – such was the chauvinistic fervour which the *Ruhrkampf* excited – who would spend their annual holidays on jaunts to the Ruhr with the object of shooting a French officer or blowing up a supply train.

In reply to all this the French and Belgians arrested, gaoled and executed, and diplomatically both they and the German government worked themselves into an impasse from which extrication without loss of face became impossible. Russian agents, as might have been expected, began to pour into the Ruhr, but in general found that the flood of paper money which accompanied them was more than a match for the weasel words of Bolshevism, at least in the beginning. By March Russian propaganda in the Ruhr had ceased because the Soviets did not want to appear unsympathetic to the popular distress.

In contrast, the French then started to act in collusion with the local Communists in order to undermine the German authorities. This stimulation by France of the *Rote Hundertschaften*, the 'Red Centuries' operating in the Rhine-Ruhr, echoed the policy which the German High Command had adopted six years before in shipping Lenin off in the sealed train to Petrograd during the war in order to hasten the disintegration of Czarist Russia.

In the matter of popular patriotism Munich distinguished itself from the rest of Germany by a rigid adherence for several months to the manifestations of mourning and indignation which had been inaugurated with the first day of the occupation. No dancing in public or private was permitted, despite the losses suffered by those classes whose livelihoods depended on such things. No Frenchman could show himself with impunity in a restaurant, shop or other public place, a practice in respect of which Berlin was far more lenient. Moreover, as Mr Seeds reported, the perpetual singing of '*Deutschland über Alles*' often entailed savage assaults on any foreigners who, by inadvertence or boredom, failed to rise to their feet.

Committed as they were to a monetary programme of unlimited printing, the government and the Reichsbank fully recognised that if the value of the mark continued to sink for ever the days in which the population of the Ruhr could be sustained in idleness must be very short. For that reason, by the middle of February large amounts of foreign bills were being thrown on to the market at home and abroad by the Reichsbank to support the rate of exchange, a policy immediately made possible by the government's having suspended reparation payments for the duration of hostilities. As excess paper was mopped up, the price of the mark rose sharply, and by February 20 recovered by more than half, moving from 50,000 to the dollar to 20,000. One encouraging consequence was a favourable reaction in wholesale prices. A distressing one was the correspondingly severe fall on the Bourse, as every speculative calculation went wildly wrong.

The main reminder, however, that sanity had not even thought of returning was the appearance of more and more paper from the Reichsbank presses. During February the note circulation was being increased by a matter of 450 milliards every week. On a single day in early March, by way of Treasury bills discounted at the Reichsbank, the floating debt was increased by 800 milliards.

The anomaly of a currency temporarily stable on the world market and roaring inflation at home – accompanied by the usual price increases – did not go unremarked. The *Berliner Tageblatt* roundly condemned the Reichsbank credit policy for 'giving advantage to individuals at the expense of the community by clinging to the fiction of a paper mark which has long ceased to be a reservoir or even a measure of value'. The main reference was to the continuing tendency of industrial and other concerns, partly in order to avoid taxation but more so as not to hold marks, to put every spare mark into extensions, renewals or improvements – a practice which for many months the French had been watching with mounting disapproval, unable to reconcile it with Germany's protestations of national poverty.

Nevertheless, the mark maintained its position at just under 100,000 to the pound throughout March and for the first two weeks of April. It survived a further incursion of the French Army on March 13 across the Rhine to occupy parts of Mannheim, Karlsruhe and Darmstadt; and the news that the Japanese were placing new shipbuilding contracts in Britain rather than Hamburg. It survived the collapse of the franc which, at between 20 and 25 to the pound before the war, now sank from 66 to 77, relieving the French rentiers of another sixth of their purchasing power.* It survived the troubles which accompanied the suppression of a Bavarian separatist plot in Munich; and the worries repeatedly expressed in the Reichstag about the manoeuvrings of 8,000 troops under the direction of Herr Hitler in the same town. It even survived the announcement of a budget deficit of 7,000 milliard marks, or £70 million (about four times the January level) which, as everybody knew, only printing would make good.

---

* By March, French coke prices were at double the January figure.

The Leipzig Spring Fair, held in early April despite the country's troubles, was a disappointment to exporters for the very reason that export prices were now too high to get orders, and that because of the mark's stability on foreign exchanges inland prices were often higher than export prices when expressed in foreign currencies. The wild fluctuations in the mark's value over the previous months when the goods were actually being manufactured meant extraordinary price differences throughout the fair – amounting to as much as 60 per cent for the same type of wares. The only products in which traders could hope to prosper were in those like toys and fine mechanical instruments where Germany still enjoyed something of a monopoly: but German leather goods, glass and crystal, for example, were now being severely undercut by the United Kingdom.

Visitors to the fair found that German firms seemed to be concentrating upon large quantities of low-class goods – the inference being that their production ensured maximum employment, would meet the greatly reduced inland purchasing power, and in addition gratify the Germans' need and urge to get rid of all their paper money. The average citizen these days preferred buying three pairs of indifferent leather boots to buying one good pair. At the fair he was being offered mouth organs at the equivalent of 17s a dozen, or concertinas at half a guinea each. His was becoming in many respects a cheapjack country.

It could only be a matter of time before the Bank's capacity to support the currency ran out. The government attempted to raise a gold loan with the issue of dollar Treasury bonds (repayable at 120 per cent three years later), but found that afer all people preferred to hold on to any foreign currency they had. When the first official results of the loan were announced in the last days of March, it turned out to be still undersubscribed by 75 per cent. The lack of confidence this news engendered led to a demand for foreign currencies greater than ever before; but it was not until April 18 when Hugo Stinnes presented the Reichsbank with a demand for £93,000 in foreign bills that the intervention policy came to grief. Support was withdrawn. The mark broke; and it was decided to let the exchange find a more realistic level. Within twenty-four hours the mark was at 140,000 to the pound, and still sliding.

'Inflation is like a drug in more ways than one,' remarked Lord D'Abernon. 'It is fatal in the end, but it gets its votaries over many difficult moments.' Hopelessly addicted, the Reichsbank ploughed on. The foreign currency holdings having failed to keep the mark steady while more and more paper notes gushed forth day upon day, the gold reserves had been thrown into the breach as well. In March these stood at 1,004 million gold marks, equivalent to just over £50 million. By the middle of May one-fifth of them had gone, good money after bad – at a time, moreover, when those reserves would almost certainly still have been a sufficient basis for the issue of a stable currency.

From the spring onwards, the gold reserves dwindled away (not exclusively in support of the mark: much was spent on essential imports of food and British coal); and more and more desperate attempts were made to control the market in foreign exchange. Such intervention as sporadically took place thereafter to stem the fall of the currency contrived at best to brake its descent for a few days at a time. Almost invariably these attempts made it easier for speculators to pick up foreign currencies at artificially low prices. The regulation in May requiring banks to report in detail any purchases of foreign currency made on behalf of their clients was simply tinkering with one of inflation's natural side-effects; and the three dozen or so separate ordinances which were to follow, governing the buying, selling and even the casual holding of foreign money, in turn did little more than hamper the normal workings of commerce.

Prices went up, and although there was no weakening of resolve in the country at large or in the Ruhr in particular, to continue the enfeebling struggle with France, morale began to sink, especially in the Rhineland. If the small Francophile party there had then decided under French backing to proclaim a Rhenish Republic, most of the population would probably have closed their eyes and accepted the situation. The separatist movement gave the Communists the opportunity to stir up trouble all the way from Essen to Frankfort. The flood of refugees into unoccupied Germany increased in size and caused there as many economic and social problems as they thought they had left behind. Labour leaders who stayed at home were now beginning to demand work in lieu of an increasingly inadequate dole. With May Day, when Hitler's attempt to use his stormtroopers to break up the traditional trade union demonstrations in Munich – and if possible force the Reich into civil war – was thwarted by the local Reichswehr commandant, von Lossow, the mark dropped past 200,000 to the pound. Curzon's endeavour* to break the Ruhr deadlock by appealing to Germany to make a new offer in respect of reparation payments came to nothing.

Ernest Hemingway returned to Kehl in late April, fortified by a visa obtained from the German consular attaché in Paris with the aid of a bribe. Since the year before, the little Rhineland town had been transformed.

> The waiter sat down at the table. 'No, there is no one here now,' he said. 'All the people you say you saw in July cannot come now. The French will not give them passports to come to Germany ... The merchants and restaurant keepers in Strasbourg got angry and went to the police because everybody was coming over here to eat so much cheaper and now nobody in Strasbourg can get a passport to come here ... Now no Germans can get passports to go across the river to Strasbourg where many worked. They could work cheaper than the French, so that is what happened to them. All our factories here are shutdown. No coal, no trains. This was one of the biggest and busiest stations in Germany. Now nix. No trains, except the military trains, and they run when they please ... We haven't had any fun since 1914. If you made any money it gets no good, and there is only

---

* In April, a month before Baldwin, to Curzon's chagrin, succeeded Bonar Law as Prime Minister. cf. Harold Nicolson, *Curzon: the Last Phase*, Chapter XII.

to spend, it. That is what we do. Last year I had enough money saved up to buy a *Gasthaus* at Hernberg: now that money wouldn't buy four bottles of Champagne.'

Hemingway recorded for the *Toronto Daily Star* that Champagne then cost 38,000 marks a bottle, luncheon 3,500 marks, a sandwich 900 marks, and beer 350 marks a stein.

I remembered that last July I stayed at a de luxe hotel with Mrs Hemingway for 600 marks a day. 'Sure,' the waiter went on, 'I read the French papers. Germany debases her money to cheat the Allies. But what do I get out of it?'

The answer was that the waiter got nothing out of inflation, and – apart from relieving itself of a further minute proportion of the remaining minute fraction of the national debt – nor now did the Exchequer. There were those, however, who were doing better than ever. A currency speculator who borrowed from the Reichsbank on January 1, 1923, enough paper marks (about 1,980 million) to buy 100,000 dollars, and on April 1 sold enough dollars (about 80,000) to repay the bank, and who again borrowed the equivalent of 100,000 dollars and continued thus until the end of May, could have made the equivalent of a quarter of a million dollars at the expense of the acceptors of pure marks. His problem then, of course, was in what form to keep his profits: if they were in marks, they would evaporate before his eyes.

That evaporation was inevitable. In March, April and May the government's income was a mere 30 per cent of its expenditure; and during May the working classes actually paid more to the Reich in tax than the assessed tax payers of the higher social classes, for the reason that whereas the former could be tapped at source, the others had to fill in returns which were long out of date by the time the administrative machine could deal with them. Between May Day and May 31 the mark fell from 220,000 to 320,000 to the pound. The First of June was celebrated with the issue of the first five-million-mark note.

Speculation in currency was in no way the exclusive domain of the financially informed. Anyone – banker, politician, businessman or workman – who observed that there were easier ways of keeping one's head above water than the now very problematic one of working for it was ready to indulge as opportunity offered. It was computed that well over a million Germans in early 1923 were engaged in exchange speculation. Their dealings took place mainly through the so-called *Winkelbankiers*, the back-street operators who had sprung up with inflation and, battening on an unhealthy economy, made a living entirely through taking advantage of the difference in the buying and selling prices of foreign currencies. Although they were not even members of the Bourse, they played a significant part in determining the daily rate of exchange – and, indeed, to the arbitrage machinations of the *Winkelbankiers* was attributed the fact that Berlin invariably closed at a lower rate than New York.

By the end of May 1923 no single reform, possibly no half dozen measures, would have been enough to avert ultimate disaster. Small reforms were made: a law was passed on May 19 to liquidate holdings of Government stock of less than 5,000 marks, because they cost too much to administer – and 920,000 holders of War Loan alone who had paid up to £250 to help the war effort were compelled to accept the nominal value (at most, 6d) for their stock. In another improvement, the Minister of the Interior permitted the substitution of paste-board coffins for wooden ones, especially for the rising number of pauper funerals. Otherwise, the Government contented itself with steps to postpone the inevitable.

Until the Ruhr invasion the inflationist policy had been mainly governed by the fear of unemployment. Now massive unemployment had come – although the revival of the national spirit had greatly mitigated its worst disruptive side-effects – and inflation was pursued more vigorously than ever. As the Ruhr unemployment was fully subsidised it had no corresponding countervailing influence on the huge additional wage claims there or anywhere else. Conjointly the minds of Berlin turned more earnestly towards reforming the tax system, which to a great degree meant persuading Stinnes and his friends to make real fiscal contributions to the Exchequer. In June, of the 511 milliard marks received in income tax, only 90 milliards came from assessed tax payers: wage-earners' prepayments accounted for the rest, and Stinnes was increasingly seen to be a maleficent influence on Germany's finances. The Exchequer's only joy that month was in the increased yield from the Bourse turnover tax, which doubled because of a new rush of orders to buy German securities.

Petty crime, the crime of desperation, was flourishing. Pilfering had of course been rife since the war, but now it began to occur on a larger, commercial scale. Metal plaques on national monuments had to be removed for safe-keeping. The brass bell plates were stolen from the front doors of the British Embassy in Berlin, part of a systematic campaign unpreventable by the police even in the Wilhelmstrasse and Unter den Linden. That members and families of the British Army of the Rhine suffered severely from burglaries probably reflected the fact, not that thieves had particular animus against the forces of occupation, but that these days foreigners were so much more robbable than anyone else. Over most of Germany the lead was beginning to disappear overnight from roofs. Petrol was syphoned from the tanks of motor cars. Barter was already a usual form of exchange; but now commodities such as brass and fuel were becoming the currency of ordinary purchase and payment. A cinema seat cost a lump of coal. With a bottle of paraffin one might buy a shirt; with that shirt, the potatoes needed by one's family. Herr von der Osten kept a girlfriend in the provincial capital, for whose room in 1922 he had paid half a pound of butter a month: by the summer of 1923 it was costing him a whole pound. 'The Middle Ages came back,' Erna von Pustau said.

Communities printed their own money, based on goods, on a certain amount of potatoes, or rye, for instance. Shoe factories paid their

workers in bonds for shoes which they could exchange at the bakery
for bread or the meat market for meat.

Those with foreign currency, becoming easily the most acceptable
paper medium, had the greatest scope for finding bargains. The
power of the the dollar, in particular, far exceeded its nominal rate
of exchange. Finding himself with a single dollar bill early in 1923,
von der Osten got hold of six friends and went to Berlin one evening
determined to blow the lot; but early the next morning, long after
dinner, and many nightclubs later, they still had change in their
pockets. There were stories of Americans in the greatest difficulties
in Berlin because no-one had enough marks to change a five-dollar
bill: of others who ran up accounts (to be paid off later in depreciated
currency) on the strength of even bigger foreign notes which, after
meals or services had been obtained, could not be changed; and
of foreign students who bought up whole rows of houses out of
their allowances.

There were stories of shoppers who found that thieves had stolen the
baskets and suitcases in which they carried their money, leaving the money
itself behind on the ground; and of life supported by selling every day or so
a single tiny link from a long gold crucifix chain. There were stories (many
of them, as the summer wore on and as exchange rates altered several times
a day) of restaurant meals which cost more when the bills came than when
they were ordered. A 5,000-mark cup of coffee would cost 8,000 marks
by the time it was drunk.

The reality behind such inflationary anecdotes, amusing in
retrospect, was exceedingly grim. The agony was displayed as much
by the shrunken-necked gentlemen to be seen in the streets with their
mended white collars and shiny suits saved from the war as by the
exhausted workmen queueing impatiently outside the pay windows
with big shopping bags in which to rush their wages away to the shops.
Badly off as wage-earners were, their standards were still at a level
distantly comparable with the past. Throughout Germany, Austria and

Hungary the old standards of salary earners, pensioners and people living on savings had often dropped almost out of sight.

Lady Listowel,* whose father held a senior post in the Hungarian diplomatic service, recalls the distress among the circle of her family's friends in Budapest:

> One used to see the appearance of their flats gradually changing. One remembered where there used to be a picture, or a carpet, or a secretaire. Eventually their rooms would be almost empty – and on paper some people were reduced to nothing. In practice, people didn't just die. They were terribly hungry, and relations and friends would help with a little food from time to time. We sent them parcels, or took them ourselves because we had no cash to pay for postage. And some of them begged – not in the streets – but by making casual visits (one knew only too well what they had come for) or by writing letters asking for help. Everyone still tried to keep up appearances: at first, early on, people looked around to see what economies they could make, what clubs to resign from, what luxuries to do without. Later it was a question of considering what necessities to do without.
>
> And when food was not the problem – after all, we lived most of the time in the country where we could get it – there were troubles because we had no money. Only one of us could afford to go into Budapest at a time. There was no way to get medical help without money. If you had toothache you couldn't afford a dentist. If you needed to go to hospital, you might get into a convent: otherwise you stayed at home, and got better, or got worse.

In June after a brief pause, support for the mark was resumed. The reason was quite openly stated – to allay popular discontent which was assuming alarming proportions. The people had reason to complain.

* Judith, Countess of Listowel, formerly Judith de Marffy-Mantuano.

In the month following May 20, the price of an egg rose from 800 marks to 2,400; of a litre of milk from 1,800 to 3,800, of a kilo of flour from 2,400 to 6,600, of pork from 10,400 to 32,000. In the Ruhr, too, while salaries doubled (a workman's wage rose from 3,300 an hour to 6,800) the cost of commodities trebled. Tradesmen could not know how to establish prices, and often simply shut up shop. For these reasons, in a single day in June, 6 million gold marks were lost to the reserves in 'another of the Reichsbank's convulsive and desperate attempts', as Mr Joseph Addison put it, 'to bolster the mark by throwing foreign currency on the market – in this case with the object of bringing the dollar below 100,000'. The government's hopes again turned out to be illusions. In mid-June, the note circulation stood at 8,564 milliard marks. By June 21 the daily increase in the circulation was 157 milliards. By June 28 the mark was at 170,000 to the dollar, the total circulation had risen to 11,000 milliards, and no notes of less than 100,000 marks (2s 10d) were being printed.

In a letter to the Foreign Office on June 29 Addison recorded a circulation increase between June 25 and 26 of 959,156,010,000 marks and between June 26 and 27 of 1,523,534,460,000: in one day, an *increase in the increase* of more than 500,000,000,000 marks. 'We are far from the modest daily increase of 160 milliards of a week ago,' he wrote, and added Mephistopheles's comment from *Faust*:

> 'Der kleine Gott der Welt bleibt stets von gleichem Schlag,
> Und ist so wunderlich als wie am ersten Tag.'*

As the circulation swelled and the value of the mark fell, less and less importance attached to revenue from taxation. The increase in the floating debt recorded on June 27 – the 1,500 milliards which had so startled Addison – was more than the Exchequer's total revenue (1,400 milliards) for the entire month of May. Although the Finance Ministry

---

* Roughly: '*Earth's little lordling stays to his casting true, As odd as on the day when he was new.*'

was working on plans to bring taxes up to a level proportionate to the mark's depreciation, the Reichsbank's policy of discounting and printing was bound to keep the mark far ahead of the game. In two and a half months government expenditure had totalled the equivalent of £15.5 million against a revenue of only £5 million. In sterling terms these sums were trifling enough: but the truth was that a nation of 60 million people was going bankrupt because (at, say, 500,000 marks to the pound) she could not raise even £30 million a year to meet expenditure of only £80 million.

Towards the end of June 1923, the government began turning with repeated, but undue, optimism to temporary expedients of all kinds. One nostrum was the multiplier, to be wielded by the Minister of Finance as he thought fit, to keep the rate of taxation on a par with that of depreciation. It worried no one in the ministry that it sinned deeply against Adam Smith's sacred canon of certainty which provides that taxpayers know clearly in advance what they have to pay. During May, income tax had been multiplied 25 times, and it was now announced that in August, when payment would be due, the multiplier would be 40. Yet it was obvious that the tax returns could never keep up with the speed of depreciation, from whatever source they came. The yield from consumption duties – for example, on tobacco, beer, wine, sugar, salt and playing cards – no longer even met the cost of their administration.

The trouble was that all taxes were levied not on real but on current values, so that the Finance Minister, Dr Hermes, was in some ways right in protesting that to bring these duties up to normal world levels would have offered 'no financial guarantee for the future'. Despair was the keynote of his approach. The lightness of the tax burden on the German economy as a whole had become painfully evident, even though individuals were often heavily hit. Dr Hermes began to discuss new taxes on bills of exchange and on traffic in capital, and – potentially more significant – the prepayment of income and corporation taxes. This last, however, seems to have been mooted mainly as a palliative to the working classes.

In the second half of June it became necessary again to double the salaries of government officials, and to give higher grants to the war-wounded, to widows, to pensioners and to the unemployed, in and out of the Ruhr. An additional reason for these increases, over and above the general fall in the mark's purchasing power, was that the poorer classes, especially the rentiers, would soon no longer be able to afford the price of bread. Agricultural interests had become angry about the 'Umlage', the forced delivery of the first two million tons of wheat produced each year which enabled half the total supply of bread to be sold cheap. From August onwards farmers were to be paid at world prices because, when obliged to sell wheat cheaply, they still had to pay the world price for fertilisers. The change in policy, from subsidising food to subsidising the needy, may have satisfied the farmers; but the extra subsidies for the poor soon became worthless again.

The third week in June produced yet another attempt to control speculation in foreign currencies by fixing the rate of exchange at which they might legally be traded. The penalties for infringing the new ordinance were unlimited fines and up to three years' gaol. Undertaken at the request of the bigger banks who were afraid of a popular attack on them if civil disorder were to break out, the measure was aimed at the continuing operations of the *Winkelbankiers*, who would now be unable to make a price for the mark before the official quotation was known. It was determined first that German industry possessed enough foreign currency to meet its needs during the month in which the ordinance was to run, for otherwise it would have made the import business impossible and trade would have been brought to a standstill.

The Rhineland High Commission, however, refused to adopt the ordinance, so that huge transactions were soon taking place in Cologne, seriously depressing the mark exchange once more. General Degoutte further declared it inapplicable in the Ruhr; and thus put France, which had frequently accused the Germans of wilfully debasing the mark, in the anomalous position of forbidding a move whose sole object was to strengthen it. The ordinance was by and large a failure, and in part had the effect – as a similar measure had had in Austria – of driving the *Winkelbankier* out of the open into the café round the corner. (In Austria the Bourse was compelled in the end to follow and then actually adopt the rates of the *Schwarze Börse*.) On July 2, the dollar opened in New York at 174,000 paper marks but closed in Berlin, under the influence of the Reichsbank, at 160,000. In other words, the Bank was selling dollars at 160,000 marks in the full knowledge that the dollar was worth 14,000 more points abroad.

The next day, July 3, there appeared a new ordinance to forbid the buying of futures. It was partly aimed at restricting imports, for stocks were now very high and importers had been able to obtain great quantities of foreign bills during the period of heavy mark support. The consequence was that the Bourse rapidly became overloaded with demands for 'sight' bills rather than three-month bills; and of these only about a tenth could be satisfied. Accordingly importers began to apply for ten times the dollars they required in the hope of getting their full quota.

This ordinance was also aimed at those who sought to buy dollars at, say, 160,000 marks each and use the dollars to buy dollar Treasury bills quoted at a very much higher rate – an obvious way of making great gains. The higher quotation of the bills had even led people to believe that the dollar rate was artificial and that the bill rate was the genuine one. Over-ordering, however, meant that many firms were caught out when the Reichsbank, with more than usual astuteness, called their bluff by requiring cheques to meet the total application. In that it revealed which of the smaller banks were condoning exchange speculation this ordinance therefore had some success.

And yet every effort to prevent foreign currency losses, every new attempt to hold the mark steady, was only trifling with the nation's troubles. The Reichsbank's Autonomy Act of May 1922 had fully persuaded Dr Havenstein that he was master in his own house. Despite pressures mounting on all sides, he showed clearly that he had no intention of resigning, and every thought of pursuing his own convictions. Believing that it was in Berlin that the mark exchange had to be kept low, whatever it might do elsewhere, he willingly satisfied the demands of his public by selling what foreign currencies he had available. During the last days of June and the first days of July, as the mark sank from 600,000 to 800,000 to the pound, nearly 80 million gold marks – £2 million – were thrown away, as Dr Bergmann, a high official in the Finance Ministry, admitted, in order to satisfy the greed of German speculators: only 1 million gold marks were meanwhile required for the more laudable purpose of supporting the mark in New York.

By July 10, Germany's free gold reserve had fallen to the equivalent of £35 million pounds, and all the Bank was doing had produced precisely the effect it was hoped to avoid. Another loss of 50 million gold marks was suffered during the week which ended on July 14 – the direct result of supporting the paper mark by rationing supplies of foreign currencies and having to cover indispensable imports from the gold reserve. If intervention continued at the then level of 10 million gold marks daily, bankruptcy would come within 60 days: the reserves had already taken as much as they could stand. If intervention ceased, on the other hand, it was broadly expected that the dollar would go to a million marks, the pound to over 4 million – and by the end of July that expectation was fulfilled. Merchants were still said to be borrowing paper marks to the value of 80 per cent of their stock, and exchanging them at the Bank for dollar Treasury bills needed ostensibly for imports. These bills were sent abroad to the merchants' buying agencies, and in most cases stayed there with no countervalue returning to Germany.

Complacency appears then to have crept into the government's financial thinking. The Finance Under-Secretary, Herr Schroeder, for example, referring to the 8,000 milliard marks discounted in June opined that it only represented £10 million sterling, which was hardly excessive seeing that the country was in a state of war. The Reichsbank nevertheless eyed the disappearance of its remaining resources with dismay. On July 19 it suddenly suspended the discounting of trade paper and refused to sacrifice any more of the gold reserve. The ordinary import trade promptly came to a standstill, and it became very hard for the Government to finance the import of coal and food – the coal desperately needed to keep the railways going.

The Bank's decision was in part a panic measure. Demands upon it from other banks had amounted that day to a sum equalling the entire paper circulation in the country. The manager of the Exchange Department produced only one quarter per cent of the total, which the banks rejected as inadequate. Two days later, the Reichsbank relented to the extent of issuing 5 per cent of the demand – but also resumed discounting interior trade bills; and at the end of July the Reichsbank had only £25 million in gold left. Attempts by the government to raise a loan abroad, in the first instance in London, to cover necessary imports were met with the old response that nothing would be available until Germany's finances had been put in order.

A number of diverging, often conflicting, tendencies were noted throughout Germany at this time, as bewilderment and depression afflicted everyone from government and business circles, who might have been expected to know what was going on, to the wage earners and clerical classes, who had no idea whatever. On the one hand, among the lower German officials who had always been intensely loyal to the government, mainly because their own fortunes were intimately linked to those of the country, an extremely nationalist spirit had developed. It had become and now remained politically impossible for the government – any government – to consider giving up passive resistance in the Ruhr. On the other hand, in the country at large, the coalition was losing support in every other way very rapidly. The leading Centre newspaper, *Germania*, announced on July 27 that confidence in the administration was 'now completely shattered', that anger was universal, and that 'the general feeling is that of the Ninth of November' (the day the Republic was proclaimed in 1918).

The Wirth government was accused of wobbling [*Germania* said] but the Cuno government makes no movement at all. They stand still. Beyond a few ordinances, such as controlling the consumption of meat in restaurants, and occasional speeches, they remain passive … The huge sums required for passive resistance were provided by the printing press … Credits were issued to industrial circles, and it is not known to what extent they were used for hoarding foreign bills …

The policy of fulfilment was only partly responsible. People abroad lost confidence when they realised that the authority of the State was being undermined in Germany itself. The first symptom was the murder of Rathenau. The real collapse of our currency began when it became evident that certain industrial circles were more powerful than the government.

In the meantime the working population were losing their patience. The withdrawal of the 1,000 mark note, although worth barely one-third of a penny at the beginning of July, had been an unhappy loss. The highest denomination as long before as 1876 and thus an old friend, its issue was repudiated, it appears, because rumours were circulating that it might be revalorised at its old gold rate. In practice, it also disappeared because (as Dr Schacht put it) in order to produce low-currency notes far more working time was required by paper-makers, engineers, printers, lithographers, colour experts and packers than was represented by the value of the finished article. In the fourth week of July the German nation was introduced to a new range of banknotes of which the three highest denominations were now 10, 20 and 50 million marks.

The workers responded in the only way they could, demanding not only higher wages but daily payment so that their income would keep its spending power long enough to get rid of it. The demands were enforced with repeated strikes, disorders and demonstrations in all parts of the country. The possibility of civil war was openly discussed in the press, and frenziedly denied by the government. A thousand arrests were made after riots and plundering on July 20 and 21 in Breslau, where organised bands of Communists prowled through the streets. July 24 produced demonstrations against profiteering, capitalism and Fascism in Frankfort, where inoffensive citizens were molested, windows were broken, and one man kicked to death. Open air meetings were forbidden in Berlin, but 10,000 demonstrated peaceably enough in Leipzig, and 5,000 in Dresden. In the last week of July demonstrators were killed in the Bavarian town of Rosenheim, and in Potsdam. There were ship-building strikes in Hamburg and a pilots' strike in the Kiel canal.

The same pattern was to continue through August, when armed strikers were to kill police at Wilhelmsburg and throw them into the water at Hamburg – all in aid of a basic wage which was inevitably out of date by the time it was negotiated and paid. Some of the troubles were Communist inspired, others not particularly so. In 1922 the Third International had laid down that policy in Germany was to be restricted to gaining influence with the workers by exploiting their serious economic situation. In May 1923 a rising in the Ruhr had been considered again, but in general now it was felt that the time was not yet.

As they discovered that a stable purchasing power for wages became less and less attainable, union leaders began to demand that wages be fixed on a gold basis. That, however, all agreed, could scarcely be done before a gold standard was adopted equally by trade and finance. An agreement was thus struck at the beginning of July between the Minister of Finance and a representative trade union committee to relate wages by indexation to the cost of living. Its principle was a weekly wage adjustment (as well as daily payments) to maintain value – the adjustment applying equally to the 'efficiency' wage (*Leistungslohn*) as to the 'social' wage (*Soziallohn*) which covered such matters as extra-family allowances. The negotiation of real wages (*Reallohn*), that is to say increased payments on the basis of the gold mark, was to be regarded as something quite separate.

In practice, as the government was aware, rises in wages – and government salaries – would always be 15 days in arrears of the rise in the cost of living, for the new adaptations would be received at the end of each 15-day wage period, the basic wage having been received at the start: a device which meant a great saving to the Exchequer as, in each successive week of July, the mark's rate against the pound mounted startlingly from 800,000 (July 7) to 900,000 (July 14) to 1,600,000 (July 23) to 5,000,000, or 21 million to the dollar, on the last day of the month, and as prices moved upwards in step.

What Lord Curzon described as 'this extraordinary and almost incredible fall in the value of the mark', which brought on an acute food crisis in Germany, also brought the German Ambassador in London, cap in hand, to see him at the Foreign Office. There he was pressed by the ambassador to use his influence to secure the long-requested loan to pay for Germany's essential fuel and food imports. As France was still titularly Britain's ally, Curzon for the present was unable to accede, and confined his refusal to asking whether it was the intention that the Reichsbank's printing presses would cease work. To that, and to the question of why the latest tax measures had not been tried before, the unfortunate ambassador had no answer. He delivered a memorandum to Curzon, however, couched in terms which *Germania* might well have approved:

It is an ominous sign that the mark following its latest tremendous collapse [*nach ihrem letzten ungeheuren Sturz*] is now beginning to lose its purchasing power in internal trade also. At the same time the Reichsbank no longer has sufficient foreign currency to make it possible for industry and for the State to procure abroad the necessities of life, especially coal and food. The dreary foreign outlook together with the destruction of the currency and the resulting chaos in the whole economic structure have produced the result that the population are beginning to lose confidence in the State and in themselves. Distrust of the depreciating currency is driving goods from the market, while the late harvest has produced an exceptionally alarming scarcity of foodstuffs in the towns, especially Berlin. The desperation of the masses is being exploited by radical agitators from both Left and Right.

In fact, the wheat crop had been rather a good one, especially in Saxony, and the scarcity was caused by the farmers' refusal to accept paper in return for their produce. However, while the government's only policy was to borrow at the maximum rate to pay wages in the Ruhr, and while the independent Reichsbank added fuel to the flames of this folly (for Dr Havenstein and the Bank's directorate were if anything more wrong-headed in these matters than the government), no loan was possible: Britain, for one, had already been stung early the year before by agreeing to part with £12 million to aid an equally profligate Austria. The phenomenal fall of the mark in the last days of July certainly caused grave embarrassment to the government. The German Ambassador's complaint that the mark was losing its internal purchasing power, though heard so often for many months, was becoming ever more real. For the present, however, traders' disclination to accept Reichsbanknotes could still theoretically be countered by multiplying both their quantity and their denominations. In practice, it was harder than ever to supply the banks with enough money to allow business to proceed on traditional lines. From Dresden to Coblenz, at the end of July, the new high denomination notes were awaited anxiously.

Between July 11 and July 20,. the floating debt increased from 28,000 milliard marks to 40,000 milliard, a daily issue, excluding Sundays, of 2,000 milliards. The taxation system had entirely broken down. Living from day to day, the government did not seem to care. Of the expenditure during those few days of 12,000 milliard marks, only 4 per cent was found from taxation – at just over 500 milliards not even enough to cover the interest (570 milliards) on the debt for the same period.

These appalling figures were no more than a foretaste of the chaos of the following weeks. The Ruhr railways, which had once provided a third of Germany's revenue from the Ruhr, now accounted for one-fifth of her outgoings, in wages and compensation. '*Wir schiessen*,' a high financial official told the British Ambassador, '*dieselben Böcke wie die Österreicher*'– ('We shoot the same goats as the Austrians'). Between August 1 and August 10, the records show, the floating debt almost doubled. But during those latter ten days, the government's general administrative expenditure rose to 40,000 milliards: a sum somewhat greater than the total nominal expenditure during the first four months of the year.

Although Austria's goats had become a very different breed since the previous autumn when Dr Zimmermann took over financial control and the Geneva Protocols had been approved by the National Assembly, Germany might well look on her neighbour with awe. That unhappy country was undergoing for all to see the full throes of the exorcism of the devil of inflation, and it was plainly the most unpleasant process.

That the necessary reforms could not be achieved without hardship and sacrifice had been made clear to the people at Christmas time. What they had not been told, and were now finding out, was that the victims of the recovery would be hardly less unfairly selected than those of the inflation. In August 1922, the official dole figure (which, as in Germany, substantially underestimated the real unemployment figure and ignored short-time working) had been 21,000. In the five months from October 1922 until February 1922, the figure rose successively from 38,000 58,000, 83,000, 117,000 and 161,000. In every case, well over half the workless were in Vienna itself, which in February meant more than 100,000 idle men receiving for themselves and their families a maximum dole of 87,360 paper kronen, worth about 5s. a week. It was a dangerous concentration, though embracing both working and official classes, in a city still politically divided, where the class war was still the popular topic.

In Austria as a whole, about one-fifth of the population depended on government money for their salaries or (if retired) for their pensions, the railways having two ex-employee pensioners for every three workers still on their staff. Although the deadwood on the railways was not properly cut away until towards the end of 1923 under external guidance,* and although railway finances represented the crux of the budgetary deficit, other essential economies, planned or forced, had started at once in both the public and private sectors, with redundancies and dismissals occurring in both. Stabilisation had brought the Austrian manufacturer face to face with reality, and serious industrial depression was setting in, stagnation affecting the iron, wood, paper and leather industries and the manufacture of metal, machinery, shoes and furniture. The first bankruptcies of businesses spawned by the inflation were beginning. Elsewhere concealed overstaffing was coming to light: in January 1923 the leading Vienna banks had one official for every £2,000 of their total reserves and deposits, compared with one for every £18,000 in London. This situation was partly due to the compulsory extra work the banks had to do to help the foreign exchange office and the tax authorities, but the banks were also finding it impossible to administer except at prohibitive cost the great number of smaller, older accounts which inflation had reduced to the value of a few pre-war pfennigs, and in some cases to less than the value of the paper they had to be written down on. Savings banks catering for the small saver and hoping to restore his confidence were particularly badly affected in this respect.

Dismissals in the public sector were governed by the public expenditure cuts called for by Dr Zimmermann's office. Generally they came in the wake of the sackings in private industry, the government being slow to implement the directives it received. It was noted, however, that those who were at last axed were first and foremost those with no political connections. One unfortunate consequence of this

---

* Sir William Acworth, chosen as technical adviser for the railways, presented his report in November 1923 and recommended that one man out of four should be dispensed with.

was that, by the end of 1923, administrative efficiency had seriously declined, for the civil service was hardly less overmanned than the railways, and the senior, more experienced civil servants were those who had traditionally kept politics at arm's length.

From March onwards, however, the economic and financial picture began to look better from the point of view of Austria's sponsors. Unemployment which reached nearly 170,000 that month began to fall substantially and regularly, dropping in August to as low as 84,000 (53,000 of whom were in Vienna). The krone remained rock-steady, and the fact that for the best part of a year it had already been more stable against the dollar than, any other currency in Europe was a solid foundation for confidence. Deposits were accumulating in the savings banks. When the long-term international loan was at last floated on June 1, 1923, it was a huge and immediate success. Austria's budget was to be balanced ahead of the Zimmermann schedule, and the whole loan was never called up. The striking increase in demand for Austrian stocks and shares, whose index had doubled between December 1922 and the following May and increased by 400 per cent in the course of the year, was a development which reflected general confidence more than it brought great tangible benefit to the economy: speculation in undervalued shares absorbed a great deal of domestic capital which might have been put to productive purposes.

The lowest point which Austria's official unemployed figure reached was the 79,000 of November 1923, still nearly four times the number before stabilisation. After November, the number of planned redundancies in the civil service, in the *Volkswehr*, the postal services and the railways began to have a real impact upon the labour position. The comparatively promising situation in the middle of 1923 was in large part owing to the increase in Austrian trade arising from the *Ruhrkampf*: foreign orders for certain goods were switched from Germany to Austria, where even a little of Germany's business would go a long way.

The dismissal of more than 23,000 officials from the State service between October and December 1923 was to be a much truer gauge of the belt-tightening that was taking place. Strikes were few – but that was because a strike policy, with or without union support, was so obviously suicidal when everyone was losing jobs and employees could be easily and cheaply replaced. The official target, after all, was a cut of 100,000 State jobs by the end of 1924, and the unions were well aware that in the autumn of 1923 the programme of reduction of government officials was falling badly behind.

It was doubtless satisfactory that foreign confidence had returned in such full measure to this European financial oasis maintained and guaranteed by the Allies; and that Austria's economy, public and private, was obviously reorganising along the correct lines. Yet they were hardly considerations which allowed, the Austrian people much scope for rejoicing, greatly as the general atmosphere of uncertainty and gloom of 1922 had improved. From January 1923 onwards and as the *Ruhrkampf* had its effect on the European economy, the cost of living began to creep upwards again and continued to do so throughout the year, adding 3 per cent in August alone. Although by December 1923 it only attained once more the previous highest level of September 1922 (after which there had come the 20 per cent drop), the rise took place in the face of higher taxes which more people than ever before had to pay. The government found it particularly unfortunate that prices (in line with world prices) went on rising while the necessary reforms and reductions were taking place; and as early as May, indeed, questioned whether it was possible at all to maintain law and order at the same time as budgetary equilibrium.

Perhaps it was not surprising, therefore, that the workers persisted in opposing the abolition of the index system under which wages could not be reduced until the index had fallen in two consecutive months. The factory worker was now relatively better off than most, and in some cases better off than he had been before the war, notwithstanding that wages were lower than anywhere else in Europe except Germany. In a country which had a great excess of educated men, the difference in average rewards between manual and intellectual workers had become very small, and the wages of a skilled mechanic often exceeded those of a factory manager, who himself received many times those of a government official.

The financial picture was sound. The economy was improving. But the social picture was far from happy. The classes who had already endured so much well understood that a far harder time might be on the way. Those whom the index had to some extent protected began to experience chiller winds than they had known possible, in some degree because until stabilisation they hardly knew how poor they had become. The days of subsidies and doles were over. People who had no work were more penurious than ever, spending their time searching notice-boards and newspapers for jobs which did not exist. State officials who remained on the national pay-roll found that on average in 1923 they received one-quarter of their 1914 spending power. State pensioners received one-third in real terms of what had been little enough before the war.

In Vienna most people lived in flats, for only the very rich had houses which they could afford to keep in repair. Because rents were kept so low (rent restriction is habitually one of the first and cheapest of government devices to restrain the cost of living under inflation) flats themselves were in short supply. Even had the Viennese municipality been well-disposed towards the landlord, it could not have been ignored that most of the middle class would have been entirely unable to afford economic rents of up to 20,000 times the pre-war figure. Though unable to raise their rents, many landlords at least had the consolation that their own mortgage payments were no more than a nominal burden to them – a consideration which had long since dismayed the depositors and share-holders of the mortgage banks. Under such circumstances, however, no new buildings at all were being put up by private developers, most of whom had been virtually expropriated. More than 42,000 families were waiting for the 6,000 or so dwellings which the local authorities built in Vienna each year. This shortage, and the regulation whereby the local authorities, not the landlords, decided who would go into any flat which became empty, led to a great deal of jobbing and corruption in an area where it was already rife.

The period of Austrian rehabilitation, of heavy taxation and drastic cuts in public spending, was one of great popular suffering, of continuing class and group hatred, and of political struggle. The State and the municipal government of Vienna appeared to compete to tax Austrian industry, so much of which was centred on the capital, to the utmost – the State in order to be able to repay the interest on foreign loans, the latter (whose activities were free from League control) in order to pursue the interests of its political supporters in the working classes. Whether or not the charge was just that the Socialists controlling Vienna did little more than hang doctrinaire reforms around the Republic's neck – 'actively concerned in the pleasing process', Germains wrote, 'of converting middle-class incomes into doles for the workers' – there is no doubt that party politics continued to rend the country in two when unity was the crying need.

Austria's reconstruction was compared to the experiment made by the gipsy to teach his horse to do without food. When he got it down to a straw a day, the horse died.

10: Summer of '23

At the end of July 1923 German shares had established themselves as a popular though unstable repository of wealth. In general, shareholders were a good deal poorer than they thought, the fact of impoverishment having been largely veiled by the gigantic increases in nominal prices. Speculation kept all shares at a high level above their interest-return value, even given that dividends were still being held artificially low to avoid income tax. A Deutsche Bank share cost £114 just before the war and yielded £6 5s; but in 1923 cost £5 and yielded a farthing. A share in Siemens and Helske, £101 pre-war and paying £6, now stood at £23 and paid 2d. Thus capital values, low as they had come, had not fallen to the same extent as dividends which were proportionately even lower than in 1922. At the annual general meeting of one large bank, an American shareholder complained that the dividend on his holding was barely worth fetching away, not merely because its value was so small but because of the high cost of transport for the volume of notes required.

Anyone who during the first six months of the year had sought a haven for money in domestic shares would at least have lost little of it in real terms. The total value of German company shares quoted in Berlin, though at a paltry £89 million in December 1922, was three times as great – at £271 million – in July 1923. This must have been a comfort to any who could overlook the comparison with the pre-war total of £1,767 million, or the £600 million in July 1921. The price (in terms of the dollar) of a number of so-called 'undiluted' shares in the first few months of 1923 was actually twice as high as during the previous October, their all-time low. At that point, in terms of the paper mark the dollar had risen 1,525 times, but nominal share prices had increased only 89 times. In fact from October 1922 onwards it was possible by choosing investments carefully actually to increase one's real capital substantially: by July 1923 the average portfolio would have risen sixteen times, by September twenty-three times and by October twenty-eight times in terms of gold.

The year's performance of the markets, albeit at a level far below pre-war, more or less complemented the hideous bear market of 1922. The fall and the climb, on the other hand, mirrored the availability of foreign currency as a means of holding real value, and the severe volatility of the market at all times made rational investment judgments extremely difficult. During the *Ruhrkampf*, moreover, an enormous number of the buying orders came from the occupied territories – backed by the very subsidies which the government was paying in order to keep passive resistance going. Many investors were dealt heavy losses because of the wild swings in market prices: others, equally, made large chance profits. The effects of inflation upon share prices generally caused immense shifts in the distribution of wealth among a now large share-holding community, and contributed to the rancour and demoralisation of the nation at large. Many who would have dearly liked to buy industrial shares when they were still absurdly cheap were unable to for want of money.*

Not only were individuals induced by the harshness of their circumstances to look after themselves. As the nation moved swiftly towards chaos every community from the states downwards began to look narrowly at its priorities. In East Prussia, for example, seeing from a distance the imminent collapse of central Germany, the businessmen and landowners of Königsberg sought to secure a backdoor for their exports. In this outwardly prosperous district, the ruling class were reported to be quite prepared to leave the ship for another refuge if it sank, and even to leave central Germany to starve if it could provide no market for agricultural produce.

---

* For further and deeper discussion of shares under inflation see Bresciani-Turroni, *The Economics of Inflation* (originally *Le Vicende del Marco Tedesco* 1931) pp 253-285.

East Prussia still enjoyed full employment. In spite of the steps they were now taking to safeguard the future, it was notable that the rich of the state had contributed generously towards the *Ruhrspende* – the fund to support the struggle against France. The isolation produced by the Treaty of Versailles, cutting the area off from Germany proper, had led to the revival of many industries, and latterly an electricity station had been built to cope with the coal shortage. Characteristically, Stinnes had bought up nearly all the shipbuilding yards, and cellulose and paper mills in East Prussia, and other investors were following his lead.

Prosperity, however, was confined as elsewhere to those in a position to benefit from the production of saleable goods. The editor of the *Königsberger Volkszeitung* claimed that there were working-class quarters in the area 'the condition of whose denizens compared unfavourably with what he had seen of the fellahin of Egypt'. As ever, the lower middle class were suffering tragically, and in July four-fifths of the 60,000 persons in Königsberg dependent on public support were *petits bourgeois* attempting to live on their savings. A schoolmaster at Insterburg, interviewed by an Allied observer, said that 70 per cent of East Prussia's schoolchildren were under observation for tuberculosis, adding darkly that 'the sight of food destroys the reason of starving people'.

Saxony was in a politically more dangerous condition. Communism was strong, and the Socialist Prime Minister, Dr Zeigner, had bought the support of nine Communist deputies in order to retain his power in the Landtag. Here there had appeared the first of the Red Centuries – the *Rote Hundertschaften*, those organised bodies of Socialist workmen, Soviet agents among them, whose overt purpose was to supplement the police. What they lacked in firepower they made up for in numbers:' probably 30,000 strong in Saxony to the 11,500 in the police force. They were a dangerous development from a national point of view, although many saw them as an element to neutralise the equally sombre expansion of reactionary societies. Basically, however, they were combustible material, the more so because Saxon factories – as everywhere else – were now pricing themselves out of business. Severe reduction in foreign orders and the necessary curtailment of output were leading to short-time working and unemployment.

The near-stoppage of foreign trade in the middle of the summer affected Germany's trading partners in varying degree. The Board of Trade in London had already recorded the impossibility of doing business directly with Germany. Now the Dutch, the Italians and the Austrians (still struggling to their feet) began to prepare grimly for the political and economic collapse of their common neighbour. Belgium worried intensely about the transit trade via Antwerp in respect of both railways and waterways. Early in August, reparation deliveries in kind ceased even to non-invading members of the Entente. The upheaval in trade and the supply of raw materials throughout the Continent appeared to all to be unending.

Of all Germany, naturally enough, conditions in the Ruhr and the Rhineland at the beginning of August were most challenging. M. Poincaré might require French newspapers to refrain from assisting the disintegration of this area by publishing articles in favour of a Rhenish republic, but France did all she could to break the spirit of passive resistance by persuading German workers in the areas she occupied either away from Germany or back to work. The Ruhr, indeed, was a sorry sight, a picture of economic stagnation. The only trains which ran were the military ones, shunting aimlessly up and down. Canals and inland harbours were blocked with all types of vessels, unable and unwilling to move. Postal and telegraphic services were hopelessly impeded, and telephones were cut off. Few cars circulated and it was hard for anyone to get about, travel difficulties rousing ugly passions in all. The coal being produced by the summer was a fraction of the normal, and now the French, who had cleared the pithead stocks and sent them to France by rail, had located the steel industry's coal stocks by spotter aircraft and were starting on those. The Ruhr's blast furnaces had mostly been damped down, and steel production was minimal.

Lack of coke had reduced the output of iron and steel to one-fifth of its 1922 rate.

In the occupied areas, in and outside the Ruhr, law and order became a fragile commodity. The mark, at 5 million to the pound on July 31, stood at 16 million on August 7. For the next eight days the frontier with unoccupied Germany was closed as a reprisal, General Degoutte announced, for the recent bomb outrages in Düsseldorf. Reprisal or not, it was also part of the French policy to weaken resistance by holding up the import of money supplies, a practice which was correspondingly more effective the more sharply the cost of living rose. The policy was not unsuccessful, for the Ruhr miners and railway workers in particular were reported to be offering to co-operate if no wages were forthcoming from their nominal employers. However, the more immediate result was to turn the populace against authority of all kind; and the unavailability of currency drove frantic not only the Ruhr workless for whom the dole, now at 2 million marks a day, was barely adequate, but the workers who struggled ineffectually throughout the rest of the occupied areas to bring home a living wage.

In the Belgian zone pillaging of crops threatened the harvest. West of Cologne, where looting, strikes and riots were increasing day by day, huge bands of protesters took to roving the countryside destroying crops and farm buildings. At Aachen, 12 demonstrators were killed and 80 wounded in local disorders arising from wage demands. The brown-coal miners of Bergheim (in the British zone) went on prolonged strike after a succession of wild-cat stoppages and threats to burn factories and smash machinery. Police had to disperse 3,000 paper workers at Mülheim, and a mob of unemployed at Solingen raided the market and forced dealers to reduce potato prices by half. The fire-brigade at Leverkusen were locked up by a band of Communists. And at Gelsenkirchen, near Essen in the Ruhr, where Chancellor Cuno and Hugo Stinnes were hanged in effigy, a full-blooded riot developed in the town after the local police force had been surrounded and attacked, with two more deaths recorded.

On August 10, on which date a printers' strike broke out to the further interruption of the supply of banknotes, the full weight of the shortage of paper money was felt. Stocks of food disappeared entirely in many communities, and factories were able to pay wages on account only. The railway workers in the British zone, with a wage tariff half that of factory workers, attempted to join the passive resisters of the Ruhr, and asked pathetically whether, if they were not allowed to strike, they could at least be guaranteed by the occupation authorities enough food at fixed prices as well as the money to buy it.

At Coblenz 300 milliard marks were needed immediately for the weekend payments so that riots and bloodshed could be avoided. Lord Kilmarnock, at Coblenz, did his best to persuade Degoutte to relax his control of the frontier; but the French, strongly suspecting that the Ruhr strikes were mainly financed from the British zone, argued that it was unreasonable for Coblenz and Cologne to receive supplies of marks while the German government refused to supply any for the use of the French and Belgian armies. In this, French suspicions were probably justified, because for three weeks Berlin had systematically been transporting paper marks to Cologne via Amsterdam and Croydon in order to avoid levies and confiscations at the frontiers of French-occupied territory. That innovation came to the notice of the Foreign Office in London because the Croydon Customs Office required guidance as to whether the packages of banknotes which accompanied the Reichsbank's representative Herr Heinrich Schlinkmeier, a quarter of a ton at a time, should be classified as merchandise or personal effects. The traffic in fact continued until the end of passive resistance, and in the meantime General Degoutte was instructed by Paris to allow money supplies into Cologne.

In the British zone things then began to look up in respect of currency. The Reichsbank promised to print locally a million notes a day, each worth a million marks. 'This should render our zone-in-dependent of supplies from outside,' telegrammed Lord Kilmar-nock on August 13 in a misplaced burst of optimism1 (for within a month the million-mark note would be worth a ha'penny), 'and should enable the bank to constitute a reserve against the possible future fall of the mark.'

The local authorities, Cologne and Coblenz included, still did their best to make up for the shortfall in supplies by printing their own currency, but were now finding that the large industrialists were unwilling to give them credits. Friction increased rapidly in local politics, encouraging workers to demand wages geared to notional future values of the mark. The dockers of Bremen were making a bid for wages related to the price of gold. The rioters of Hamburg, where public assembly was forbidden in vain, demanded a base wage of 4.65 million marks (about 7 shillings) a day. On August 13, a Monday, most firms gave rises to their employees ranging from 5 million to 15 million marks a week; but the bulk of the wages had to be paid by cheque, leaving an average of only 5 million (6 shillings) in cash. Cheques took longer to dispose of than cash; and on August 14 the employees of Wupperman surrounded that firm's directors' houses demanding 50 million marks (£3) per head immediately, while a crowd of 10,000 made the same demands from Bayer. Within the week police in Cologne were assaulted with iron bars and stones, mobs were patrolling the streets in Wiesdorf, Ohligs and Hilden, and tremendous unemployment was setting in.

Meanwhile, back in Berlin, far from the bitterness of the Ruhr and the Rhineland, life was scarcely any better. The political crisis had come to a head. When the printers' strike broke out, large crowds furnished with baskets and wheelbarrows surrounded the Reichsbank head office calling angrily for banknotes. There was growing fear of new disturbances in all parts of the country if wages could not be paid, for it was no longer a question anywhere of meeting a weekly deadline, but a daily one. For a fortnight Berlin had been like a beseiged city, the country districts having practically stopped all supplies of meat, eggs and vegetables to the capital. All that could be said about the currency was that it was still current, nothing having replaced it: but it was no serious measure of value, and hardly a medium of exchange.

The complications of daily life in the city by this time were such as to require an extended mathematical knowledge merely to keep body and soul together. In the press each morning would be published a list of the day's prices:

Tramway fare	50,000
Tramway monthly season ticket	
for one line	4 million
for all lines	12 million
Taxi-autos: multiply ordinary fare by	600,000
Horse cabs: multiply ordinary fare by	400,000
Bookshops: multiply ordinary price by	300,000
Public baths: multiply ordinary price by	115,000
Medical attendance: multiply ordinary price by	80,000

There was a different index or multiplier for every trade and for every class of goods in each trade. The most ordinary purchase in a shop demanded three or four minutes of calculation, and when the price had been ascertained several more minutes were usually needed to count out the notes in payment. The queues grew longer and longer. Lord D'Abernon wrote:

> It is hardly to be wondered that a great deal of discontent prevails. It is vexatious enough for a foreigner to be asked for a green fee at the golf course of one million marks, but he can console himself that in his case it amounts to about a shilling. The unfortunate housewife charged similar rates for household articles can make no such reflection. To boot, she has to stand in a queue for several hours to get some articles like butter.

The government, ever desperate to make sense of taxation and to drain back into the Exchequer the paper marks – 'Havenstein roubles', as they were called – which the Reichsbank poured forth (so that the need to print would diminish), tried all it knew. The struggle in the West had to go on, and the *'Rhein-Ruhr Opfer'* (or sacrifice) was instituted to oblige income tax payers to make it possible. The new tax was based on 1922 assessments multiplied fiftyfold for the first payment and by much more for the two subsequent payments. It devolved principally on trade, industry and farming, but anyone earning more than a milliard marks a year (say, £150) or owning a motor-car had to pay it – the latter at 50 times the automobile tax. By August 14 depreciation was so great that the old multipliers of 25 and 35 applying to pre-paid tax were out of date, and even the new proposals for raising income and company taxes respectively by 100 and 140 times had to be super-ceded. Three days later still, it was decided that corporation tax would have to be raised 600 times. Even had these taxes worked, they would not have reduced the budget imbalance by more than half.

The problems of indexation and under-charging were equally evident in the postal services, which were notoriously used to camouflage unemployment. Although Treasury officials freely admitted that the service would work much better if half the employees were dismissed, there was no political possibility of such a measure. The post office fell back on raising the tariff rates from the derisory to the inadequate: letters were now to cost 400 marks (one-eighth of a penny) for inland postage and 1,000 marks for foreign. The expected postal deficit would still be nearly 6,000 milliards. So with the railways, whose administration for four months had failed to adjust prices to the fall of the mark. When first and second class fares rose by 300 per cent on August 1, third and fourth class fares by 250 per cent, and freight charges by 150 per cent, the public outcry was more remarkable than the returns. In fact, in no government department was there any hope of balancing a budget while banknote-printing went on.

As the national debt doubled once again, a gold loan was projected (repayable at 50 per cent premium in 1935) with the express object of mopping up paper notes. It provided for two sorts of investors, the parent who wished to leave something for his children, and the entrepreneur who wanted to keep working capital in stable form. Although this measure was briefly hailed as the first serious attack on the printing press, it was as much use as a broom for keeping back the tide. The Reichsbank was unstoppable. Whole denominations of mark notes were worthless almost on leaving the presses. The entire currency of the country as autumn came had to be renewed again and again, whenever the price of a single tram fare – typical of the value of the lowest unit in circulation – soared on its unflagging upward career. Even from this point of view the policy of inflation must have been a most costly business.

The incapacity of the Bank's directorate at this stage passed the belief of many. On August 3, 1923, observing as though for the first time that the market rate on loan money was 1 per cent a day, the president raised the Bank's discount rate from 18 to 30 per cent per annum and on loans from 19 to 31 per cent. The move, against the advice of the Bank's central committee who considered that it was truckling to market conditions, was however insisted upon by Dr Havenstein's fellow directors; and Havenstein himself opined that it was the Reichsbank's duty not to make rates of interest but to follow them. Had he meant – or at least understood – what he was saying, he should have set the Bank rate at 360 per cent, for even the 3 to 4 per cent a week pertaining to current accounts represented 200 per cent a year. The new rate had no impact whatever.

In an atmosphere of gathering fury and frustration, and with attacks on the Reichsbank's policy being launched from all sides, Dr Havenstein plunged on. Day and night 30 paper mills, 150 printing firms and 2,000 printing presses toiled away adding perpetually to the blizzard of banknotes under which the country's economy had already disappeared. Havenstein spoke of the efficiency – the *Leistungsfähigkeit* – of his printing system, and saw the greatest inflationary danger in the private state banks who were permitted to issue up to 15,000 milliard marks not daily, as the Reichsbank was doing every day of the week except Sundays, but as a once-and-for-all legal limit, and who were demanding the right to print more. This, he said, proclaiming once more his mission to relieve Germany of its dearth of currency, would 'render nugatory the whole credit policy of the Reich and of the Reichsbank'.

The strain of Havenstein and the *Ruhrkampf* together was more than the government could take. Dr Cuno's future was already in doubt when the mark's precipitous slide at the beginning of August began. Without a loan from abroad, with a supplementary estimate before the Cabinet for 6,000 milliard marks (about £400,000) because of the Ruhr subvention, and knowing that to end passive resistance would mean not only political death but probably physical death as well, the coalition began to founder. 'It is not a choice between capitulation and chaos,' explained the Foreign Minister, Dr Rosenberg. 'Capitulation would mean chaos. If things go on much longer without relief, we shall have chaos without capitulation. It comes to this: the alternative is chaos with honour or chaos with dishonour.'

Despair, indeed, was consuming Germany. It was believed that the disturbances in the Ruhr and the Rhineland might lead to the French marching upon Berlin; and the French did not discourage such talk. Violent Communist-led outbreaks were occurring in Saxony and Thuringia, and the reactionary movement under Hitler in Bavaria was palpably growing in strength and size. On August 8 in a speech to the Reichstag largely inaudible because of the noise by Communist deputies, Dr Cuno warned that imports would now have to be curtailed more than ever, that taxation would be 'unrelenting', and that national unity was needed as never before. Although the feature of this sitting was the hostility shown between the Communists and the Majority Socialists, together with the increased insolence of the former towards everyone, the Chancellor was heard in silence at last as he claimed that the seven months of passive resistance in the Ruhr had shown to the world that Germany was worthy of respect. The house listened with approval to his call for the fight to be carried on; but it was Cuno's last effort. He had the air more and more of a scapegoat.

In an avalanche of paper marks, and crashing exchange rates, under the threat of a general strike, in the universal misunderstanding of a Note sent by Curzon stating more or less baldly that France had no right to be in the Ruhr, the Cuno Cabinet fell. It was replaced by that of Dr Gustav Stresemann, the leader of the constitutional, anti-socialist, businessman's Volkspartei.

11: Havenstein

The new Chancellor's first action was to publish Curzon's Note and distribute it for all to read. The threatened general strike was cancelled and heart was almost instantly put into the German people in regard to the *Ruhrkampf*. But Stresemann could not immediately win support from a nation unable to forget for an instant the financial anarchy in which they all lived. The Right, including some of the industrialists who had a marked aversion to taxation, began to suspect and accuse him of following a Socialist line. Disorderly sections of the people – the Communists and, in Bavaria especially, the 'patriotic' organisations – became less ruly than ever.

Fears grew, or were nourished, that Stresemann's appointment spelt an end to passive resistance and capitulation to the French, so that Hitler came within an ace of his aim of welding the forces of reaction into unity: the issue that now divided Munich was whether to shake Bavaria loose from Berlin or to march on the capital. By contrast, anti-Hitler Communist disturbances were launched in Stettin, Lübeck and other towns, and labour riots occurred all over Germany.

No situation, however, was so bad that summer that Dr Havenstein could not make it worse. Nor was anyone in the government who ostensibly knew less about these things than he disposed to remonstrate with him, the guardian and leader of orthodox German financial opinion. He held firmly to his view that money supply was unconnected with either price levels or exchange rates; saw his duty as having to supply to the limit of his ability the medium of exchange for which, because of the mark's ever-tumbling purchasing power, his countrymen were crying out; and was spurred to renewed activity by the latest enormous price rises with which they were beset. The sheer logistics, not to speak of the incredible expense, of printing and distributing time and again the amounts with which he was dealing appeared to be his greatest worry: and although notes of adequate denomination were only transiently available these days, no one in the banking world or in the Reichstag ever suggested that someone else could have better mastered the difficulties of providing them.

The full enormity of Havenstein's policies was duly revealed in the speech he made – published immediately afterwards – to a Council of State on August 17. 'The Reichsbank,' he said, with evident pride and satisfaction, 'today issues 20,000 milliard marks of new money daily, of which 5,000 milliards are in large denominations. In the next week the bank will have increased this to 46,000 milliards daily, of which 18,000 milliards will be in large denominations. The total issue at present amounts to 63,000 milliards. In a few days we shall therefore be able to issue in one day two-thirds of the total circulation.'

How he would bring all this paper into circulation was the least of the questions raised. Havenstein had been completely unconscious of the disastrous effect his intended action and, even more, its proclamation, must have upon the mark's value, not to speak of the whole financial, trading and industrial structure of the country. Before he spoke the mark was at 3 million to the dollar, 12.5 million to the pound (there had been a recent small improvement): within 48 hours it fell to 5.2 million to the dollar, 22 million to the pound. The circulation in August 1923 had an exchange value of £9 million, less than one-thirtieth of what it had been ten years earlier, and no amount of printing contrived to increase its value by a penny. On the contrary, the hole in the budget was getting bigger; but it was on this phenomenon that Dr Havenstein's beliefs about the relationship between money supply and prices were based.

'No one could anticipate such an ingenuous revelation of extreme folly to which ignorance and false theory could lead,' Lord D'Abernon wrote to the Foreign Office. 'The Reichsbank's own demented inspirations give stabilisation no chance.' And in his diary he noted:

Forty-six billion marks [12 noughts] represent a face value of £2,300,000,000,000 and the note circulation £3,150,000,000,000 … The Council of State is supposed to contain financial and economic experts, yet none criticised the policy stated or referred to its insanity. The speech was largely reproduced in the German press, and provoked neither outcry nor astonishment.

That was not quite true. *Vorwärtz*, of which Hilferding, Stresemann's semi-enlightened Finance Minister, had been political editor until 1915, roundly accused Dr Havenstein of spoiling the government's latest attempts to make paper marks scarce – not so much by printing marks as by allowing people to hold on to their foreign bills or, worse, by lending paper marks to them with which they could buy more foreign bills. Under the heading 'Havenstein the Eternal', *Vorwärtz* protested:

> Germany is a Republic but the Reichsbank is a Monarchy! Wilhelm is in Doorn: Havenstein is still in Berlin! He is here for life. He owes that to the Entente – it was an English delusion that the Reichsbank needed strengthening, that inflation was taking place against its will, that an autonomous Bank would refuse to discount Treasury bills. We need an Abdication Law for Havenstein!

The Chancellor seems to have been shocked by Havenstein's performance, but being, with Stinnes, who had greatly influenced him, an inflator himself, he was clearly more taken aback by the fact of the publication of the speech than by its substance, whose stupefying purport he can hardly have grasped. The Socialists demanded Havenstein's dismissal, which was enough to make it politically impossible – and Havenstein's friends said that if he retired the chance of a loan from London, where they believed he was respected, would go. In any case, if called to resign, Havenstein would have been within his rights in refusing.

In the cities, in the towns, in the villages, Havenstein's voluminous, inadequate banknotes, far too many yet far too few, multiplied the already manifold difficulties of existence and drove people further to despair. In Berlin the tramway system ceased to run through lack of means. In villages where no municipal or other emergency currency was available, a sudden drop in the value of the mark would leave the community with too little money to carry on at all: and in isolated villages this would occur without any warning. The sight of shoppers with baskets full of banknotes was now common in every town.

'You could see mail carriers in the streets with sacks on their backs or pushing baby carriages before them, loaded with paper money that would be devalued the next day,' said Erna von Pustau. 'Life was madness, nightmare, desperation, chaos.'

Owing to the shortage of banknotes, which continued in spite of the introduction on August 22 of the first 100 million mark note, numerous firms had begun to issue illegal, unfunded emergency money without any Reichsbank guarantee: and much as Havenstein condemned what he called 'an important new source of inflation' which he was trying to stop, it was clear that the Reichsbank would always redeem them.

Statute books on taxation formed a mountain several feet high, and none could tell who was liable to pay what, when or to whom. The tax receipts for August, though nominally 98 times greater than in April, were in real terms worth half as much, for the mark had fallen 200 times in the same period. Thus between August 20 and 30 receipts represented 0.7 per cent of expenditure. It would in fact have made little difference by then had the tax system been capable even theoretically of meeting a budget whose balance was now continuously being violently upended: in human terms, the imposition of unpayable taxes to settle an impossible debt had at last destroyed tax morals at every level of society. The national unity of the spring had all but evaporated, and hardly anyone was willing any more to make sacrifices for the State.

The useless fight to remove Havenstein crackled on. The Berlin *Börsen*

Courier called to Hilferding to show a strong hand, and wondered whether 'with his pliable Austrian manner' he would fill the role.

> If the *Geheimrats* [meaning, in this case, the senior officials of the Reichsbank] want to dispose of the new Minister they know what they can do about it. First by giving him too many documents so that he is unable to ascertain the simple facts, and then by giving him too few in order that he may know nothing. The currency struggle is personified in the battle between Hilferding and Havenstein; and the struggle about the presidency of the Reichsbank sums up the German situation today.

Did a Prussian estate owner like Havenstein understand, the newspaper inquired, that the German worker could starve? Or was there something more sinister than stupidity at work; was the aim to spread desperation through the masses, to destroy the Republic's authority, and to prepare the way for a dictatorship of the Right? The Stresemann government, the *Courier* thought, was the last effort to save Germany by legal parliamentary methods.

Hilferding made an important speech stating that the mark had to be stabilised, but admitted he could find no better way of meeting the situation than his predecessor, Hermes, had found – and the new gold loan was attracting few subscriptions. The Minister of the Interior attempted uselessly to draw up a budget on a gold basis on the ground that no one understood the meaning of the present figures which in any event were always changing.

On August 25, apparently because the imposition of the *Rhine-Ruhr Opfer* was obliging commerce to cash foreign currency holdings to pay it, the mark staged an abrupt recovery from 25 million to the pound to 12.5 million, so that for 48 hours real wages suddenly exceeded peace-time levels and prices of imported raw materials exceeded world prices; but the rally, long enough to throw the retail price system into complete confusion, was a mere flash in the pan. Havenstein, now on the defensive, insisted that inflation came not from granting credits but from what he called the boundless growth of the floating debt – which was to say he thought it was the government's fault. To the reproach that he had not refused to discount the government's bills, he replied that 'Even a threat by the Bank would have been a useless gesture,' adding that if the Bank's discount rate had been raised to meet the depreciation such a policy would have harmed all branches of industry – and would have had a 'catastrophic' effect, too, on prices.

Havenstein's speech, made in the closing days of August to the central committee of the Reichsbank, ended with a description of what he still regarded as the most serious task in hand:

> The whole extraordinary depreciation of the mark has naturally cre-
> ated a rapidly increasing demand for additional currency, which the
> Reichsbank has not always been fully able to satisfy. A simplified pro-
> duction of notes of large denominations [including printing on one
> side only] enabled us to bring ever greater amounts into circulation. But
> these enormous sums are barely adequate to cover the vastly increased
> demand for the means of payment, which has just recently attained an
> absolutely fantastic level, especially as a result of the extraordinary
> increases in wages and salaries.
>
> The running of the Reichsbank's note-printing organisation,
> which has become absolutely enormous, is making the most extreme
> demands on our personnel. The dispatching of cash sums must, for
> reasons of speed, be made by private transport. Numerous shipments
> leave Berlin every day for the provinces. The deliveries to several banks
> can be made ... only by aeroplanes.

On September 1 the Reichsbank issued a note with a face value of 500 million marks; the new word 'billiard' was coined, joining three more noughts to the old milliard; and 50 million marks were needed to buy one pound sterling.

Circumstances rapidly grew more favourable to the forces of Fascist darkness operating in the south. Externally, perhaps, they were encouraged first by the success of the military party in Spain, but more by Mussolini's successful defiance of the League of Nations following his bombardment and occupation of Corfu at the end of August.* Internally, the all-pervading economic, financial and political uncertainty which had effectively smothered the old national spirit was now the food of extremism. The most moderate persons declared that firmness – a strong hand – was required. They would have agreed with Stresemann that '*In dringenden Notfälle muss geschossen werden*' ('In pressing emergency there must be shooting'). To many, however, Berlin had become synonymous with weakness, the Republic with misery. Thus on September 2, 1923, a hundred thousand demonstrators gathered for the Nazi rally at Nuremburg, where Hitler stood at Ludendorff's side and launched yet another virulent attack upon the government which, he alleged, was about to surrender Germany's honour to France. After the parade, the *Deutsche Kampfbund* – the German Combat Union – was formed with Ludendorff as its president. Within the week, speaking sometimes five or six times a day, Hitler was calling for the installation of a national dictatorship. All he thought he required now was a final national catastrophe in the Ruhr to prove him right and to carry him to power.

Extremism was no less evident on the Left. Stresemann stated privately his belief that the Communists could not let the present opportunity pass without making a desperate effort to upset the existing order: they would never get such a chance again, and the German working class, at heart inclined against Communism, had had its vision clouded by the terrible stresses it had undergone.† Hamburg,

---

* A measure taken precipitately in retaliation for the shooting by brigands on Greek soil of the Italian member of a commission delimiting the frontier between Greece and Albania.

† Not for nothing was Stresemann heard quoting a new verse to the National Anthem, beginning:

'*Deutschland, Deutschland, über alles, und im Unglück nun erst recht,*
Erst im Unglück lässt's sich sagen ob die Liebe frei und echt.'

('*Deutschland, Deutschland, über alles*, and more than ever in distress: to be first in misfortune lets one say whether charity is free and true.')

where bourgeois families were taking steps to protect themselves from outbreaks of revolutionary looting, simmered with discontent, the more so as 600 workmen who had been conspicuously active during the recent shipyard strikes had not been allowed to resume work and were now resorting to crime for a living: the unemployment dole of 700,000 marks a day (about $3^1/_2$ d) made no serious contribution to the needs of a married man with two children. There were many there and elsewhere to heed the cry of 'Hands off proletarian Germany!' now emanating from Radek in Moscow and Zinoviev in Petrograd.

At Dresden in Saxony on September 9 there took place a rally of Socialist and Communist so-called 'self-protecting organisations', in which 8,000 men exercised and manoeuvred for two hours under the command of a local demagogue, Stadtbaurat Sierks, an ex-warrant officer. The Police President, Herr Mehnke, who had once done two-and-a-half years' penal servitude, stood by applauding as Sierks proclaimed: 'We are here to protect the dictatorship of the Left ... If the workers do not join us in their masses, they must be brought out at the point of the bayonet ... It is better that I should do this than that the same task should be left to Hitler's hordes: I must anticipate his actions.'

It was notable, too, that the parade took place with the connivance of the Prime Minister, Dr Zeigner, who had countenanced the formation of the Red Centuries, dragons' teeth which were at last beginning to sprout. Wherever lay the political sympathy of Herr Mehnke's police, however, it did not prevent them from wounding 13 unemployed rioters in a fracas in Dresden two days afterwards.

The nation was also threatened with territorial disintegration beyond that being engineered by France in the Rhineland. From Stettin came the warning of a plan to set up a dictatorship in Pomerania, East Prussia and Bavaria: it would have been a somewhat disjointed arrangement with Herr Noske, the former Defence Minister and now Provincial President of Hanover, as its leader, and Hitler as his

Bavarian deputy; and since, though monarchist in flavour, it would have been Socialist in outlook, Ludendorff would not have been used. How developed was this plot is hard to say. Among the evidence was the concentration in large amounts of foodstuffs, especially potatoes, done with an eye, perhaps, to establishing confidence in the movement's efficiency; the result in Pomerania at least was a shortage of potatoes in spite of a good harvest.

Financially and constitutionally, in the meantime, new measures were being hurried forward, too little and too late, to cope with events of which nobody was in control. The new taxes and the gold loan had in no worthwhile way improved or even altered the situation (although gold loan *'coupures'* became negotiable instruments, credited by the public with constant value). More links were added to the long chain of legislation against traffic in foreign currency, each of which people in the main had no choice but to ignore, since marks were hardly exchangeable except over government counters.

On September 8 a Commissioner for the Control of Foreign Exchange was appointed, with the widest powers to seize foreign currency wherever he could find it, and to oblige holders of bills of exchange or of gold securities to deliver them against gold loan scrip. The appointment required the suspension of various portions of the constitution with regard particularly to postal secrecy, domestic inviolability and the expropriation of goods or property generally; and within ten days the new *Devisenkommissar* had assumed the right also to seize gold, silver, platinum and alloys, whether in coin or raw metal. This move was in part occasioned by the realisation that as 200 million gold marks had been set aside to guarantee the Reich dollar Treasury bills, Germany's gold reserves were effectively down to the equivalent of less than £14 million, too little now with which to establish a new currency in which people could believe.

Thus under the commission's auspices the *Wucherpolizei* on September 20 raided the cafés and restaurants of Unter den Linden and the Kurfürstendamm in Berlin, forced every customer to produce his wallet or purse, and extracted all foreign money therein. The yield of the day's raids, for which receipts were duly given, consisted of 3,120 dollars, £36 sterling, 373 Dutch guilders, 475 Swiss francs, 200 French francs, 42,523 Austrian kronen, 37 Danish kroner, 30 Swedish kronor, 1,402 Czech koruna, 800 Hungarian korona, 143 Serbian dinars, 18,000 Bulgarian lewa, 30 Estonian marks, 5,100 Polish marks and 500 Soviet roubles.

The exercise went not only to show the futility of the new policy, but to underline the desperation of an advanced industrial nation which was unable to find accommodation in a foreign market to the extent of £6 million, the amount Germany then needed to borrow. 'It is,' Addison had written in a private letter to Miles Lampson,* 'as though I was unable to borrow a farthing.'

Unknown heights have now been reached [ran that letter, dated September 11, 1923]. The floating debt increased this morning by 160,000 milliard paper marks. Efforts to calculate in something else are vain: it all comes back to paper marks. The shops are demanding pounds, francs, Danish crowns and any other foreign currency you may care to enumerate, and then take half an hour ascertaining how many thousand millions they require in paper marks: hence an increase in prices quite beyond the fall in the mark. Except for things like tram fares, we are now charged for most articles a few hundred millions more than the same would cost at present exchange rates in London. It is natural, for the shopkeeper discounts a further fall. He has become unaccustomed to thinking in simple figures, so it is thought that forty or sixty shillings must be nothing without millions at the end of them. The Adlon Hotel charges the equivalent of £4 or £5† for a bottle of wine.

---

* Later 1st Lord Killearn. He had just returned to the Foreign Office from Siberia.

† Ten or twelve times the London price: a bottle of good claret at the Savoy Hotel in 1923 cost about 10 shillings.

Addison felt that Germany was 'marching with giant strides towards something very unpleasant' – yet people were still arguing about the responsibility of the industrialists for the nation's woes, or about the form which self-help should take. He had met Germans who appeared genuinely to believe that because conditions had been getting worse for four years they could go on getting worse for ever.

> But obviously something goes on only until the moment when it cannot, and that comes suddenly. Nobody thought the war was near an end in March 1918. Nobody in France anticipated the French Revolution because the shop of Réveillon Frères was sacked by the Paris mob.
>
> You should see the long queues of people standing for hours on end in front of the Berlin provision shops. The housewife cannot clean her home or look after her children if she has to stand from 8 a.m. to 1 p.m. for a piece of sausage which in the end she does not get. The patience of the people is marvellous, but a German crowd when angry is ugly.

He had personally been to take a look at the situation first-hand in Bavaria where food was short in the towns but plentiful in the country. However, he was unable to buy an egg from a farm with paper marks, having been told by a peasant '*Wir wollen keine Judenfetzen von Berlin*' ('We don't want any Jew-confetti from Berlin' – the popular description for Reichsbanknotes). Bavaria was pining for the good old thaler, given up in 1870 – the coin from which the dollar itself derived its name.

Addison's letter had a post-script:

> Since writing the above the pound has gone to 500 million, a drop of 200 million in less than 24 hours.

The new danger was that when the peasants finally refused to deliver produce to the towns, the towns would go and fetch it. It had happened in Austria during the blockade. It had happened in the Ruhr and the Rhineland under the provocation of French militarism and enforced idleness. Now there were reports from Saxony – unoccupied Germany – that bands of several hundred townspeople at a time had taken to riding out into the countryside on bicycles to confiscate what they needed.

Anna Eisenmenger's diary included a first-hand account of the plunder of Linz and its neighbourhood in Austria – the place which Hitler regarded as his home town. She transcribed a letter from her daughter who had been staying there for a few weeks with cousins who ran a small farm with eight cows, two horses, twelve pigs and the usual poultry:

I had driven with Uncle and Aunt to church at Linz. The nearer we approached the more crowded became the usually deserted high road. All kinds of odd-looking individuals met us. One man wearing three hats, one set on top of the other, and at least two coats, excited our amusement … We met people drawing carts piled high with tinned foods of every description … A man and a woman were seated in a ditch by the side of the road and, without the least embarrassment, were changing their very ragged garments for quite new ones. 'Hurry up,' the woman shouted to us, 'or there'll be nothing left!' We did not understand this remark until we passed the first plundered shops.

Peaceful Linz looked as if it had been visited by an earthquake. Furniture smashed beyond recognition littered the pavements. But not only provision shops, inns, cafés, and drapers' shops had been looted. Jewellers and watchmakers, too, had been unable to defend their wares. We saw that the inn at which Uncle and Aunt usually stopped after Mass was completely devastated. The old innkeeper caught sight of us and hurried up, almost in tears. He could not open his inn because all the furniture had been smashed and all the provisions stolen; and he strongly advised my uncle to drive home, since the ringleaders of the mob were inciting their followers to ransack the neighbourhood …

My uncle urged on the horse … In the lane which winds to my uncle's farm … we noticed a troop of about 80 or 100 men and and women. They were bawling and singing and driving in their midst a cart harnessed with a brown horse. Uncle exclaimed: 'They're driving away Hansl and our cart!' Without another word he leapt to the ground, but could only advance slowly with his stiff leg across the field towards the road where he meant to intercept the troop.

A lorry load of gendarmes turned up at that moment. A few shots were fired, and the mob dispersed into the hills, the horse and cart left behind.

In the cart I saw three slaughtered pigs. In addition, some pieces of slaughtered cows and pigs and a few dead hens were lying in an untidy heap. 'My God, my God,' wailed my aunt. 'What will things be like at home?' … Two gendarmes accompanied us in order to ascertain the damage. 'If only they didn't always destroy everything,' said one of them. 'As for their being hungry, that's not surprising.' We were prepared for the worst. The gates of the farmyard were wide open. There was not a sign of the servant girls. A pig seriously injured but still living was lying in its own blood in the yard. The other pigs had run out into the road. The cow-shed was drenched in blood. One cow had been slaughtered where it stood and the meat torn from its bones. The monsters had slit up the udder of the finest milch cow, so that she had to be put out of her misery immediately. In the granary the store of grain and fodder were in a state of wild confusion … a rag soaked with petrol was still smouldering to show what these beasts had intended. In the kitchen-living room of which my aunt was so proud not a thing had been left whole. Uncle estimates the damage at 100,000 peace kronen, and no insurance company will pay him any compensation for his loss.

The towns were starving. The countryside had had a bumper harvest, but there it remained because of the farmers' steadfast refusal to take paper for it at any price. Something had to be done to shift it. On September 18 were published the plans for the new Boden Credit Bank, later to be known as the Rentenbank, a bank of issue backed not by gold (it was too late for that) but by mortgages on both agricultural land and industry. It was fundamentally an expedient to induce the farmers to co-operate in feeding the nation: and the *Bodenmark* was by way of a solid form of *Kontomark* – the units of account worth ten cents each which the Reichsbank was now using to express the real values of current accounts: at last the old fiction of *Mark gleich Mark* had been formally abandoned.

The most usual comment on the new scheme was that, having found the printing press almost played out as an instrument of inflation, the Reichsbank was looking round for a new one. The Bodenmark was, after all, in no way intended as a means towards stabilisation. Like the gold loan which preceded it, and like the rye loan – to be issued and repaid according to the going price of rye – which was proposed simultaneously, it was merely a stop-gap: nor was it suggested that the printing presses should stop. Indeed, ten and twenty-milliard mark notes were just coming into circulation, the larger falling from a theoretical exchange value of perhaps £50 on the day of issue (September 15) to £30 within seven days. By this time there was an acute divergency of up to 40 per cent between the official exchange rate and the free market rate. The paper mark was finding fewer and fewer takers and every industry was fixing its prices according to different indices.

In the first half of September, the Ruhr was responsible for five-eighths of the daily increase in the floating debt: 50 milliard marks a day spent to maintain the workers there in idleness, somewhat – but not much – more than the phenomenal costs of subsidising the German railways and postal services. To some extent, the Ruhr financial operation was actually supporting the franc, for marks were being used there to buy up that much less sickly currency.

The *Ruhrkampf* had turned sour. No doubt the idea of it still roused patriotic fervour in many parts of Germany: certainly the suggestion that surrender might be the more practical solution was still worth more than any politician's life. In the Ruhr itself, though, demoralisation among the working class was deep, the result of acquiring the habit of idleness while on insufficient pay. In national terms, coal was the crux of the struggle: Germany could not carry on without it, and for that reason it had become certain that, whatever one chose the expression to mean, Poincaré would 'win'. A Pyrrhic victory for France would be of no more than academic comfort to the losers: nor would Stresemann be allowed by the reactionary movements to exploit it.

By the end of the third week in September, therefore, the Government's control of the political, let alone the financial, situation was strained to breaking point. So were the ministers: according to Beneš, then Czech Foreign Minister, they were so exhausted that they were incapable of any real consideration of the problems they had to deal with, 'the decision of which depends on which minister had most sleep the night before'. The proclamation of September 19 threatening a month in gaol and unlimited fines to anyone who hoarded food or money, or prevented the paying of taxes, or impeded the distribution of food or fodder, though signed by the Chancellor, the Minister of the Interior and the President himself, was a useless act of desperation: everyone, ministers included, was hoarding all he could; no one made any effort to pay taxes; and the only impediment to the distribution of food was the lack of a negotiable currency to pay for it.

There was, however, no doubt about Stresemann's determination. His problem was how to abandon passive resistance without the loss of Germany's dignity. It was a problem without a solution. Following an apparent agreement between Poincaré and Baldwin that no point of policy divided Britain and France, and learning of the illegal declaration of a State of Emergency in Bavaria, Stresemann, who had been fully prepared to act on his own if the Reichstag should stand in his way, at last looked facts in the face.

On September 26 he suspended seven articles of the Weimar constitution, himself declared a State of Emergency, and gave executive powers to Herr Gessler, the Defence Minister who had succeeded Noske after the Kapp *Putsch*. This transfer was a formality. Effectively, from then on, for five months, General von Seeckt, Commander-in-Chief of the Reichswehr, was the supreme executive and administrative power in the land.

Germany had become a military dictatorship, no less, and by the choice, at that, of a largely Socialist cabinet. The country was divided into seven military districts, with a local military dictator over each. Simultaneously President Ebert announced the end of passive resistance in the Ruhr.

12: The Bottom of the Abyss

Here, perhaps, was the strong hand that moderate Germans had wanted for months. They had it at a cost beyond the imagined loss of international dignity. There could now be restrictions on personal liberty, freedom of expression, freedom of the press and freedom of association. The army and the police might interfere at will with postal, telegraph and telephone services, indulge in house searches, and confiscate property. Incitement to disobedience could be punished with imprisonment or a fine of up to 15,000 gold marks. If lives were endangered the punishment would be penal servitude. Death would meet death – and would also be the penalty for the ring-leading of armed mobs, treason, arson or damage to the railways.

The Right, presumably, would have wished for no less. However, Berlin was only catching up with the game. Bavarian leaders had already questioned Beneš about Czechoslovakia's attitude in the event of a declaration of independence. Beneš told them (he reported to Curzon) that he would remain neutral provided there was no union of Bavaria with Austria, and 'provided the movement was left in the hands of Hitler and Rupprecht [the Wittelsbach crown prince of Bavaria] and that Ludendorff had nothing to do with it'.

Munich's rulers knew Hitler rather better than Beneš did. The Bavarian emergency had been proclaimed mainly in response to Hitler's putting 15,000 SA troopers on the alert and assuming leadership of the *Kampfbund* – no one knows whether or not he intended a *coup d'état* at that moment. Now the Bavarian cabinet, equally unconstitutionally and in violation of the Treaty of Versailles, appointed the anti-Republican politican Gustav von Kahr as State Commissioner-General with dictatorial power over the state. Von Kahr thereupon sat on a furious Hitler, and the situation was soon regularised, in name if not in practice, by Gessler's appointing von Lossow, the local Reichswehr commander, as the official government commissioner with von Kahr as his civil arm. Because from then on communication between Berlin and Munich became progressively more sticky, the new reality was that Germany had two dictators, one in either city. Von Seeckt rapidly reduced an ill-organised Right-wing *Putsch* at Küstrin in Prussia to impotence, taking the opportunity finally to suppress the 'Black Reichswehr' (the remnants of the Free Corps), and would treat equally firmly the Left-wing movement in Saxony. Much though Helfferich, the leader of the Nationalists, might fume in the Reichstag against Germany's new capitulation to France, the fact remained that a way out of the diplomatic and economic impasse was at last opening up.

It is a matter for record that at this desperate point in Germany's fortunes at least some sectors of the economy were trying to maintain business as usual. A case in point was the motor industry who decided to go ahead with their October motor car exhibition in Berlin, designed to show that the German manufacturers were still a world competing force. Critical opinion held that this was not proved. The main difference since the last motor show in 1921 was the huge increase of small cars and cycle-cars, the majority ugly and of doubtful quality. The well-known makes had developed very little.

> Euler still shows his fantastic car shaped like a drop of water [the *Tropfenauto*], blunt end at the front [reported the British Commercial Attaché sourly], Maybach again his gearless chassis, Benz and Mercedes their usual types, and the only other make worth mentioning is the Audi, which has possibly improved. All the bodywork is inferior, the colour schemes are painful, and the shapes are monstrous where not stereotyped. The fittings are shoddy and in bad taste. There is no intelligible basis for prices.

A strong hand at the centre, or centres, brought none of Germany's tangible problems nearer solution. Indeed, in almost every way things were rapidly worsening, with accelerating inflation at the root of every trouble. In the last week of September the Reichsbank issued 3,267 million million marks, a sum with a current exchange value of £5.2 million a day. Duly responding, the mark, at 315 million to the pound on September 11, reached 1,500 million to the pound on October 2, and 5,700 million on October 9. The Reichsbank stepped up its output.

These extraordinary figures betokened terrible distress. The average pre-war wage had been about 36 gold marks – £1 16s – a week. In October 1923 the purchasing power of the average wage fell to less than 20 per cent of normal. The situation hardly required extremists to whip up revolutionary feeling. Sums of less than one million marks were no longer dealt with, and, indeed, as Lord D'Abernon reported to Curzon, 'a beggar would hardly accept any smaller note'.

And yet the distress was not only physical. For eight months the German people had been assured by their Government, and taught to demand, that passive resistance would never be given up. To the ignorant this implied that it could go on for ever. Every window and every kiosk was still placarded with exhortations to stand firm, or with appeals for funds, or with pictures of French troops beating the population. Now all this suddenly ceased, and the people were calmly informed that their Government had been making fools of themselves and that they must surrender unconditionally over a matter which had cost them trillions of paper marks and an immeasurable amount of inconvenience and suffering. Contempt for the Republic and its servants now became almost universal.

'The population is ripe,' Joseph Addison wrote home to Alexander Cadogan,[*] 'to accept any system of firmness or for any man who appears to know what he wants and issues commands in a loud, bold voice.'

Addison had another significant point to make:

---

[*] Later Sir Alexander Cadogan, O.M., Permanent Under-Secretary of State for Foreign Affairs, 1938-1946.

Economic distress is leading the people to be much more amenable to authority as representing the only hope of salvation from the present state of affairs. Unemployment is taking the gilt off the gingerbread of democracy, while the working classes realise that striking is useless since nothing would be more welcome to employers.

At the beginning of October, just after the passing of the new Currency Bank Law, Stresemann tried to push through an Enabling Act, taking further extra-constitutional powers for the government. His Volkspartei had seen the opportunity to give a death-blow at last to the eight-hour day, a piece of revolutionary legislation which business interests still condemned with peculiar hatred: and the new proposal was the very negation of Social Democracy. The issue split the Ministry, and now even Hilferding, who had clung to his post of Finance Minister like a limpet, felt obliged to resign with his Socialist colleagues. The government fell.

Stresemann's new Ministry which took office on October 6 was inevitably further to the Right, seeking a formula for making people work harder and German industry more productive. It was a programme with which the working people were disposed to agree. They had little enthusiasm left for democracy, and were themselves moving towards authoritarianism through sheer weariness of spirit and an almost complete indifference to anything except their own lack of material comforts. The Chancellor was to get his Enabling Act on October 13. The Volkspartei's manifesto of October 4 therefore only reflected national predilections when it asserted that 'the helm of the Ship of State must be put over to the Right ... Marxism has ruined Germany ... An end must be made to this policy of compromise. Away with the Socialists out of the government!'

Away they went, though not without a counterblast from the unions: 'Obey only the instructions of your organisation! Maintain discipline! Down with the enemies of the working class! Long live the Republic!'

The workers, however, accepted that the Ruhr struggle was over.

On September 30 the *Kölnischer Zeitung* (price 5 million marks) had published a copy of the declaration that workmen had to sign on returning to work for the French *régie* – an oath of service to the Belgians and the French. On October 6 the German government abandoned the *'Rhein-Ruhr-Hilfe'* – aid to the area – but prepared to carry on paying the dole to those who could not find work: until November 1 the dole was to be twice the amount payable elsewhere, after which it would be the same, which was to say equal to half the estimated basic requirement of whoever received it. The pressure was already on: and on October 7 a number of industrialists, including Herr Stinnes and the director of the Prussian State Mines (but not Herr Krupp von Bohlen, who was still in gaol), approached the French Commander-in-Chief with a view to resuming work. Discussions continued, and a week later the German government instructed the railway personnel to return to their posts.

It remained as true as it had even been that no settlement of any kind was possible until German finance had been restored. The resumption of coal deliveries to France and any other deliveries in kind could only be paid for by the government. The only means of paying was increasing the issue of banknotes. On October 10 the pound stood officially at 7 milliard marks – but on the free market one could get 18 milliard for it. On October 15 the official rate was 18.5 milliard and the free market rate into the 40 milliards. Every kind of plan for currency reform was in the air, based on gold, or rye, or foreign exchange, or 'material values'. The. great question was whether foreign control of Germany's finances would be acceptable. The formula of a small loan, a new bank of issue, and supervision by an external agent would probably have worked in Germany even better than it had done in Austria: the great advantage for any country whose currency had gone to pieces was that one could start with a clean sheet, public and municipal debts wiped out. The talk went on as the mark shot downwards meaninglessly from worthless to very worthless, as poverty, hunger and now cold gripped the nation. The working classes were at last undergoing what the middle classes had been suffering for three years.

When the Rentenmark Ordinance was published on October 15, creating the Rentenbank, it was hailed as radically unsound. The Rentenmark was the *Bodenmark* rechristened, in essence a modified *Roggenmark* (or rye-mark), the device propounded by Karl Helfferich; and it was designed to win support from Helfferich's agrarian Nationalists as well as from the Left who found the *Roggenmark* politically suspect. Whatever might be said against the Rentenmark – especially about the reality of its backing – it met the fundamental principle of releasing the Reichsbank from the fatal obligation of having to finance the government. If it worked, it would carry Dr Havenstein back to the currency framework of 1913, when every banknote meant what it said. The Rentenmark was the contrivance of Hilferding's successor at the Finance Ministry, Dr Luther, and of Dr Schacht, the managing director of the Darmstadt & National Bank who was soon to be appointed the new Currency Commissioner. However, in the middle of October, the Rentenmark scheme was just one more of the currency plans which, as Addison had it, 'simply smudge one's brain with ink'. There was no new bank of issue, still less any new banknotes which might replace the old.

Although Munich and the municipalities of Bavaria were suffering no more than the same economic rigours as anywhere else, it was evident that here was the most explosive mixture in Germany. The new British Consul-General at Munich, Mr Robert Clive, noting that numerous press correspondents had gathered in the Bavarian capital, ventured that so far as he could gather 'nothing for the present is likely to happen'. New decrees were issued daily prohibiting public meetings and strikes, and there was no doubt that the two authoritarian friends, von Kahr and General von Lossow, were in full control. So confident were they, indeed, that they were calculatingly ignoring instructions received from Berlin. Their posture even went to the lengths of refusing Berlin's order to ban Hitler's newspaper, the *Völkischer Beobachter*, on October 2, but none the less suspending it for ten days from October 5 for publishing a treasonable article.

'Bavaria prefers Kahr,' wrote Clive. 'The eclipse of Hitler is almost complete.' Von Kahr, in fact, was tearing leaves wholesale out of Hitler's book, deliberately fostering the war responsibility lie (the *Kriegschuldlüge*) and expelling dozens of Jewish families, from paupers to profiteers, from the state: when the *Münchner Post* accused him of taking this action expressly to please Hitler, it, too, was suppressed.* Von Lossow was no more amenable to central discipline than Kahr. Kahr did not answer letters. It was reported by Addison, to whom Stresemann had poured out his woes:

> Lossow is always protesting that he is doing his best to carry out instructions as *Reichsdiktator*, but somehow something invariably happens to nullify those excellent intentions: his instructions arrive too late, or he is out at lunch, or he is burying his aunt ... For practical purposes Bavaria is no longer part of the Reich.

On October 20 Kahr overruled Berlin's dismissal of Lossow.

The central government's difficulties can hardly have affected the populace on the spot, least of all those whose minds were not permanently fixed on political or military adventure. 'The distress is very great,' said Clive's report of October 18.

> Few families can afford meat more than once a week, eggs are unprocurable, milk terribly scarce and bread already sixteen times the price of a few days ago when the maximum price was abolished. It is no doubt true that the expensive restaurants are full of well-dressed people drinking wine and eating of the best in Munich – but they are either German-Americans mistaken for locals, or Ruhr industrialists ... No one expects political disturbances, but hunger riots are another matter ... and the cold: no one can afford central heating. No one imagines the Rentenmark will help.

---

* The *Post* probably was unfair to Kahr, who was something of a pietist, unreasonable to deal with, and considered himself the Providential instrument chosen to deliver Germany from Socialists as well as Jews.

So, too, Herr von Haniel, Berlin's representative *Reichsminister* in Munich:

> The desperate economic conditions are mainly responsible for these recurring troubles. Things could not be worse. Demoralisation and irresponsibility are rampant, and will continue until some light appears on the horizon and the feeling again begins to grow that there is something to live for, beyond the value of the dollar and the necessity to get rid of paper marks before they are worthless.

Elsewhere the people were equally resorting to direct action where the government was failing them. Troops with machine-guns patrolled the streets of Bremen whose cotton-spinners and shipyard workers were all on another cost-of-living strike. There, and in the surrounding province of Hanover, unemployment was increasing by about 10 per cent every week, and prices were rushing upwards in terms of gold as well as of paper. Mr Elphick, the Consul at Bremen, had just arrived there:

> The first thing that strikes one is that the days of German cheapness seem to be practically over. One comes to this country full of stories of the wonderful value to be obtained for one's money in all directions. On arrival one finds that prices in Germany have not only reached the world level but are already outstripping it, so that it is actually cheaper to buy in England than locally. The reason is that even in Germany it is now fully realised that the mark is absolutely valueless and all prices have been placed on a gold basis.
>
> Generally speaking a 'ground price' is fixed on gold marks at double the pre-war figure, and this is multiplied by a multiplicator fixed by the retailers themselves, according to their own free will, and which increases not only day by day but frequently even hour by hour in an effort to keep pace with the Gadarene downward

rush of the paper mark – rather, to keep ahead as, in order to provide against the rapid depreciation on their hands of the resultant 'gold' price in paper marks, an enormous rate of profit is included.*

On October 24 the Bremen Senate took it upon itself to issue gold notes to a total value of 1 million dollars, not in marks but in denominations of a quarter, a half and one dollar, with smaller values of five and ten cents expressly to be used for daily purchases without the necessity of exchanging them for paper marks. Gold certificates had already been issued as part of wage packets, and were repayable in five months time either in Bremen State 5 per cent dollar bonds or in Reichsbank currency at the middle official New York rate. The one-dollar note, on the other hand, was redeemable at any time in paper marks at the full official rate without the usual tax on foreign exchange transactions. As the issue was backed by all the receipts and resources of the rich state of Bremen – an important gateway to Germany in the event of the nation's breakup – it seemed to be as stable a currency as it was then possible to devise in any part of Germany.

Bremen took the calculated risk that the continued issue of paper marks would put into operation Gresham's Law, that bad money drives out good; and so that the new gold notes would merely be hoarded. However, by the autumn of 1923, a new factor was at work – the absence of any ability to hoard. Workers and *petits bourgeois* alike had been reduced to penury, their realisable resources gone. Stocks of retail goods badly needed replenishing so that small trade might revive; but pockets were empty. It seemed improbable that anyone would continue to handle a currency which nobody wanted, so that, contrary to theory, the better medium would actually drive the inferior out of circulation. One result hoped for from the gold issue was a fall in prices as retailers no longer had to allow for depreciation.[†]

---

* The envelope of Elphick's letter to London, postmarked October 22, bore stamps with a face value of 148,000,000 marks.
† On February 10, 1923, Professor J. Shield Nicholson pointed out in *The Scotsman*:

Separatism of the financial variety was the least of the government's worries. Territorial separation threatened in Prussia, Saxony, Bavaria and the Rhineland. There was even a Guelph secessionist plot in Hanover, with its figurehead the Duke of Cumberland – the English title of the grandson of the deposed Elector of Hanover. The most menacing, after Bavaria, was the Rhineland separatist movement which had been gaining strength for many weeks – at least, it had been increasing noticeably in the numbers of its marchers and rioters and in the volume of their cries. At Düsseldorf on September 30, twenty thousand separatists had gathered, marched and killed eleven policemen – the crowds imported by train with French permission and encouragement while the local population locked its doors and stayed at home.

Further outbreaks with and without French support occurred throughout the following three weeks, and at last, on October 21, a Rhenish Republic was proclaimed in the Belgian zone, at Aachen. It was immediately quashed with a sharp note to Belgium from Curzon. However, supported by French troops, separatist administrations were instantly declared at Bonn, Trier, Wiesbaden and Mainz in the French zone. The leaders of the new Republic quarrelled, the German civil service refused to co-operate, and the regime and public services collapsed. The French then turned their attention to the Palatinate, an integral part of Bavaria, intimating that it had become an autonomous State.*

Simultaneously with the Rhineland diversions came serious and dangerous Communist-encouraged trouble in Hamburg. Fundamentally the cause was the old one: when the week's wages were

---

'After a point in the depreciation of paper money the reverse of what is called Gresham's Law comes into play: the legal tender in spite of penalties loses its purchasing power. The better money drives out the worse … The feeble efforts of the German Government to restrain speculation in paper marks are as useless as the chains and death penalties decreed to support the Assignats [of the French Revolution, which were made legal tender in 1790 but abandoned in 1796 as unworkable].'
* The story of how Curzon knocked this one on the head is retailed in *Curzon: The Last Phase*, Harold Nicolson, Chapter XII.

received in the tail of another currency collapse they were entirely inadequate for people's needs. On October 15 the authorities withdrew the bread cards which had enabled people in need to buy bread at less than half the market price. A week later the dockers and ship-builders went on strike again. Police stations were rushed, trees felled across the streets, trenches dug, and the few open food shops which the rioters could find plundered. One *coup* had already been suppressed in Küstrin; and the government were taking no more chances. The German cruiser *Hamburg* arrived accompanied by torpedo boats and put ashore enough marines to stamp out the rebellion and arrest 800 of its Left-wing activists.

On October 15, the mark's rate against the pound passed 18 milliards. On October 21, after the mark had moved in three days from 24 milliards to 80 milliards to the pound, Lord D'Abernon noted with some statistical glee that (at 60 milliards) this was 'approximately equal to one mark for every second which has elapsed since the birth of Christ'. At the end of the month the banknote circulation amounted to 2,496,822,909,038,000,000 marks, and still everybody called for more. On October 26, the Reichsbank in Berlin (where there had been no bread for some days as bakers were short of flour) was surrounded by a crowd demanding milliard-mark notes which were carried off in baskets and carts as soon as they were printed. The first billiard, and 5-billiard, and 10-billiard notes would be ready on November 1.

Thus the Hamburg disturbances at the end of October, although worked on by the Left, were the product of the most genuine frustration and despair. Depreciation had taken place so rapidly that wages could no longer be readily adjusted by the use of index numbers and multiplicators. Workmen who had been receiving 405 million marks a day on October 1 (about 6s 8d at the then rate of exchange) and 6,500 million on October 20, suddenly found that their new packet (with the exchange at 80 milliards) represented only is 7½ d. Prices, on the other hand, had pretty well kept pace with the exchange rates: in the main, the speed with which retail prices moved was a protectiv measure. Business had become virtually impossible, and shopkeepers who kept going were subject to a new ordinance – promulgated on October 22 – compelling them to keep their shops open and to offer goods in exchange for paper marks.

As elsewhere, the cry remained in Hamburg for wages of fixed value. It appeared to be a long time since the unions' single demand had been for ever-higher wages – enough marks to meet the increase in prices. On October 26 the very men who were clamouring for fixed wages turned down the offer of a wage rendered in the new Hamburg gold mark notes on the dual grounds that their employers were in no position to pay it and that, in any case, they needed paper marks to meet their living expenses. People hardly knew what they wanted. On November 1, after the Hamburg assembly had voted 500,000 milliard marks (nearly £2,000) to relieve distress, Hamburg went back to work again, with payment in the port being made after all in the municipal 'gold' currency.

The arrangement was far from perfect, because the notes had to be converted into paper marks before they were spent, and outrageous advantage was frequently taken by the moneychangers. However, general relief that the Communist uprising had been suppressed was so great that the seriousness of the industrial situation in the city was widely unappreciated: Hamburg's 100,000 unemployed included 30,000 shipbuilders, 6,000 longshoremen, and some 60,000 others.

It was the same story all over Germany, better in some places, worse in others, and worst in the Ruhr. Dismissals continued everywhere. A contingent of marines from the *Hamburg* was despatched to the Ruhr because of the trouble feared following the decision by Thyssen, Stinnes and other industrialists to close down many of their factories. Their discussions with the French had been amicable, to mutual advantage, but in conflict with the requirements of Berlin.

The Chancellor visited the Ruhr and returned, appalled, on October 27. The run-down of the official dole in the occupied areas was all but complete, but even at its risible national level the government could no longer afford to continue subvention of any kind. The trade unions were reporting an over-all German unemployment figure of 18.7 per cent of their members, with another 40 per cent of the work force on short time which varied from 4 or 5 to 30 or 40 hours a week. Apart from the 2 million workers in the occupied territories, the government was paying unemployment relief to 877,262 in unoccupied Germany (where union unemployment was at 10 per cent) and short-time relief to nearly 1,700,000 others. There were as many more whom no relief was reaching. Practically all the stagnation in unoccupied Germany was due to the shutting down of the rest.

For November, Stresemann said to D'Abernon, there was the prospect of 5 million workers without work, without government support, and largely without food. More riots were inevitable. Stinnes and his colleague Vogler were to continue negotiations with the French, but it seemed certain that the Nationalists, with Stinnes behind them, were determined as their first priority to destroy the present government. That was only half of it. The coal tax demanded by the French as part of the price of a return to normality simply could not be paid. The Rhineland had become the domain of lawlessness, anarchy and the unrestrained terrorism of armed separatist bands, occupying the town halls and, with French support, defying the police. In the country in general, the population would no longer accept a currency in any form which lost half its value every successive day. Nor was this all.

Dr Zeigner's Communist ministers in Saxony had issued a manifesto setting up a red dictatorship, and Zeigner had declined Berlin's ultimatum bidding him to restore order. Furthermore, knowing that his only hope, and perhaps Germany's only hope of surviving as a complete nation, was the introduction of a stable medium of exchange, the Chancellor now expressed his doubts that the Rentenmark would be effective even as a stop-gap. Most surely, the pips had squeaked.

On October 30, with the mark at 310 milliards to the pound, the Berlin government faced five immediate crises: Bavaria, Saxony, the Rhineland, the question of resumption of work in the Ruhr, and the financial chaos.* On a successful outcome to the Ruhr negotiations depended further negotiations with New York for the supply of sufficient credits to buy essential imports of food and fuel. If the loan were large enough, it might be possible, in conjunction with Germany's remaining reserves, to start a new currency. Otherwise the government had nowhere to look for the oxygen that might keep it going a little longer.

Its troubles, however, were not coming in single dozens. On November 1, Hitler's Bavarian levies were understood to be mustering on the border of Thuringia (with much moral support from Brandenburg and Pomerania), threatening to deal with the Communist insurgents there if the Republic would not. The military Commissioner-General in Saxony, meanwhile, to whom reinforcements had been sent, proceeded with such force (as well as success) against the Red Centuries and their sponsors – Zeigner and his ministers were arrested – that it provoked an adverse reaction from the Socialists in the Reichstag and contributed to the brewing Cabinet crisis. On November 2 there was violent panic on the Berlin Bourse – not because of Bavaria or the Cabinet crisis, nor merely because of the mark which had just lost four-fifths of its value in three days, but rather because of the realisation that there were no fewer than eight official kinds of paper in circulation, outside the numberless issues of emergency money made by municipalities, industrial firms and the federal states. The official tokens ranged from the Reichsbank notes and railway *Notgeld* to gold loan '*coupures*' and Reich dollars. It was a period (said Lord D'Abernon) of 'chaos the like of which had not been seen in economic history'.

On November 5, the military authorities considering that the action against Saxony was complete, the Reichswehr turned upon Thuringia, drawing more protests from Socialist deputies, many of whose constituents were now in the line of fire. On November 6, the looting of foodshops – with strong anti-Semitic overtones – started in

---

* The taxation system remained largely based on paper values until December 1923. In October a passport at the Polish border still cost 2 paper marks, the tariff never having been raised since the war.

the poorer quarters of Berlin, where the population was once again in the acutest distress because of the farmers' reluctance to sell their produce in the cities. A British businessman, Mr J.C. Vaughan, passed through Berlin and wrote a letter of protest to the Foreign Office in London:

> I was sickened by the sights I saw. I happened to pass through the Arcade between the Friedrichstrasse and Unter den Linden, and in that small space I saw three almost moribund women. They were either in the last stages of decline or starvation, and I have no doubt it was the latter. They were beyond asking for alms, and when I gave them a bunch of worthless German notes, it shocked me to see the eager way in which they seized upon them – like a ravenous dog at a bone. I am no pro-German, but that we should tolerate such a state of things five years after the Armistice is to my mind appalling. I cannot help doubting whether persons who have not seen these miserable things really realise what they are … Of course one sees motors and crowds of well-to-do people in profusion in Berlin, but do we know what is going on in the poorer quarters? The waiting queues tell their own tale.

This was the common lot in the industrial areas and in the towns everywhere, except in the municipalities whose *Notgeld* based on gold values had proved acceptable and whose basic needs could be supplied by their immediate agricultural neighbourhoods. Such havens were few. In Breslau, another foreign businessman who had lived since September largely on bread and weak tea found that he could get 'one square meal a day by crowding into a restaurant in the early morning and waiting until luncheon was served some hours later'. Although he had money to pay for what he ate, he went hungry to bed each night.

The fact was that although the farmers' barns all over the country were bursting with unsold food, Germany was suffering from widespread famine. Every Zurich provision shop had a placard saying: 'Send food parcels to your friends in Germany.' As ever, and worse than ever, the conditions and prospects of the middle and professional classes were fearsome. Only two remedies seemed possible, the one preposterous, the other elusive to the point of absence: food from abroad, or a stable medium which would persuade Germany's farmers to release food in exchange for paper.

The Thuringian action held the lid down for two more days on the boiling Bavarian kettle. Hitler's hopes that a pitched battle with the Communists of Thuringia or Saxony would lead to Bavarian troops marching on Berlin were dashed. Tension in Munich mounted hourly as Kahr and Lossow toyed – or so it was believed – with proclaiming Bavaria's secession as an independent monarchy. This danger, with the necessity to do something positive in order to ride with the revolutionary momentum which had been building up ever since the end of the *Ruhrkampf,* persuaded Hitler to attempt his *Putsch* on the night of November 8.

The course of the Bürgerbräukeller *Putsch* and its ignominious end the following day after one volley from the Munich police guarding the Odeonplatz is not strictly part of this story, and has anyhow been related often enough.* The important considerations are that Hitler and the Nazi Party were able shamelessly and facilely to use the miseries inherent in a severe inflationary situation to drum up nation-wide opposition to authority and to persuade many thousands of people that the fault and the blame lay directly in many places where it palpably did not: with the men who had signed the Armistice, with the French, with the Jews, with the Bolshevists. Inflation played into Hitler's hands, and was no more the invention of the Communists, who were also taking advantage of the social wreckage it was causing, than of Hitler and the Nazis.

Inflation is the ally of political extremism, the antithesis of order. At other times – in post-revolutionary Russia, in Kadar's Hungary

---

* The accounts in Wheeler-Bennett's *The Nemesis of Power* or in Bullock's *Hitler: A Study in Tyranny* seem to need no embellishment.

– it may have been deliberately engendered in order to destroy the social order, for chaos is the very stuff of revolution. In Germany at this time, however, the inflationary policy was the consequence of financial ignorance, of industrial greed and, to some extent, of political cowardice. It therefore produced hothouse conditions for the greater and faster growth of reactionary or revolutionary crusades. Hitler set his hopes in 1923 on 'the revolt of starving billionaires'.* He gave the Bavarian authorities and, perhaps to a lesser extent, the Berlin authorities a very nasty turn during that second week of November. To the Reich government for twenty-four hours, as sympathy for Hitler mounted in East Prussia and Pomerania, there appeared to be a real danger of civil war not confined to Bavaria. And yet the Communist rising that had just been suppressed in Hamburg a few days before was regarded – at least until Hitler's trial in February 1924 – as the much more sinister and dangerous episode. In fact the danger of a workers' revolution other than under Communist sponsorship was what had hurried the Communist Party, in due consultation with Moscow, into promoting its ill-co-ordinated national insurrection.

The bloodletting in Bavaria – where martial law was declared – hardly served to cool passions or relieve the unhappiness anywhere else. Von Seeckt set about suppressing all the extreme parties, armed with the powers of the latest presidential decrees. In the interest of calm, the President and the Chancellor issued a proclamation condemning the treasonable outbreak in the south and pointing out that the latest currency measures had improved the mark manifold within 24 hours; but this sumptuary triumph was short-lived. The first 100-billiard note† was already out. Dr Havenstein's presses were giving of their bounty to the record tune of nearly 74 million million million marks a week, quadrupling in six days the previous total circulation. The cost-

* Konrad Heiden, in *Der Führer: Hitler's Rise to Power*, explains fully how Hitler played on the economic fears of all classes at this time.

† The highest denomination ever printed: 100,000,000,000,000 marks, referred to in Germany (as in Britain) as one hundred billion.

of-living index, taking 1914 as 1, had risen from September's average of 15 million to 3,657 million in October and now, on November 12, was at 218,000 million.

The women of Cologne, where there were nearly 100,000 work-less, sent an emotional but hardly exaggerated appeal addressed 'To the Women of the British Empire':

> During the times of passive resistance we existed, not by industry, but through the paper money doles sent from unoccupied country. Now these have ceased and we face starvation. Industry cannot recover, and there are millions, literally, out of work … tens of thousands of our leading citizens have been banished or imprisoned … our newspapers have been suppressed … armed hordes of adventurers have now been let loose on our disarmed and helpless population in the name of separatism and Republicanism … Winter is before us, and we have no coal.

In fact the German government was preparing to leave the finances of the occupied zone to their own fate. It was something that might have been done rather than embarking on the suicidal path of passive resistance, but of course the previous January humanitarian and patriotic considerations had made it impossible. The danger now was that the end of financial aid would throw the area into the arms of the separatists: a proposal to set up a new bank of issue for the Ruhr and the Rhineland was viewed with great dismay for that reason, unless it could be absorbed into the new Rentenbank when it came. Negotiations between the French and the industrialists continued unavailing. However, it was certain that the Rentenmark would go the way of the paper mark if unproductive payments in subsidies and doles to the Ruhr were to be prolonged. To avoid that, even the payment of old age pensions was to be abandoned – although for the present, still, paper sums to the amount of millions of gold marks were being despatched daily to occupied Germany to save the population.

The industrial firms and the muncipalities in the occupied areas did their best to cushion the effects of the coming change. The district of Solingen, for example, made an issue of gold-based marks with cover provided by the foreign exchange balances standing to the credit of members of the Solingen Chamber of Commerce. Höchst dye works made their second issue of gold-mark currency covered by the deposit of more than 400,000 Swiss francs in a Zurich bank. Several firms made large purchases of milk and potatoes to sell to their own workers, but could only afford to pay them 70 gold pfennigs, about $8^{1}/_{2}$ d or 20 cents, an hour. The margin between skilled and unskilled labour had been reduced to about 10 per cent throughout Germany. Labour was more demoralised than ever, and the output per working man less than pre-war.

13: Schacht

When Dr Schacht was appointed Commissioner for National Currency on November 13, the questions were still being asked, in what form of stable currency was the paper mark to be redeemed, and at what rate of exchange. They were academic questions, because no one nursed more than a hope that the Rentenbank scheme could work. Every day was seeing some new order issued to direct the still mounting financial, economic and administrative chaos, the net result having been to confound the confusion further. The absence of newspapers because of a printers' strike from November 10 to 16 considerably augmented consternation, rumour and panic, as people were in general ignorant of the latest prices, the news from Bavaria, or even the desires of the administration.

Schacht was faced with incredible disorder. During the previous ten days expenditure had exceeded revenue by 1,000 times. The floating debt had been increased fifteen times. The government would shortly be unable to pay cash wages to the Army, to the police, or to its own officials. Already the officers of the Ministry of Finance itself were being paid partly in potatoes. The budgetary estimates included on every page the outrageous reminder, in brackets, that all figures were in quadrillions.* The Rentenbank Directorate tended unashamedly to the Right, comprised of large landowners, big industrialists, agricultural interests and the like – the class of people whom the inflationist policy had enriched and who had escaped paying their just dues to the State – so that there was not much hope of a democratic outcome.

---

* US notation, with 15 noughts. Government expenditure at this time amounted to 6 quintillions (US notation, with 18 noughts) to which revenue had contributed a mere 6 quadrillions, one-thousandth as much.

What followed Dr Schacht's appointment and the fledging of the Rentenbank on November 15, exactly a month after the original Ordinance, was astonishing. On that day, when the discounting of Treasury bills was at last halted by the Reichsbank, Dr Havenstein had unparalleled resources coming to the rescue of the mark which only the previous day had fallen to 6,000 milliards to the pound. According to Dr Schacht the unissued paper marks then in the hands of the Reichsbank and its branches would have filled 300 ten-ton railway wagons.

The engine of inflation had been put out of gear, but still the country's finances hurtled downhill under their own stupendous momentum. In the course of the next five days, as the first Rentenmarks appeared, the mark in Berlin fell, and was allowed to fall, to 12,000 milliards on November 15 to 18,000 milliards to the pound on November 20, the equivalent (for sterling had recently been depreciating in New York) of 4,200 milliards to the dollar. The face value of the total circulating notes doubled again in those five days, and the paper mark became worth exactly one-million-millionth of the gold mark. It was at that point, when it was only necessary to strike off 12 noughts to effect a simple conversion, that the paper mark – still the only legal tender – was at last stabilised.* A million million marks equalled a gold mark. A gold mark equalled a Rentenmark. *Mark gleich Mark*, once more: the vital question was whether anyone, whether everyone, would believe it. Confidence was all. Dr Luther, the Finance Minister, compared the exercise to building a house beginning with the roof.

There were problems, many of which had already been thrashed out at the end of the summer. The gold and gold-equivalent reserves had been so frittered away during the *Ruhrkampf* that they were inadequate to back the new currency. The Rentenbank's notes were therefore guaranteed in equal amounts by mortgages on landed property and by bonds on German industry – trade, commerce, banking and transport – to a combined amount of 3,200 million gold marks, about £160

---

* Had the mark been stabilised at its rate on November 15, the unworkable and difficult coefficient of 1.66 recurring would have been needed for all conversions.

million. The maximum note issue in Rentenmarks was to be 2,400 million. The Rentenbank was independent (as the Reichsbank had been) of government interference. In return for special credits of 1,200 million to the Reich – including 300 million Rentenmarks at nil per cent to pay off the floating debt – the government guaranteed not to discount any more Treasury bills with the Reichsbank. During the five days following November 15, when the paper mark was allowed to lose another half of its value although discounting had stopped, the gold-mark equivalent of the discounted Treasury bills fell from 320 million to 191.6 million. By the device of waiting for a round number, the Rentenbank had done the Reich a most advantageous turn.

The pause, in fact, struck another blow at the insensible, many-times-overkilled national creditor, from the War Loan lender to the mortgage granter, from the life insurance policy owner to the co-operative society member, from the savings bank depositor to the debenture holder, all of whose chances of justice now finally crumbled to dust. For them the extinction of the National Debt was the extinction of hope. Germany's debtors, public and private, had been relieved of their obligations to a value estimated at £10,000 million.[*]

Even at the time outsiders were astonished that the German middle classes, as well as the more organised bodies such as savings banks or trade unions, acquiesced unmoved in a remedy, however efficacious, which consecrated their spoliation by extinguishing all debts and annihilating the savings of the great majority. The seal of permanence had been put on the people's losses; as Bresciani-Turroni described it, 'the vastest expropriation of some classes of society that has ever been effected in time of peace'. These classes, wrote Addison from Berlin in 1924, 'accepted both approaching and accomplished ruin with no less stoicism than the first painful symptoms of convalescence – heavy taxation and widespread unemployment'.

Perhaps they did so because their despair was complete; but more

---

[*] Philip Snowden, Chancellor of the Exchequer, in 1930 estimated that the war had cost Great Britain an identical sum.

likely because most of them simply did not understand what was happening. The Rentenmark was, in its literal sense, a confidence trick. The real value of the mortgage guarantee was exceedingly doubtful, if not entirely illusory. Moreover, although the discounting of Treasury bills ceased, the discounting of trade bills had to continue, and did so apace. The 'miracle of the Rentenmark' was that from November 20 onwards the price of the paper mark remained steady while the number in circulation did not stop growing. Depreciation stopped, in other words, but the inflation of the money supply went on.

It was what had happened in Austria. The real value of the Reichsbank's circulating medium in November 1923 was still at less than a thirtieth of what had been found necessary in the stable years before the war. There was a desperate physical shortage of cash, of which the Rentenbank, if it were stretched to its legal limits, would only have been able to make good about a third. There were hundreds of authorised and illegal issues of *Notgeld* to be replaced, and an immense amount of foreign exchange to work out of the system: the sum of the former has been estimated (with no certainty) at 1,000 million gold marks and of the latter at 2,000 million – together adding perhaps £150 million to the official issue.

By November 30, 1923, 500 million Rentenmarks had gone into circulation; 1,000 million by January 1, 1924; and 1,800 million by the following July. These issues were in addition to the paper marks still being added to the 93 quintillion,* now equivalent to 93 million gold marks, circulating on November 15. The paper mark circulation rose to 400 quintillion on November 30, to 690 quintillion at the end of March 1924, and to 1,211 quintillion in July; a sum not far short of £70 million, or two-thirds of the value of the Rentenmark circulation. It was well to remember, admonished Costantino Bresciani-Turroni, the economist member of the Reparations Commission writing in 1931, that

---

* The British and German 'trillion', or 1,000,000³. Confusion internationally about what anyone meant when speaking of the value of the mark led the British Embassy and others to adopt the American (and French) style for the larger amounts. This muddled people more than ever.

the stabilisation of the German exchange was not obtained by means of contraction, or even by a stoppage of the expansion of the circulation of legal money. On the contrary, the quantity of the legal currency rose considerably.

It was an essential prerequisite of recovery: but to have announced that the Government would be issuing within eight months more than twelve times the total amount of paper marks circulating at the moment when the Rentenmark was introduced would have had a psychological effect nowhere short of disastrous.

The Rentenmark's own position was anomalous. It was not legal tender but, rather, 'a legal means of payment'. It was not convertible into gold, still less into the agricultural or industrial assets which were supposed to back it, although 500 Rentenmarks could be converted into a bond with a nominal value of 500 gold marks. The legal tender was still the mark, dead but mummified, and negotiable because its constancy at a million-millionth of its nominal value was guaranteed in people's minds by the Rentenmark, itself only another piece of paper with a promise on it. The legal reduction of the paper mark to this extreme fraction was not sanctioned until the monetary law of August 30, 1924, which permitted the conversion of the note inscribed 'Eine Billion Mark' (with the addition, in the interests of clarity, of the further inscription '1,000 Milliarden') into a Reichsmark.

The immediate basis of stabilisation, therefore, was not the closing down of the printing presses so much as the rigorous disciplining of State expenditure by the refusal of further credit to the government and by a return from a floating mark to a fixed parity against gold and the dollar.

As it was, the confidence trick worked. The Rentenmark, the stopgap designed to shift the 1923 harvest, became the weapon which held the field for the billion-mark note until the Reichsmark was brought in a year later. 'On the basis,' said Bresciani-Turroni, 'of the simple fact that the new paper money had a different name from the old, the public thought it was something different from the paper mark ... The new money was accepted, despite the fact that it was an unconvertible paper currency. It was held and not spent as rapidly.'

The same experience had already been found, not only in Austria, but with the spurious gold loan issue of August in Germany: it had had no genuine cover but, because the gold loan bonds had been labelled 'stable-value', it was enough to make the public not only accept but hoard them. The velocity of the circulation slowed from a mad gallop to a sedate walk. In the case of the Rentenmark, the fact that it was to win the confidence of agriculture was the most important advance of all. From the day of stabilisation onwards, there was at last the prospect that food might again flow back into the cities, and that one day the nation's budget might again be balanceable.

Dr Schacht had two immediate problems in establishing the new medium. One was the black market – on which the dollar was fetching in the last week of November up to 12,000 milliard marks, nearly three times the new official rate. The other was the *Notgeld*, the emergency money which was largely on an equal footing with the paper marks and which was the severest threat to continued stability. 'Everyone his own Reichsbank' was a system which Schacht determined to end. The announcement that the Reichsbank would no longer accept new issues of *Notgeld* aroused a storm of protest from those who, at the Bank's expense, had grown used to, and fat on, the practice of printing their own currency.

At a boisterous Cologne meeting on November 25, the National Currency Commissioner resisted the supplications and threats of a large assembly of industrialists and municipal officials – all aimed at restoring the acceptance of *Notgeld* – and declared that the decision stood, and that they would once more have to accustom themselves to budgeting with stable figures. The day of reckoning had dawned. With every cause for misgivings, Germany now peered fearfully forward into the December murk.

The black market was dealt with automatically, but no less brusquely. Speculators closing their books at the end of November, when the black-market dollar rate was at its highest, had not the money to meet their commitments. Credits which the Reichsbank would formerly have gladly given were no longer to be had, so that anyone who had bought dollars at 12,000 milliard marks each was now forced to sell them back at 4,200 milliard, losing two-thirds of their outlay. Before December 1, £10 million in foreign currency had returned to the Bank in this way. The speculators took off for Paris and went to work on the franc, their departure the first signal that stabilisation was a fact.

Dr Schacht sat in a single room which had once been used as a charwoman's cupboard, looking on to a backyard in the Ministry of Finance. From this post he transformed the German financial system from chaos to stability in less than a week. His secretary, Fräulein Steffeck, was later asked to describe his work as commissioner:

> What did he do? He sat on his chair and smoked in his little dark room which still smelled of old floor cloths. Did he read letters? No, he read no letters. Did he write letters? No, he wrote no letters. He telephoned a great deal – he telephoned in every direction and to every German or foreign place that had anything to do with money and foreign exchange as well as with the Reichsbank and the Finance Minister. And he smoked. We did not eat much during that time. We usually went home late, often by the last suburban train, travelling third class. Apart from that he did nothing.

The arcane, abstruse financial manipulations in the Finance Ministry passed largely unnoticed by most of the population, whose preoccupations on November 15 were hunger, cold, and the steadily mounting social unrest and misery. Rioting and highway robberies were occurring all round Berlin. The passage of Stresemann's Enabling Act had made it possible to give greater powers of action to von Seeckt, who now instructed the military authorities to aid the civil ones in controlling food prices; but even so it had been thought wise to send home the female staff of the Reparations Commission.

Three days after the official stabilisation, no more food than before had appeared in the markets. The high price of beef and mutton, which were plentiful, made eating it out of the question. No pork was being delivered because, said the reports, the farmers were eating it themselves. Owing to the absence of artificial oils from abroad there was a shortage of cattle feed, and milk yields were falling off. Berlin's daily milk consumption of 1.8 million litres had fallen to 130,000, and the city's biggest dairy, Bollo, was selling only 25,000 litres a day against more than a million before the war. Butter was not obtainable, and would anyway have been too expensive for most people.

More than financial collapse, the Socialist politicians were worried by the collapse of Germany's new democracy. Ever since the suppression of the Left in Thuringia, the Reichstag had been bubbling with indignation against the Chancellor. The Socialist vote brought his Ministry down on November 23 on a motion of no confidence and on the ground that he would not end the State of Emergency; yet there were other reasons for their disgruntlement. Stresemann had come to office in August in order to stop inflation and, by implication, to depose Dr Havenstein. Havenstein, by an odd quirk of fate, had actually died on November 20, the very day of stabilisation, and only resigned his effective management of the Bank by doing so. The appointment by Stresemann of Hilferding as Finance Minister had done nothing to stem the tide – and as Stresemann stepped down there was little real sign that Hilferding's successor, Dr Luther, was achieving any more. Stresemann, it was also recalled, even by his supporters, had taken office in the wave of optimism following the British Note of August 11, declaring that passive resistance in the Ruhr would not cease:* but he had personally stopped it, and still no settlement had been reached with the French. The Ruhr was the final sticking point: the possibility that the workers there would be abandoned to their fate after so many months decided the vote, even

---

* The dramatic introduction of half-starved poor into the precincts of the Reichstag in August also led to Cuno's fall.

at the risk of exchanging one administration for another further to the Right.

No confidence in Stresemann, dead tired as he was, did not imply any confidence in anyone else. Lord D'Abernon described von Seeckt's operations as moderate and tactful, dictatorial as they were: but in the last week of November he also found the confusion in the political world 'indescribable', the Ruhr problem more acute than ever, and the financial difficulties no better. Apart from the fact that the Communists in Hamburg and Dresden, where they had been exceptionally strong, now seemed to be completely cowed (von Seeckt's latest decree had abolished the extreme parties of Left and Right, to the reconciliation of moderate opinion), he could see no light on the horizon.

Yet sanity was slowly returning. Stresemann's fall and the political problems it posed obscured the more promising developments, but did not endanger them. An agreement of a sort was suddenly cobbled together between the Ruhr mine-owners and MICUM, the Franco-Belgian Commission of Control which had replaced the German Coal Syndicate when the Ruhr basin was occupied, to the effect that the mine-owners would make full deliveries of reparation coal and coke and would pay $15 million in arrears of coal tax. Thus, at obvious cost to the prospects of economic recovery in Germany, were Poincaré's 'productive pledges' secured; and the way opened (although it was not followed: Poincaré had to fall first) for a French evacuation.

Nor was external agreement all. The decision to put postal charges on a gold basis; the announcement of the dismissal within two months of 10 per cent of the railway personnel, together with other drastic economies; the agreement of the miners to work (for the time being) an eight-hour, rather than a seven-and-a-half hour day underground, and of State officials and employees and even of the iron and steel industry to go back to a nine-hour one; the reduction of official salaries to below pre-war levels – these were all substantial straws in the new cold winds of realism that were starting to howl across the country.

Such moves were reinforced, first, by the collapse of the provisional government of the Rhenish Republic and, second, by the assumption of the Chancellorship by Dr Marx of the Centre Party, who formed a Cabinet on November 30, with Stresemann as Minister of Foreign Affairs. When on December 8 the Reichstag adjourned until the middle of January, it marked the end of the Cabinet and parliamentary crisis which had begun when passive resistance was abandoned in September.

The overriding issue was the swelling unemployment. The extent to which the act of stabilisation contributed to the number of workless is not easily determinable. Already Germany's finances and economy had deteriorated too far for any measure to have slowed or even arrested the rapid upward trend: and the time when palliatives might again have postponed the evil day of mass idleness had certainly passed. The old currency having been reduced to total unacceptability, there was no way whereby printing money could keep anyone in his job any more. The choice had simply become between unemployment and financial chaos or unemployment and monetary discipline. Either alternative meant misery, but the second at least held the promise of food, and a way out of the cul de sac. It was not that Germany's unemployed noticed the distinction at first. The week of the interregnum between Strese-mann's and Marx's administrations produced a recurrence – largely Communist inspired again – of the endemic disorders in Düsseldorf, Essen and Gelsenkirchen, with armed fights against the police and much bloodshed. Food was the problem.

The first signal that stabilisation was a fact may have been the exodus of the international parasites to Paris, lured by the depression of the franc; but the subsequent signs were far less welcome. Taxation now began to weigh heavily. Interest rates remained high, at 100 per cent. Shortage of capital and credit meant high prices and closing factories. The cost of living crept up and up, now in real terms. Certain real costs rose very suddenly, such as university tuition fees, which caused student enrolment to fall. State and municipal relief was even less adequate than it had been. The trade unions, whose funds had vanished with the paper mark, were in turmoil.

During the earlier phases of inflation, workers' wages were low but on the whole enough. As exchange movement became violent, working-class hardships became greater. The sudden shock of stabilisation brought almost intolerable strain. By Christmas the registered unemployed total in unoccupied Germany, mounting all the time, was more than 1.5 million – twice the figure of early November; but the real total was probably a million more, and the number on short-time or on reduced pay embraced the majority of the work force. Arthur Rosenberg, from the far Left, estimated that only 30 out of every 100 workers were in regular employment. Workers soon had to accept employment on any terms of wages or hours – a condition of which hard-pressed employers took full advantage, backed by the government's benevolent, weary neutrality.

The government, indeed, having put the screws on the nation and made Schacht President of the Reichsbank for life, could do little but hope the cure would work, prepare its new tax ordinances, and make such directions to ease people's difficulties as cost nothing. Trial by jury, for example, was temporarily abolished because of the financial hardship to jurymen. A greater act of faith, as well as of necessity, was the decision that only half of the salaries of officials would be paid on the week ending December 17, and that the balance would be made up when taxes furnished the revenue. But here there was reason for confidence. Taxes had been quickly put on a gold basis. Whereas immediately before stabilisation the budgetary deficit between receipts and expenditure had been 99 per cent, in the period after November 20 it dropped to 92 per cent, and in the last ten days of December to 44 per cent. December's revenue was 33 million gold marks; but the following January's was to be 440 million, or 95 per cent of outgoings. After a lapse in February 1924, the budget finally balanced in March.

Although its success in restoring order to German finances was to be far greater than had ever been hoped, the Rentenbank's most important immediate triumph was in achieving that first object of a universally acceptable currency: shifting the harvest. The 1922 medical reports had shown that every great town in Germany had substantial pockets of desperate undernourishment. Throughout the urban nation, lack of food, clothing and warmth had produced all their concomitant ailments, from ulcers to rickets, from pneumonia to tuberculosis, all pitifully aggravated by the soaring costs of medicines and medical supplies. Another year of infinitely greater deprivation had taken a more terrible toll, and now there was the certainty of the demoralisation of prolonged unemployment to come.

Food, however, was beginning to appear again in the towns half way through December; and to the Rentenmark alone was this development due. In 1923, before November, the only increase in animals slaughtered for food had occurred in dogs:* after stabilisation, the consumption of every article of daily need – beer, pork, coffee, sugar, tobacco – increased regularly, except dogmeat. On Christmas Day 1923, Lord D'Abernon wrote of the 'magical wand of Currency Stability':

> Not even the most fanatical advocate of stabilisation – and this title
> I yield to no one – could have anticipated more remarkable results
> from its attainment than those which are now manifest. Food has
> become abundant in the great towns; potatoes and cereals are brought
> to market in large quantities; while butter, which was obtainable
> only in the better quarters, is now offered at stable, if at high prices.
> Animals crowd the abattoirs and queues have disappeared from
> before the shops of butchers and provision merchants. The economic
> détente has brought in its train political pacification – dictatorship
> and *Putsches* are no longer discussed, and even the extreme parties
> have ceased, for the moment, from troubling.

The euphoria of the immediate post-stabilisation months communicated itself to Bresciani-Turroni, writing six years later of the beneficial influence of the reform:

---

* Mainly used to supply a deficiency in pork.

Commerce revived, the food situation in the cities was eased, the purchasing power of many classes was increased, the factories reopened, unemployment declined rapidly, and a refreshing wave of confidence revived the energies of the people.

It was all true – for a space. In February 1924 Dr Kuczynski, a leading German statistical authority, confirmed that a sea-change had come over German life:

> The difference in public feeling compared with two months ago [he told the British Ambassador] is absolutely astounding. Then everyone was depressed and thought a catastrophe imminent. Today they are full of confidence. There is no adequate physical or economic reason for this – the change is mainly psychological. You may say it is based upon the Rentenmark, but that is more or less a fraud, and it would be more correct to say that it is due to the moral effect of the mere cessation of printing banknotes, or more correctly to the belief by the public that printing has at last stopped. This has given them so much confidence that they keep the circulating medium in their pockets and tills – £125 million there today against £5 million last September.

Sanity had returned to Germany's finances; and no doubt 1924, a period of often extreme monetary stringency, consolidated the financial recovery. But it was too much to hope, after the Dawes Plan was adopted in August and unemployment dwindled encouragingly throughout the summer and autumn, that years of reckless profligacy could be so easily paid for, or what the country had passed through would have no lasting effects on the people's minds. The destitution of the middle classes, of whom the resilient would recover in due course, was only part of the price. The economic reckoning was still to come. Some would say that the political reckoning did not come until 1933, when economic recovery had to begin again.

14: Unemployment Breaks Out

Dr Schacht, the author of the reform, had no illusions about its shortcomings. He understood that the Rentenmark could hold the tide only so long, that new credits from abroad were essential, and that for that reason no departure could be made (despite the pleadings of the government, desperate for money) from the strictest discipline. Nothing could be done that would put at risk the currency stability or the budgetary balance. 'After a long devaluation,' Schacht held on January 24, 1924, 'stability can only be regained at the cost of a severe crisis. We are in the midst of this crisis. External commerce is at a standstill. The balance of trade is active [i.e. in Germany's favour] only because imports have ceased as importers have no means of paying. Industry is living on old stocks.'

He had already seen Lord Norman, Governor of the Bank of England, about funding his *Golddiskontbank*, a project which successfully headed off the establishment of a new Rhineland bank of issue supported by the French; and at the end of January he went off to Paris where the Dawes Committee (under Dawes, the American financier) was starting its hearings on help for Germany and the future of the reparations question. His icy meeting with M. Poincaré showed him that France was still insisting on her pound of flesh, and no less anxious than before to promote separatism in the Rhineland.

The confidence that had returned to Germany hardly affected the industrialists in these western provinces. Hard-pressed for funds from home and abroad, they now began to turn to the French for terms, considering (as Stresemann put it) that a patriot's first duty was to make money, not to become bankrupt. It had been their guiding thought for many years past, and Stinnes was more dangerously ready than most to agree to whatever Paris proposed. It concerned him little that a French-backed Rhenish bank in opposition to the Reichsbank would give a further boost to separatism.

Nor had the new confidence, or even the new plenty, worked itself through to the poor or the workless, least of all in the Rhine-Ruhr area. Stabilisation was having devastating effects on many sections of the food trade, especially the food importers. When the mark was still falling, the merchants had been able to charge high prices with the justification that they had to cover themselves against the fall. As the money received was in practice often converted into stable values, an unhealthy kind of business had developed. Not only did these merchants (along with most farmers) find it hard to return to a world of dull, small profits: many were being caught out by the availability of cheaper imported food, which left them with large, expensive, often perishable stocks on their hands. The biggest importers, who had ordered when depreciation was in full spate hoping to repay in depreciated marks at the Reichsbank's expense, found themselves threatened with bankruptcy, panicked, and began to throw their stocks on to the market.

Thus from Cologne in the third week of January 1924 came reports of 'abundant supplies' of vegetables and fruit, domestic and foreign: German potatoes, eggs and butter; Italian cauliflower, Canary tomatoes, Spanish grapes, American apples, French nuts. A fortnight later, abundance had become a glut. People were being begged to buy milk at 36 pfennigs a litre (less than 3d a pint). There were mountains of Hawaiian pineapple, Colombian salmon, and American corned beef – all the product of bankruptcy or near-bankruptcy. Cheap as the prices were – beer was coming down 25 per cent at a time – the goods remained unsold, because the mass of the population were simply unable to buy. There was in fact much suffering, in part because a great many workers were on strike over the return of the ten-hour day, but more because so many of the larger factories had closed down. In the Ruhr and the Rhineland, unemployed were to be seen in crowds in every town.

There, food was cheaper but few were earning or receiving enough to be able to buy it. In the rest of Germany, although vegetables were still at a premium, the prices were coming down for more orthodox reasons. At Christmas 1 billion marks (a million million, the equivalent of a Rentenmark) would have bought two or three oranges, but in February the same sum would have bought 20 or 30 from the unemployed who, to the annoyance of shopkeepers, were hawking them in the streets. Margarine could be had for 500 milliards a kilo, having been as high as 800 milliards. Frozen meat had come down from 600 to 450 milliards a pound, although fine cuts still cost 4 billions (4s) a pound.

From an economist's point of view, a new era had dawned; but as the British Embassy reported home:

> The poor are not really getting a proper amount of food, as they haven't enough money to profit from the cheaper market – owing also to strikes and unrest, the stagnation of industry, and cessation of exports. There has been a general increase in the cost of living for such things as heat, light, and housing – all more than in Britain.

People needed work. The unemployment allowance was not enough; and the wages of part-time workers were too low even for necessities.

Bavaria quickly settled down politically once Hitler's 24-day trial, which started on February 2, 1924, was over. The trial itself, having given a national and international platform to the protagonist, ended in minimum sentences for all the accused – to the affront of many, including Ludendorff whose own acquittal disgusted him, or so he maintained. At the end of the year, looking back at the events he had witnessed, the British Consul-General in Munich, Mr Clive, noted that

> National Socialism had thrived in the existing depression of 1923. There was a don't-care feeling in the air. The greater fiasco of the trial

disillusioned the minds of more reasonable people, although Hitler's party a little later got one-fifth of the Landtag votes ... Hitler's greatest enemy is the Rentenmark. It is impossible to overestimate the beneficial effect of the stabilisation of the currency on the Bavarian, and I suppose also on the whole German outlook. When the London Conference [on the implementation of the Dawes Plan] assembled in July 1924, six months of stabilisation had already had a calming effect on the Nationalist hotheads.

Von Kahr and von Lossow resigned in mid-February, permitting the re-establishment of agreement between Bavaria and the Reich.

In Bavaria, too, of course, the middle classes had gone to the wall. That was the story throughout urban Germany, although whether they felt harder hit, as well as hungrier and colder, at the end of 1923 than at the end of 1922 is hard to say: Christmas 1919 had brought destitution to so many. People who lived on savings, or pensions, or war-disability grants, or assurance payments, or otherwise on fixed incomes, had to continue to make do on the proceeds of what chattels they could sell or what small, unaccustomed work they could find. Municipal soup kitchens often had to feed them.

Their numbers amounted to millions, and none was on the list of receivers of unemployed or short-time relief. They were the ones who had had their wealth shot away by the war, without knowing it. They looked in vain for charity to help, but the charitable institutions and the religious societies, just like the literary and scientific foundations and many of the universities and hospitals, had equally had the fountains of their incomes reduced to a trickle or less. Any who had held industrial debentures had lost their capital, to the benefit of industries who redeemed those debts with worthless paper. Any who had held industrial shares in 1913 would have had their capital reduced by three-quarters, and a pittance paid in dividend totals over the years – but in practice most people had panicked long since and sold the bulk of their shares for what they could get for them to the industrial profiteers and speculators who amassed the nation's wealth to themselves, paying themselves not dividends, but 'fees'. Germany's capital had been redistributed in the most cruel way, no longer spread reasonably evenly among millions, but largely in coagulated blobs among the new plutocracy.

It was widely remarked that the destitution inflicted by the inflationary process was not general. The very evidence, indeed, of great wealth – ostentatiously flaunted by the new rich who had it – misled many observers, including the French, into supposing that Germany's refusal to pay reparations on the nail was Teutonic knavery. The existence until the Ruhr invasion of full employment, an obviously prosperous working class, a buoyant economy, a booming home market, a strongly competitive position in foreign markets, factories bursting with production – all made possible by the vast scale of Germany's borrowing – could have fooled anybody.

But inflation shed its deadly rain discriminately, so that for some the reality of pauperisation lay hardly below the surface. The rentier classes – the people whose livelihoods depended on their savings, or on annuities or pensions – have already been mentioned. They included the poorly paid professions – judges, army officers, parliamentary deputies and the like – whose positions and dignity had traditionally been supplemented by private means. There were other groups, mainly the professional people, whose services turned out to be expendable in what their clients would have seen as the short-term. Civil litigation, for example, became a luxury. Who would buy books? Who was in a hurry for architectural advice? Art and tuition could wait. There was no rush for any but emergency medical treatment, and even that could not always be paid for as soon or in such amounts as doctors would have wished: private patients were slow to come forward, and health-insurance companies could not pay the full fees because of what inflation had done to their funds. No one could tell how many dependants of these professional people went short on account of such a recession in business.

The common assessment that it was the middle classes who were left destitute is only part of the story. Certainly they had savings to lose, and they lost them, whether in paper form, or in the form of the jewellery, silver, furniture, pictures or other precious possessions with which they were obliged to part. Certainly the landlords were reduced, if they had no other source of livelihood, to beggary through the restriction of rents to nominal sums or through having to sell off their property at knock-down prices simply to stay alive. Some householders survived by renting off apartments at realistic rates.

But not only the middle classes were going through the mill. Whereas the organised, unionised workers had managed by and large to keep their wage-packets at acceptable (although scarcely opulent) levels at least until the Ruhr struggle began to stifle the whole national economy, the unorganised workers had gone down with the middle classes. They ranged from tailors and cab-drivers to chimney-sweeps and domestic servants: painters, gardeners, chauffeurs, carpenters, shop assistants, printers, laundrywomen, cabinet-makers, porters; skilled and unskilled, male and female, from the self-employed to the sackable. A third group, which probably comprised a proportion of the foregoing, were the people who received small subsidies and pensions from the central or local governments – whose age and disability entitled them to an income from the public purse. But the social insurance contributions of years amounted in the end to no assurance whatsoever: the public purse in 1923 was paying them at rates which ranged upwards from the insulting to the disgraceful: and their numbers, excluding the unemployed, were reckoned at the end of the year at more than 5,600,000.

Stabilisation brought as little relief for the middle classes dependent on fixed incomes as for the working classes who could find no employment. A year of stability in Austria, it was observed, had gone far to prove the proposition that inflation had imposed a deeper, more devastating social change than anything the revolution achieved. The closing entries in Frau Eisenmenger's diary give some idea of what she had undergone:

Foodstuffs which three years ago were entirely unobtainable in Vienna and the rest of Austria [she wrote in December 1923] can now be bought everywhere. But who can buy them? Whose income has kept pace with the tireless activities of the banknote printing-press? Although my holding in shares is worth at today's quotation more than 10 million kronen, I am at my wits end to know where to find money to buy food ... today the value of our krone is quoted in Zurich as 0.00705 centimes.

On January 2, 1924 the full implications of the Austrian currency reforms dawned upon her:

The kronen and heller have been changed into schillings and groschen.* It is a drastic change. For 15,000 kronen we get – one schilling! Thousands of Austrians have been reduced during the last days to beggary. All who were not clever enough to hoard the forbidden stable currencies or gold have, without exception, suffered losses. An old married couple with whom I have been friendly for years had a holding of government stock amounting to 2 million pre-war kronen which brought them in interest 80,000 pre-war kronen a year [more than £3,200]. They were rich people. Today their stock brings them in *8 new schillings a year*. Panic has seized the Stock Exchange. My millions have dwindled to about a thousand new schillings. We belong to the new poor. The middle class has been reduced to the proletariate. More fighting – daily, repeated, exasperated, demoralising, offensive and defensive fighting of man against man. I feel that my strength is deserting me. I cannot go on.

Times were scarcely better in Hungary, for whom the year 1923 had been dismal. It began with a severe outbreak of anti-Semitism

---

* Their issue in silver and copper coins rather than paper was to encourage thrift and restore confidence. The change of style was to get rid of large figures.

in January and with Count Bethlen's government coming more and more under the influence of the Right-wing nationalists whose numbers swelled as rumours of impending foreign interference gained ground: the '*Move*' and the 'Awakening Hungarians', which were run by M. Gömbös, Minister for War, had students and ex-officers as their main elements. The country's finances went from bad to worse, the government in many ways sharing, for want of any notion of how to put things right, the view propounded by M. Bruno Balogh, director of the British-Hungarian Bank, that

> The only proper policy is that pursued by Germany where private undertakings are supported and developed without regard to the State finances. This is Germany's strongest point and France's greatest sorrow.

The korona fell from 14,500 in March 1923 to 92,000 in August and to 120,000 to the pound in October, the free rates always being much higher and prices going at last to twice the level in the United Kingdom. Farmers had long ceased to hoard currency and now hoarded corn and cattle, to the desperation of the townspeople. A year after Dr Seipel's successful tour of Europe to find help for Austria, Count Bethlen, the Prime Minister of Hungary, set out, cap in hand, to ask for international charity himself.

In October 1923 the Reparations Commission did for Hungary what it had done the year before for Austria in waiving its first lien on the national assets; and in December more Protocols were drawn up in Geneva to arrange an international loan to restore the country's finances. Mr Jeremiah Smith, the American financier, went to Budapest as the League's Commissioner-General, and carried out his work on the lines that Dr Zimmermann had pioneered in Vienna. No less than in Austria did the population, especially the public servants, suffer the deprivations and ignominies of financial reconstruction. To these miseries were added during the pre-slump years both great land hunger among the peasantry and the lack of the strict democratic rights, including freedom of the press, which, for what they were worth, existed next door in Austria. The currency reform of 1925 permitted 12,500 korona to be changed for one new pengo.

In Germany a few of the victims of inflation actually obtained a minimal restitution. By 1922 the unfairness with which wealth and incomes were being redistributed had become extremely noticeable, the more so as the rights of creditors were being so outrageously usurped by the absurdly wide distinction between nominal and market values: the real value of a mortgaged property, for example, was no comfort to a creditor who had to accept paper rather than gold while the property itself remained securely in the debtor's hands.

As the clamour grew, with support from the Courts,* against the iniquities which inflation had caused, the government attempted to redress what grievances it could. By the decree of February 14, 1924, known as the Third Taxation Ordinance (one of more than 70 ordinances issued during the period of the Enabling Act), industrial debentures and mortgages were revalued at 15 per cent of their original gold price. Mortgage bonds, savings bank deposits and other obligations were revalued at slightly higher rates. Meagre as these terms may have been, they meant nothing to people who had been obliged to part with their securities or whose credits had been paid off in paper earlier on. A further law of July 1925 therefore introduced a retrospective element to cover extinct mortgages and debentures which had been held in good faith since at least five years before, and raised the rate of mortgage revaluation to 25 per cent.

The 1924 decree also imposed a modest tax on the grosser profits which inflation had made possible, for example through the depreciation of industrial debentures – it amounted to less than 2 per cent of their original gold value; and an even smaller one in respect

---

* Most notably by a judgment given by the Supreme Tribunal at Leipzig on November 23, 1923.

of rural profits – 1.7 per cent of the original amount in gold of the mortgages whose shrinkage had so hugely contributed to them. These taxes were earmarked either for the Reich or for its constituent states. A move to revalue the government's own loans became law in 1925, which resulted in the stockholders' receiving $2^1/_2$ per cent of their original investment subject to reparations having all been paid (!), with an annual lottery for long-term holders who with luck would have their loans redeemed at $12^1/_2$ per cent without waiting for the reparations settlement. The public outcry that led to such slender satisfaction of creditors' demands was accompanied by violent speculative trading in government stocks and bonds on the Bourse, a practice already proceeding unhealthily in respect of the plunging French franc.[*]

Economic recovery, and a fall of interest rates from January's 100 per cent to May's 30 per cent, reduced the number of unemployed to half by April 1924. The great increase in imports during this period, however, led to such dangerous signs of weakness in the Rentenmark that Schacht intervened at once with drastic credit restrictions. The *Reichsbankspräsident's* unpopularity was enormous: stability was immediately restored, but not without a return to higher interest rates, more bankruptcies, and more unemployment. Marks became practically unobtainable. At that juncture the Dawes Committee presented its plan, which was adopted by the Allies in August, for reparations to be paid only to the extent that Germany's currency could stand the strain. The new payments schedule, still without any specification of what the total settlement would be, was to be helped off the ground with a large foreign loan and the evacuation, at last, of the French and Belgians from the Ruhr. The Dawes Plan also provided for the introduction of the Reichsmark to replace the old currencies.

There was once more an immediate return of confidence, the success of the Dawes loan being followed by other foreign loans, all of which helped to revive trade, to send shares up and the unemployment

---

[*] For a fuller account of the restitution programme and the behaviour and revaluation of stocks and shares, see Bresciani-Turroni. Caps. VII & VIII.

figures back down. By December 1924, the figure for the registered unemployed – about half the real number – was as low as 436,000. Until the arrival of Hitler in power in Berlin, there would never be so few out of work again.

Once more, however, here was a false dawn. Germany's trouble was that the inflation boom had never been liquidated. Stabilisation had ended the period when entrepreneurs could borrow as much as they wished at the expense of everyone else. A vast number of enterprises, established or expanded during monetary plenty, rapidly became unproductive when capital grew short. More realistic transport, fuel and food prices, and the return of rents to economic levels meant that wages, too, had to be raised substantially in real terms.

Firms that mushroomed during the inflation now found that the real interest they paid on loans for the first time was positive rather than negative, lower though the rates appeared to be. Perhaps most significant, for the first time they were obliged to pay real taxes, many of which were extremely high because of the necessity rapidly to balance the budget and to bring official salaries, which had fallen disastrously, up to an acceptable level again. Companies were often unable to buy new machinery after stabilisation came, so much so that huge stocks of unsold iron and coal began to build up in the Ruhr. Not even the foreign loans flowing in were able to prevent the seizing up once again of the Ruhr mining industry where pit after pit, especially any producing poor quality coal, was forced to close. Workers were to flock from pit to agriculture, from mines and quarries and engineering to the production of food and direct consumer goods, and to building. Hugo Stinnes himself had been deceived by the artificial prosperity of inflation into a fanatical confidence in the future of coal. It was the post-stabilisation depression in the coal, iron and steel industries, contriving even the depopulation of Ruhr townships, which led eventually in June 1925 to the collapse of the Stinnes empire.

That event finally pricked the abscess. The great groups who had resisted over-expansion during the depreciation – Krupp, Thyssen, Gelsenkirchen – were able to ride the storm. Others such as the Sichel and Kahn groups foundered. The defects of 'vertical' industrial concentrations, embracing all stages of manufacture from raw material to finished article, had been revealed, the strength of horizontal combines confirmed. The speculators, in a word, found they had to pay for their folly, improvidence and greed; and the old captains of industry resumed their sway.

The Stinnes débâcle demonstrated above all that great industrial possessions could not be held without adequate liquid resources (as early as June 1924, Stinnes had been trying to pledge Bochumer Verein and Gelsenkirchen shares against Dutch loans); and that vertical combines were inefficient and unprofitable except under the exceptional conditions which had bred them.

Germany which had undergone almost every conceivable form of collapse during the previous six years – military, political, social, financial, economic – now crashed downwards again just as her many times demoralised people had supposed that, with international help, she was beginning to rise from her knees. Confidence was shattered. The flow of foreign money slackened. The Reichsbank policy of credit restriction was maintained as firmly as ever to counteract a net outflow of gold and foreign exchange. The shifting of the working population was accompanied by a new, terrifying increase in unemployment and short-time working. Because labour was a buyers' market, those with work were nonetheless often compelled to work a 54-hour week. There was such an alarming rise in the cost of living that to prevent agitation the index had to be cooked. And there was a new, spectacular toll of bankruptcies. Much though public works were instituted to try to mop up labour, the unemployed figure had passed 1,300,000 by December 1925, and was gathering pace daily. The return of rational conditions had brought a necessary but brutal slimming of the immensely swollen public services: those who had been dismissed from the posts and the railways were now being joined not only by former miners and steel-workers but by the many who had started businesses on their own.

In the inflationary period new factories were built, old establishments reorganised and extended, new plant laid down, participations in all fields of industrial activity bought up, and the great amorphous concerns founded. Too late, it was found that this process had undermined the capital structure of the country: capital was frozen in factories for which, because of the extermination of the rentier and the reduction of the real wages of so many of the great consumer classes, there was no economic demand. Once the demand for goods was shut off and the flow of cash dammed, the fate of the productive apparatus was sealed. Even in 1924, firms of undoubted solidity and large assets were unable to pay out trifling sums of money. In 1926 that apparatus was still too great in relation to the working capital and the nation's power of consumption. Thus, whereas in 1913 there were 7,700 bankruptcies, and in 1924 only 5,700, the figure for 1925 was 10,800; and between the third quarter of 1925 and the second of 1927, bankruptcies numbered 31,000 – a rate of 15,000 a year.

In practice, furthermore, a great many bankruptcies were refused by the courts in the absence of assets with which to meet claims. Between May and November 1925, the number of protested bills per week doubled from 2,691 to 5,406. Many banks were immobilised by having had to lend to their industrial customers who had had to be kept alive but now could not repay. The banks found it prohibitively hard and unrewarding to liquidate securities, and under those conditions were unwilling to take over bankrupt factories in lieu of money. With shares now at far below value in a moribund Stock Market, there were endless sellers and no buyers.

Where some firms went into liquidation, many others rationalised at the expense of the work force. The picture in the first week of December 1925 presented the politicians' nightmare of 1922: the approach of the genuine, unhidden mass unemployment that the policy of inflation had so largely been designed to avoid. The mark stood steady. The franc, which before the war had been equal to the gold mark, was threatening to hit 150 to the pound. With France dumping currency and producing iron and steel more cheaply than her neighbours, Germany was experiencing exactly what she had done to others, and finding it very unpleasant. Krupp had just dismissed 12,000 men, and dismissals on the same scale were being pursued by Mannesmann, Gelsenkirchen, Phoenix, the Prussian State Mines, and numerous other works. Thyssen was restricting output everywhere. Gasmotorenfabrik Deutz of Cologne had sacked hundreds and would close on December 15. Osram, the lamp makers, were on short-time. Various huge firms were winding themselves up for ever, while others were closing down for a number of weeks to await eventualities – Rheinische Stahlwerke, for instance, and Bochumer Verein, some of the biggest names in German industry. The locomotive industry was producing 2 per cent of its pre-war output. The motor industry was in severe difficulties, too, with Benz deciding to close its works for a month and Opel dismissing 5,000 of its 7,000 workers.

During the first half of November there had been 145 bankruptcies in the textile industry, and now came report after report of closures and sackings. They were not confined to the Rhine-Ruhr area. In Saxony 179 factories producing metal, textiles, and machinery had been temporarily shut. In the Black Forest 65 per cent of the clockmakers were unemployed or on short time. The shipbuilding industry was employing half its pre-war and four-fifths of its 1924 numbers, and the tonnage launched was down accordingly. By February 1926 the number of registered unemployed soared above 2 million, with depression reaching from Hamburg to Bavaria. The average number of registered unemployed stayed at more than 2 million throughout 1926 – otherwise a year of rationalisation, and of economic and industrial recovery – and was still at nearly 1.5 million in December.[*]

---

[*] The average figure for both 1927 and 1928 was 1.4 million. The 1926 figure, which seriously under-represents the true total of workless, would have been much greater had not the British miners' prolongation of the General Strike in the United Kingdom so enormously boosted the fortunes of the Ruhr mines.

The industrial crises of 1926 at least spared the professional classes who had suffered so greatly in the financial one. By May of that year the circumstances of doctors, lawyers, professors, writers and the like had radically changed. They were again able to live in a fashion appropriate to their cultural environment: their fees were being paid, and their services were required in full measure. By 1927, when all Germany in an outburst of physical exercise and gymnasticism attempted to become 'strong and beautiful', the standard of living of the masses, too, had become very high, with individual affluence as superficially evident as the municipal and national prosperity. Only the legions of unemployable whose substance had been dissipated and the hundreds of thousands of workers for whom there was no work bore the outward scars of the great inflation and spoilt an otherwise happy picture.

15: The Wounds are Bared

The depth and permanence of the inward scars borne by the whole nation were perhaps harder to judge. The scourge of inflation, it must be emphasised again, followed the scourge of defeat in war, so that one must hesitate to affirm that the psychological trauma of the early 1920s would have been absent but for the social and economic insecurity which the endless depreciation of the currency brought. National disintegration and social upheavals unconnected with the money supply, after all, are in general enough to promote ethical degeneration and contempt for the old standards of behaviour in any community. It remains the case that those who lived with, or who observed, the inflationary process and the crisis of the recovery readily attributed what they saw first and foremost to the inflation: the fear, the greed, the immorality, the demoralisation, the dishonour.

Throughout the later inflationary years the shrill argument had gone on over who was to blame and what was the cause of the unceasing, increasing financial crisis – never a true crisis because instead of coming to a head it always did the impossible by getting even worse. Month upon month every excuse was found for it but the right one; every attempt made to stem the fall of the mark but the fundamental one. Mirabeau would have been no more heeded then than he was when, a few months before his death and a year before the Revolution's notorious *assignats* were introduced, he delivered the famous peroration to his speech on the French financial situation: '*La banqueroute, la hideuse banqueroute, est là. Elle menace de consumer vous, vos propriétés, votre honneur – et vous délibérez!*'.

What Frau Eisenmenger had observed in Austria, Judith List-owel, not yet grown up, watched in Hungary – how want and loss of status had led to the fall of ethical standards, to family quarrels, and to communal hatred, especially against the Jews. Judith Listowel retains no illusions about how her family reacted to the financial crises that lasted into 1924 and beyond, and rejects the generalisation that during the inflationary months everyone spent their whole time looking around for material goods in which to reinvest their savings.

My relations and friends were too stupid. They didn't understand what inflation meant. They didn't rush to get rid of their money (that was what the Jews and the Germans did). All my relations thought it would stop the next week – and they went on thinking so.

They woke up very late. They started selling their valuables because they couldn't buy food – the china from the mantelpiece, the furniture, the silver. That made them think – it made them think when the price of a set of old silver spoons went up from 20,000 to 40,000 crowns in a matter of a week or two. And if you had to sell a valuable writing desk for money which was worth only half as much a week later, of course there was ill-feeling.

It was resented when Jews bought these things. The Jewish women would turn up at parties or at *thé dansants* when we were all broke, wearing the silver fox furs – three at a time for ostentation – and diamonds which they had bought from our relations for a song – or what, when they saw them again, had become a song. My relations didn't know the value of anything. They were stupid. Our solicitors were no better. My mother's bank manager gave her appalling advice – he didn't know what he was talking about either.

Anti-Semitism had been negligible before inflation. Although Bela Kun's revolution had been mainly run by Jews, the White Terror had largely purged political resentment. The Jews had been badly treated in Hungary since the 1860s, and were not received socially for many years. Nine out of ten bore grudges, and when the opportunity of impressing the arrogant gentiles arrived at last, who was to blame them for taking it? When they made a success of inflation, they were hated. When they were ostentatious about it, they were hated even more. It may have been stupid of them, and of course the wiser Jews, especially the older ones, were greatly upset, and remonstrated with the younger, because they foresaw the antagonism their behaviour would create.

The Jews probably paid fair prices for what they bought – but that wasn't the point. Except for my father and many of his generation, people hated the Jews. My father realised that the fault did not lie with the Jews but somehow much higher up. Of course, it would be wrong to give the impression that there were not many impoverished Jews in Budapest and other places who had got things just as wrong as everybody else.

Compared with elsewhere, the elite branches of the Hungarian civil service – the Army, the diplomatic corps, and the financial administration – usually maintained the old traditions of integrity; and they suffered for that. The families of senior civil servants who tried to stick to the ethics of the Austro-Hungarian Monarchy often met disaster – unless they had land with which to support their convictions – and the attitudes of such parents were often resented by the young who found the maintenance of uncomfortable principles objectionable while their friends' families were obviously making compromises.

Real corruption was found less in the central government than at county level. This was something entirely new. When my father protested about the irregularities that were permitted – the keeping of two sets of books, the acceptance of bribes, the payments in cash, the extra jobs taken on which left less time for official work to be done – the reply was: 'Your Excellency, will you feed my children?'

There was communal hatred, which was new. There was social resentment, which was new. There was bribery and corruption: that was new. It was the same in Austria and Poland. If you get the same fever, you get the same symptoms.

Nor was German honour inflation-proof. The corruption among officials in 1924, Lord D'Abernon reported, was 'appalling', whereas before the war bribery had been almost unknown, and a high degree of uncorruptibility evident in public and private, if not always in commercial, life. There were few in any class of society who were not infected by, or prey to, the pervasive, soul-destroying influence of the constant erosion of capital or earnings and uncertainty about the future. From tax-evasion, food-hoarding, currency speculation, or illegal exchange transactions – all crimes against the State, each of which to a greater or lesser degree became for individuals a matter of survival – it was a short step to breaching one or other of the Ten Commandments. Whereas the lower classes with the further goad of unemployment might turn to theft and similar crimes (the figures up by almost 50 per cent in 1923 over 1913 and 1925) or to prostitution, the middle and upper classes under a different kind of strain would resort to graft and fraud, both bribing and bribable. Once bribery was the norm, by definition normal people resorted to it, the more so in the months of abject scarcity. No people could be expected to remain unconcerned while huge profits and riotous luxury were ostentatiously being enjoyed by the few. Corruption bred corruption, and the Civil Service caught the infection even in the war years. Counterfeiting was widespread.

As the old virtues of thrift, honesty and hard work lost their appeal, everybody was out to get rich quickly, especially as speculation in currency or shares could palpably yield far greater rewards than labour. While the anonymous, mindless Republic in the shape of the Reichsbank was prepared to be the dupe of borrowers, no industrialist, businessman or merchant would have wished to let the opportunities for enrichment slip by while others were making hay. For the less astute, it was incentive enough, and arguably morally defensible, to play the markets and take every advantage of the unworkable fiscal system merely to maintain one's financial and social position.

As that position slid away, patriotism, social obligations and morals slid away with it. The ethic cracked. Willingness to break the rules reflected the common attitude. Not to be able to hold on to what one had, or what one had saved, little as it worried those who had nothing, was a very real basis of the human despair from which jealousy, fear and outrage were not far removed.

The air of corruption in business, politics, and the public service, then, was general. The share capital abuses that became common as more and more shares were concentrated in the hands of profiteers were no more than an example, although a serious one, of the moral deterioration caused by inflation – they largely disappeared when stable money was restored. In an article in the *New York World* written in the summer of 1923, Stresemann rather defensively suggested that 'our whole business life has acquired the character of dishonesty and corruption because the value of the mark in June does not happen to be the same as the value in July'. More privately he admitted that the substance and the shadow of improbity were the same.

Most people were aware that willy-nilly their standards had fallen. 'It is the ordinary conditions of our life that make a woman evil,' said Erna von Pustau. Agonising over a peccadillo, she supposed that her 'callousness was just part of the general moral decay'. Frau von Eisenmenger's diary equally contained repeated regrets about the deceits into which life was forcing her. Her stock of good cigars enabled her to obtain a transport permit from the *Volkswehr*, normally forbidden to the bourgeoisie: but business was done in transport permits as in anything else. She shared philosophic resentment about the behaviour of others:

> The growing lack of consideration for one's fellow men ... impresses me very painfully. I can understand, however, that the instinct of self-preservation in people whose very existence is threatened should overcome all moral laws ... It has become common for better and more warmly clad people to be robbed of their clothes in the street, and obliged to go home barefoot.

However, she had less sympathy for the President of the Salzburg Provincial Government who was arrested for illicit trading in government property – food, leather and clothes: 'These are the enemies in our camp, but how few of them are detected!'

In Germany not until well after the return to stability did the nature and extent of the corruption in high places begin to be known. Events like the sentencing in March 1924 to three years' gaol of Dr Zeigner, the egregious ex-Premier of Saxony, for corrupt practices and bribery had raised scarcely a ripple. The end of the year brought to light a far more formidable array of financial scandals, enough to confirm the view that the old universal integrity had sunk in the whirlpool of inflation, and to deliver another stunning blow to the nation's morale.

The Barmat and Kutisker affairs which then rocked the country and shocked the world unfolded backwards like an Ibsen drama, the ramifications of malfeasance going further and higher the more stones were lifted up. A curious feature was that with each fresh series of arrests a *démenti* was issued by the incriminated declaring their innocence, in every case only to be confronted by irrefutable evidence to the contrary. The press, particularly the Nationalist newspapers, tried to make political capital out of the grave embarrassment of the government, many of whom were personally involved – until the arrest of highly-placed Prussian officials of the old regime showed all too plainly that corruption was not a Republican monopoly.

Iwan Kutisker was a Lithuanian Jew who moved into Germany at the time of the German revolution and recognised at once the characteristic principles of inflation. Starting with the modest sum he had amassed at home in dollars during the German occupation, he acquired a bank and directorships of a number of well-known firms, and immediately became financially influential in his new milieu. By 1923, the bank was hard hit by inflation, but not so hard that it could not be very accommodating towards the Chief of the Passport Office of the Ministry of the Interior, one Herr Bartels. Kutisker was also obliging to Bartels in the matter of indicating to him which aliens should be expelled from the country. One such alien was a fellow Lithuanian called Holzmann who in 1924, although he had provided a security worth half a million gold marks, could not repay Kutisker a sum of 200,000 gold marks advanced in the heady days of the inflation. Unwilling to be sent home on such a pretext, Holzmann preferred to take public issue with his countryman, and from then on the inglorious tale of graft and blackmail began to unfold. In November 1924, Bartels was arrested for bribery and corruption.

Julius Barmat was a notorious swindler who, though no less than Kutisker a Russian Jew of Lithuanian extraction, acquired in 1921 a certificate from the Prussian Ministry of the Interior instructing the authorities on the Dutch frontier that he and six other members of the Barmat family belonged to the Dutch legation in Berlin and that the usual customs formalities were to be waived in their case. The minister in question was later to assert that he had only acted on a direct request from the then Chancellor Fehrenbach's office.

The four Barmat brothers were directors of the Barmat Konzern, which had interests in 45 industrial and banking businesses. One brother had given a good deal of public offence by ostentatiously occupying a mansion in the lake-girt island of Schwanenwerder where he kept a flotilla of motor launches. Each of the others owned one or more palatial residences; and the vulgarity of all was a byword, noted even by those leading Social Democrat deputies who (according to the Right-wing *Vorwärts*) frequently enjoyed their hospitality.

Inflation profiteering had consisted of borrowing paper marks, converting them into goods and factories, and then repaying the lenders with depreciated paper. It was a process of which both Kutisker and the Barmats were pastmasters. Deflation profiteering, whose possibilities these Lithuanians (unlike Stinnes) rapidly saw, consisted of selling everything available for the new stable marks and – in this period of the tightest imaginable credit – lending the proceeds at extravagant rates of interest.

It was not entirely necessary to sell something first. Julius Barmat and a Frankfort Jew named Jacob Michael, one of the few postwar speculators whose pile was mainly made after stabilisation and who had been among the first to unload shares in exchange for cash,* found themselves in ostensible dispute about a certain sum of money. Together they approached the president and board of directors of the Prussian State Bank with the request that they would arbitrate between them in return for a small percentage of the money involved. The bank itself was among the oldest and most respected in the country, the epitome of financial discipline and rectitude, and one which, because of its strict avoidance of speculation, had not had its solidity undermined by the inflation. Its higher officers, too, the elite of the old order, enjoyed a very special confidence.

Perhaps none was more surprised than the bank's president, Herr von Dombois, and the two bank directors, Geheimrat Rühe and Ministerial-Director Hellwig, who together were to form the arbitration panel, to find that the sum in dispute was extraordinarily big and that the percentage they eventually received amounted to nearly 40,000 gold marks. Be that as it might, large credits from the *Seehandlung* – the common name for the Prussian State Bank – began to flow in the direction of both Barmat and Kutisker, and at a time when money was so scarce that the Finance Minister and the President of the Reichsbank, Luther and Schacht, were daily appealing to commerce and industry to respect the restrictions imposed. Elsewhere, when even the best securities would not release a pfennig, the two families of Lithuanian Jewish adventurers on the most questionable securities were able to borrow 50 million gold marks from the *Seehandlung* at from 10 per cent to 18 per cent, and to re-lend them at between 100 and 200 per cent.

Following up the leads discovered in the process of the arrest of Bartels, the bank's president and the two directors were apprehended

---

* and who was a sometime owner of the notorious dump of war material at Hanau, some miles in extent, popularly used as co-lateral for massive loans.

just after Christmas 1924. The most prominent of these gentlemen, Dr Rühe, the Financial Director of the Prussian State, was charged with conspiracy with Kutisker. The president of the bank was removed from his post, the *Seehandlung* accounts having been found to be showing a loss of some 15 million marks; and Kutisker and the Barmats were arrested as well.

These scandals led to more disclosures. The *Seehandlung* was not the only concern which had enjoyed the Barmats' patronage. It was found that the Reich Post Office had in the course of the year advanced to Julius Barmat a total of 15 million gold marks, and that credits had been issued personally by the Minister of Posts and Telegraphs, Dr Höfle, although three signatures were officially required on the cheques. Höfle resigned his position on January 9 and was suspended from membership of the Reichstag along with another prominent member of the Centre Party.

Three hundred police took part in the 30 or 40 arrests which followed – 13 of State officials. Other bankers from the *Seehandlung* were hauled in, including Herr Kautz, formerly a councillor with the Ministry of Finance. Herr Richter, the Social Democrat President of the Berlin Police, admitted to having opened an account with the Barmat bank in the same circumstances as Bartels. Herr Friedländer of the old-established bank of Hoffman and Friedländer killed himself with an overdose of Veronal on learning of the arrest of his stepson, a director of one of Barmat's offshoots.

On and on along the higher corridors of power went the trail. It was discovered that a confidential report on the Barmats had disappeared from the Foreign Office; and so had a minute to the former Chancellor Scheidemann from Reichspräsident Ebert himself, asking him to help Barmat. It was found that the Post Office had lent 5 million more gold marks to another unspecified client. The bank's loans to Jacob Michael were discovered too. Although President Ebert himself was only implicated by rumour, his son was deeply involved.

Our good friend 'der brave Joseph' [wrote Addison in reference to Dr
Wirth, the ex-Chancellor] who posed as the embodiment of Parsifal-
like ignorance of the wicked world and of transparent honesty, is
said to be in it up to the hilt, in as much as through his agency his
own company succeeded in extracting a trifle of 14 million gold
marks out of the Post Office funds. To name the others would be
to give a complete list of all the Social Democrat leaders and of the
most highly placed officials … The Right are biting their fists with
rage that all this didn't come out before the December election.

Yet it was equally believed that the Nationalists were involved
as well. The sums involved were immense – upwards of £2 million
in bribes over and above initial loans. The veniality of the bank's
permanent officials facilitated the *Seehandlung* transaction, and bribery
or political influence those of the Post Office. Subversion, in short, had
been general, and no one questioned that much of the iceberg still lay
below the surface. The whole miserable story was to have its echoes four
years later when the Sklarek Brothers scandal broke, involving massive
bribery of the Berlin municipality, including the Chief Burgomaster,
by a firm of tailors. The Barmat-Kutisker episode, at any rate, indicated
an advanced state of corruption in the higher official class, doubtless
due to the general demoralisation that the prolonged financial chaos
had produced as well as to the inadequate salaries which were paid
during the months which immediately followed Germany's financial
reconstruction.

The year 1925 was otherwise marked by two events important in
German history, the succession of Hindenburg in April as President of
the Reich and the Treaty of Locarno, signed in December. Neither was
viewed with much more than minority approval. The flow of American
funds into the country, however – £200 million between 1924 and
1926 alone, £1,000 million by 1929 – though interrupted from time to
time, from then on induced a spirit of state and municipal – and then

personal – extravagance as to make the American Mr Parker Gilbert, the Reparations Agent-General in Berlin, wonder how the country's foreign debts were ever going to be repaid, however much those loans were being used to meet reparations payments under the Dawes Plan as they became due. Dr Schacht was loudly critical of public spending policy. Dr Stresemann, the Foreign Minister, wrote to the Mayor of Duisburg:

> The fact that the Prussian State has granted 14 million marks for the rebuilding of the Berlin Opera House, and will perhaps raise it to 20 million, creates the impression in the world that we are rolling in money … Dresden builds a Museum of Hygiene with the help of a Reich subsidy … Please tell me what I am to say to the representatives of foreign powers when they tell me that all these things awaken the impression that Germany won rather than lost the war.

No one was disposed to take much notice. Traders asserted, of course, that business had been made unprofitable owing to the heavy charges of the State, but there remained among those who had survived the shake-out of 1925 both a deep satisfaction at the improvement in the country's finances and a firm confidence that henceforward life would be better. It was in this mood not only that the savings habit returned to a people who had learnt the hard way as individuals to rid themselves of cash at the earliest opportunities, but that the habit of borrowing, acquired during the inflationary period, set in more fiercely than ever.

That the federal states should have taken the lead was not an unnatural development, for with the solid proceeds of a working taxation system boosted by lavish foreign loans, public spending sprees were possible on a scale unknown since before the war. The states and the municipalities were making up for what they had missed during the inflationary period when roles were reversed and private industrial interests had flourished at their expense. Much expenditure on public building programmes was designed expressly to mop up unemployment.

The high interest rates of 1926 may have given businessmen cause to hesitate, but hardly prevented the wholesale 'rationalisation' which was to characterise the pre-slump years. The big industrialists formed cartels, first nationally and then internationally, to keep prices high. The federal states could only hope to make their own interest payments on foreign loans provided that more loans kept on coming – and soon the easy long-term loans were replaced by stiffer short-term ones. In the practice of borrowing, smaller firms and entrepreneurs were obliged to follow the lead of the big industrialists and the public bodies; and before long even the peasants were as badly in debt as the municipalities. Public and private light-headedness about money matters, in a word, was one of the legacies of inflation, and a deadly one to have acquired.

A member of the British Foreign Office staff returned from a travelling holiday all over Germany in August 1926. The German middle and lower classes, he reported, had money to spend freely. They were able to travel about in multitudes. All were 'decently and newly though hideously clad' in clothes dearer in Germany than in Britain. The cafés and places of amusement were full to the brim, although neither refreshments nor amusements were noticeably cheap. Museums, picture galleries and castles were crowded with German trippers, paying entrance money of sometimes two or three marks a head. Festivals of all kinds were being organised by both municipal and state governments, all putting up expensive new exhibition buildings and depending on German, not foreign tourists to survive. Although he observed that there were many formerly well-off still in straitened circumstances, he saw no reason to reduce the annuities payable under the Dawes Plan: Strese-mann's fears of jaundiced foreign eyes were entirely justified.

The false prosperity of post-inflation Germany, the second onset of massive economic self-deception within the decade, but in this case flowering over great unemployment below, was a poor psychological prelude to the slump conditions to come. Indeed, the inflation experience itself had ensured that the human emergencies of an economic depression could not be met by any German Government with even a modicum of monetary flexibility. 'It is easy enough to understand why the record of the sad years 1919-1923 always weighs like a nightmare on the German people,' ran Bresciani-Turroni's summary.

Democracy may have survived inflation, but there was little enough evidence of universal gratitude for that deliverance. Monarchism was the more popular creed, and it may be that the exposure to the air of Germany's moral wounds – the financial scandals of the inflationary years – contributed greatly to the strengthening of the disciplinarian side of the nation's character. Lord D'Abernon, who with Dr Stresemann had been a principal architect of the Locarno Pact which was designed to bring Germany back into a world of civilised co-existence, viewed the country through spectacles of the bleakest realism:

> If one drives on a Sunday afternoon through any German province there is always the same sight to be seen – men of every age and every corpulence, similarly dressed, marching rigidly in rank, accompanied by bands and banners, and the applause of their attendant womankind and young. They represent every school of political thought, and one will see in the same hour companies of country squires with their tenants and retainers and 'proletarian centuries' performing the same evolutions and carrying with the same invincible solemnity the emblems of Imperial Germany and Revolutionary Russia. It is thus not astonishing that there are in this country great numbers of ordinary mankind – excellent fathers and husbands of families – who can think of foreign politics only in terms of war.

Lord D'Abernon found the same atavism still more crudely illustrated in the treatment of treason cases in the German courts, in which the judges, ordinarily men of broad views and enlightened humanity, would inflict sentences of a savagery (he said) that would leave Englishmen aghast.* 'It would be straining ambition too far,' he concluded, 'to hope that in such a paste as this the leaven of Locarno will work anything but slowly.'

The aggressive posturing of the extreme, reactionary, militarist groups may have cooled somewhat since the disappearance of the inflationary conditions in which they had so notably flourished; but party discipline was still strong, and the political strength of the Nationalist parties in and out of the Reichstag grew steadily. Reparations, the 'war guilt lie', and the continued occupation of the Rhineland were still the targets and rallying causes of the Right. Hindenburg's election, though perhaps primarily the result of national sentimental sympathy for an old field-marshal who had had the misfortune to lose a great war, as well as of clever timing and a measure of ruthless machination, had given a decided fillip to the Nationalist and monarchist movements. To some he appeared to herald a reversion to a 'Prussian' Germany.

Germany, wrote General Wauchope† in a memorandum to London at the beginning of 1927, was morally mobilised for a war in the future to right the wrongs of the Treaty of Versailles.

> The greatest loss which Germany suffered was the ruin of her middle classes. If her 'natural leaders' are now to be found in the present party of the Right, Germany may again become a danger. It is common knowledge that great numbers of factories could be rapidly reorganised as in 1914-1915 for the production of war material if the government wished. Many are so overbuilt at present that they could produce a large military as well as a large commercial output. The last war showed that in time of need output per man could be made to increase.

---

* It is of course a commonplace that crimes threatening the survival of a society are found more odious by that society than those which threaten, or actually end, the survival of its members; and that in many communities, including Britain, treason has remained a capital offence where murder has not.
† Later General Sir Arthur Wauchope. He had commanded the 2nd Bn the Black Watch, and was from 1924-1927 Chief of the British Section Military Inter-Allied Commission of Control, Berlin.

Already, Wauchope pointed out, output per man in Germany, although 40 per cent below that in the United States, and only 90 per cent of what had been achieved pre-war, was 40 per cent *above* output per man in Britain. He deduced that there was a fair chance of having to fight a new war with Germany 'within the life of this generation', and had watched with awe the great attempts at physical culture going on throughout Germany to prepare the nation for future struggles.

It was, indeed, a matter of general remark among Allied observers that the German labourer worked for considerably longer for less than his British counterpart, and did so unremittingly, except for the usual pauses, during the whole of his working hours, unhampered by any trade union restrictions as to the quantity of his output. For the French particularly, the confinement in the middle of the disunited, work-shy, war-weary western nations of an energetic, well-organised block of 60 million industrious and martially-minded people, overflowing with self-justification and aspiring to the position of pre-eminence they thought their due, constituted a serious cause for alarm. The existence of ill-suppressed revanchism and the highly expert nuclear Reichswehr which von Seeckt had salvaged from the wreck of the war were additional reasons for the fears which, of course, events were fully to justify.

Epilogue

The economic causes of the German inflation appeared long before the Treaty of Versailles. Its psychological effects were felt long after the Treaty of Locarno. Where did the story end? Not with the stabilisation recovery, for that, too, was an episode in a human tragedy; not in the following years of sham prosperity founded on foreign loans which were at last called in; not in the disastrous years of 1930, 1931 or 1932, when economists, historians and politicians were even then rushing into print to write *finis* to the aftermath of the Great War.

More than any other thread that links the two world wars, the history of the inflation is a reminder that for the nation which supremely promoted both of them, the second was merely an extension of the first, reinforcing the adage that the seeds of battle are planted in peace treaties. Inflation for Germany was an unwitting part of the process of stoking the emotional boilers for a resumption of hostilities when the power to wage war returned. Not only did the loss of their former affluence and status, and the destruction of the old moral ethic, sour and humiliate the human pillars and foundations of German society: in German minds democracy and Republicanism had become so associated with financial, social and political disorder as to render any alternatives preferable when disorder threatened again.

When war came back, so did inflation. With inflation alone, noted Günter Schmölders,* can a government extinguish debt without repayment, or wage war and engage in other non-productive activities

---

* 'The German Experience', essay in *Inflation* (Ed. C. Lowell Harriss, The Acad. of Polit. Science, New York, vol 31, IV, 1975).

on a large scale: it is still not recognised as a tax by the tax-payer. Thus did Hitler resume deficit spending to finance armaments in 1938, and the experience begin again. As in the first case, the second inflation was a ten-year affair, although huge price inflation did not start in earnest until the eighth and ninth years, when cigarettes took over as the medium of exchange.

In terms of public perception, however, the second inflation travelled much faster. By 1948 the Reichsmark was abandoned, and ten Reichsmarks were traded in in cash against the new Deutschmark, while bank accounts were credited with only 6.50 Deutschmarks for every 100 Reichsmarks. Disaster had struck the holders of money values once again, but the agony was contained very much more quickly. The pass to which the Reichsmark had come in 1947-1948, the loss of nine-tenths of its value, had been achieved by its predecessor, the mark, as early as 1919.

Her new war indemnities apart, Germany was once again an almost debt-free country; and once again, with stability regained, great foreign loans were available to haul her out of her economic difficulties. Once again the repudiation of debt, conscious or unconscious, had been shown to be no more than a stage on the hyper-inflationary road. In the *Toronto Star Weekly* in December 1923, Ernest Hemingway described a street auction of inflation banknotes – German marks, Austrian kronen, Russian roubles – which the citizens of Toronto were being urged to buy in the hope, of which Germans, Austrians and Russians had long since been brutally robbed, that when sanity returned the banknotes, too, would retrieve their old values:

> No one explained to the listening men that the cheap-looking Russian money had been printed in million-rouble denominations as fast as the presses could work in order to wipe out the value of the old imperial money and in consequence the money-holding class. Now the Soviet has issued roubles backed by gold.

To say that inflation caused Hitler, or by extension that a similar inflation elsewhere than in a Weimar Germany could produce other Right- or Left-wing dictatorships, is to wander into quagmires of irrelevant historical analogy. The comparable, coincidental, financial and social circumstances of Austria and Hungary do not, in any case, support such a notion, telling in other matters as are some of the parallels which may be found. On the other hand, the vast unemployment of the early 1930s gave Hitler the votes he needed. Just as the scale of that unemployment was part of the economic progression originating in the excesses of the inflationary years, so the considerable successes of the Nazi party immediately after stabilisation and immediately before the recession were linked (*pace* the observations of the Consul-General Clive) with its advances in 1922 and 1923.

It is indisputable that in those inflationary years Hitler felt his political strength as a national figure and first tried his fingers for size on the throat of German democracy. Indeed, as Mr Clive perceptively reported, 'In the course of 1923 he succeeded in rousing more passions and stirring up more bad blood than far greater men than he have done in a lifetime.' The Consul-General might with justification have added that Hitler should go far. Germany only needed a new dose of economic misfortune for the Nazis to seize power, quasi-constitutionally, the second time round.

Inflation did not conjure up Hitler, any more than he, as it happened, conjured it. But it made Hitler possible. It is daring to say that without it Hitler would have achieved nothing: but so is it daring to assert that, had enormous post-war unemployment not been held at bay for years by financing the government's deficits and by an ungoverned credit policy, bloody revolution would have occurred, leading presumably to an equally bloody civil war whose outcome can only be guessed at. In all these matters, it was anyway touch and go.

That Germany inflated deliberately in order to avoid the costs of reparations is not a proposition that bears examination. The evidence is wholly against it. First, the rate of inflation was enormous long before reparations were an issue. Second, industrial pressure to inflate, largely self-interested, had nothing directly to do with the war debt. Third, it was correctly recognised that, although customs receipts by the Allies were perforce in paper money, reparations had to be paid either in kind or in gold equivalents: British and French war debts to America had themselves to be rendered in gold or gold equivalents, America's high tariffs making payment in goods impracticable.

Fourth, at no time did Germany's financial authorities so much as hint, privately or publicly, that their policies derived from cynicism (which would have had to be shared by their counterparts in Austria and Hungary) rather than incomprehension and incapacity. That the government and the Reichsbank were dominated by the notion that a huge 'passive' balance of payments made constant devaluation inevitable hardly seems sufficient explanation of their total, blind refusal to connect the mark's depreciation with the money supply – yet, as Lord D'Abernon wrote even in 1922: 'Knowledge of currency laws – particularly of the quantitative theory – is incredibly absent in all German circles'; or, as Bresciani-Turroni noted, the budgeting deficits of Reich and states alike were considered by writers and politicians 'not the cause, but the consequence of the external depreciation of the mark'.

It is irrelevant to this that the German workers who produced the reparation payments in goods or in bills of exchange were paid for their efforts in depreciating paper, with considerable though transient advantages for German industry and commerce – and frequently to the disadvantage of their foreign competitors. To that extent, reparations encouraged inflation. The 'transfer problem', involving the adverse economic effects of reparations on creditor countries, was only hesitantly being recognised by the Allies in the spring of 1923; and until then it was not suggested by them (or feared by German industrialists) that the excessive sale of subsidised exports for reparation payment purposes might lead to the erection of tariff barriers against Germany, much as other forms of 'valutadumping' were castigated.*

While the reparations burden and the uncertainties it led to were advanced as a cause of inflation, so was inflation pressed as one of the conditions which made reparations difficult to pay – and in both claims there was a certain justice, although neither told more than a fraction of the story. D'Abernon, who did not exonerate the French government under Poincaré from some of the blame for Germany's financial troubles (he accused Paris alternatively of 'Shylockism, bad information or, possibly, profound policy'), roundly condemned Berlin's 'folly and ignorance'. Indeed, it was inconceivable that Germany ever knowingly embarked on a course of economic and financial suicide to escape war indemnities, or that such motives were entertained by Rathenau. In practice, inflation proved no means of escaping foreign obligations except in so far as it contributed to the economic collapse of 1932 which wrecked the reparations programme for good.

The Reichsbank's display of naïveté in its credit policies of 1922 and 1923 should finally dispel any suspicions of financial Machiavellianism on the part of Havenstein and his associates. They staunchly denied that higher discount rates would moderate the inflation and, on the contrary, opined that they would merely raise the costs of production and push up prices further. Loudly as they later asserted that these inexplicably cheap credits were given principally for 'profitable' projects, the favoured firms who benefited from this largesse turned the money to their best advantage – either by turning it into material assets or into foreign exchange, or simply using it to speculate against the mark and drive it downwards. The only financial conditions which Havenstein understood were those which prevailed before 1914.

---

* Schacht, in *My First Seventy-Six Years*, Chap 21, reports Reginald McKenna, formerly Asquith's Chancellor of the Exchequer and then, in 1923, Chairman of the Midland Bank, as saying: 'Since Germany can only make payments by means of exports, she would be compelled to export to such an extent that British industry would suffer intolerably.'

How great does inflation have to be before a government can no longer control it? Most economists accept that mild inflation has certain therapeutic advantages for a nation which must deal with the social and economic problems to which industrial democracies are usually subject. Most electorates still accept the statements of their politicians' pious intentions in regard to controlling ever rising prices: and yet the Deutschmark, the currency of the country which had most reason to fear inflation, lost two-thirds of its purchasing power between 1948 and 1975. The pound lost almost half its purchasing power between 1970 and 1975. In neither instance, however, did such depreciation represent a deliberate, cynical policy; which, no doubt, would also have been claimed by the German bankers and governments of the early 1920s, who looked for causes of their monetary difficulties beyond their own printing press and tax system – and found them, without difficulty and to their complete intellectual satisfaction. It remains so that once an inflation is well under way (as Schmölders has it) 'it develops a powerful lobby that has no interest in rational arguments'. This was as true for Austria and Hungary as for Germany.

There was no moment in Germany between 1914 and the summer of 1923 when in theory currency stability could not have been secured, if necessary by the establishment of a new bank of issue for which sufficient backing was still available. Until the later date, despite the demands made by the Entente and the necessity to find substitutes for the Ruhr's iron and coal, German gold and foreign currency reserves always constituted a substantial proportion of the exchange value of the circulating paper, no matter how fantastically its volume grew. After the war was over, however, there were always practical difficulties which had little to do with the refusal of Germany's monetary authorities to see the connection between depreciation and money supply.

Long before the Ruhr invasion, and perhaps even before the preliminary meetings of the Reparations Commission, there came a stage when it was politically impossible to halt inflation. In the middle of 1920, after the brief post-Kapp *Putsch* period of the mark's stability, the competitiveness of German exports declined, with unemployment beginning to build up as a result. The point was presumably not lost on the inflators. Recovery of the mark could not be achieved without immediate repercussions in terms of bankruptcies, redundancies, short-time working, unemployment, strikes, hunger, demonstrations, Communist agitation, violence, the collapse of civil order, and thus (so it was believed) insurrection and revolution itself.

Much as it may have been recognised that stability would have to be arranged some day, and that the greater the delay the harder it would be, there never seemed to be a good time to invite trouble of that order. Day by day through 1920, 1921 and 1922 the reckoning was postponed, the more (not the less) readily as the prospective consequences of inflation became more frightening. The conflicting objectives of avoiding unemployment and avoiding insolvency ceased at last to conflict when Germany had both.

The longer the delay, the more savage the cure. Austria by the end of 1922 was in the hands of the receivers, having regained a stable currency only under the absolute direction of a foreigner. Hungary, too, had passed any chance of self-redemption, and later on was to undergo an equal degree of hardship and suffering, especially for her public servants. Stability returned to Germany under a military dictatorship when much of the constitution had been suspended – although the State of Emergency was only indirectly necessitated by the destruction of the nation's finances. To all three countries stability and then recovery came. All had to be bailed out by others. Each was obliged to accept a greater degree of economic disruption and unemployment than need ever have been feared at the time when the excessive printing of banknotes might still have been stopped. In all three cases, after inflation reached a certain advanced stage, financial and economic disaster seems to have been a prerequisite of recovery.

The take-off point in the inflationary progress, after which the advent of hyperinflation was but a matter of time, the point indeed when it became self-generating and politically irreducible except for short periods, was not indeed to be found on the graph of the currency depreciation, or of the velocity of its circulation, or of the balance of payments deficit. Nor in Germany's case did it notably coincide with some ultimate crisis of confidence in the mark, at home or abroad – Rathenau's murder, or the occupation of the Rhine ports, or the London Ultimatum, all of which had immediate seismic effects upon it. Rather it lay on the falling curve of political possibility, with which was closely linked the degree of political power and courage that the government, sorely pressed as it was, was able to muster.

What really broke Germany was the constant taking of the soft political option in respect of money. The take-off point therefore was not a financial but a moral one; and the political excuse was despicable, for no imaginable political circumstances could have been more unsuited to the imposition of a new financial order than those pertaining in November 1923, when inflation was no longer an option. The Rentenmark was itself hardly more than an expedient then, and could scarcely have been introduced successfully had not the mark lost its entire meaning. Stability came only when the abyss had been plumbed, when the credible mark could fall no more, when everything that four years of financial cowardice, wrong-headedness and mismanagement had been fashioned to avoid had in fact taken place, when the inconceivable had ineluctably arrived.

Money is no more than a medium of exchange. Only when it has a value acknowledged by more than one person can it be so used. The more general the acknowledgement, the more useful it is. Once no one acknowledged it, the Germans learnt, their paper money had no value or use – save for papering walls or making darts. The discovery which shattered their society was that the traditional repository of purchasing power had disappeared, and that there was no means left of measuring the worth of anything. For many, life became an obsessional search for *Sachverte*, things of 'real', constant value: Stinnes bought his factories, mines, newspapers. The meanest railway worker bought gewgaws. For most, degree of necessity became the sole criterion of value, the basis of everything from barter to behaviour. Man's values became animal values. Contrary to any philosophic assumption, it was not a salutary experience.

What is precious is that which sustains life. When life is secure, society acknowledges the value of luxuries, those objects, materials, services or enjoyments, civilised or merely extravagant, without which life can proceed perfectly well but which make it much pleasanter notwithstanding. When life is insecure, or conditions are harsh, values change. Without warmth, without a roof, without adequate clothes, it may be difficult to sustain life for more than a few weeks. Without food, life can be shorter still. At the top of the scale, the most valuable commodities are perhaps water and, most precious of all, air, in whose absence life will last only a matter of minutes. For the destitute in Germany and Austria whose money had no exchange value left existence came very near these metaphysical conceptions. It had been so in the war. In *All Quiet on the Western Front*, Müller died 'and bequeathed me his boots – the same that he once inherited from Kemmerick. I wear them, for they fit me quite well. After me Tjaden will get them: I have promised them to him.'

In war, boots; in flight, a place in a boat or a seat on a lorry may be the most vital thing in the world, more desirable than untold millions. In hyperinflation, a kilo of potatoes was worth, to some, more than the family silver; a side of pork more than the grand piano. A prostitute in the family was better than an infant corpse; theft was preferable to starvation; warmth was finer than honour, clothing more essential than democracy, food more needed than freedom.

Bibliography

Among the sources consulted in the preparation of this book were the following:

Foreign Office files for the years 1920-1927

An Ambassador of Peace, the diary of Viscount D'Abernon, Berlin 1920-1926, in three vols. (Hodder & Stoughton, 1929)

Gustav Stresemann, Diaries, Letters and Papers, edited and translated by Eric Sutton, in two vols. (Macmillan, 1935)

My First Seventy-Six Years, by Hjalmar Schacht (Wingate, 1955)

The End of Reparations, by Hjalmar Schacht (Cape, 1931)

The Stabilisation of the Mark, by Hjalmar Schacht (Allen and Unwin, 1927)

The Truth about Reparations and War-Debts, by David Lloyd George (Heinemann, 1932)

A History of the German Republic, by Arthur Rosenberg, translated by Morrow & Sieveking (Methuen, 1936)

Blockade, the diary of an Austrian middle-class woman, 1914-1924, by Anna Eisenmenger (Constable, 1932)

The German Inflation of 1923, edited by Fritz Ringer (Oxford University Press, 1969), which includes valuable excerpts in English from:

How It Happens: Talk about the German People 1914-1933 with Erna von Pustau, by Pearl S. Buck, 1947

Der Führer: Hitler's Rise to Power, by Konrad Heiden, 1944

The German Economy, 1870 to the Present, by Gustav Stolper, Kurt Haüser and Knut Borchart, tr. 1967

The Nemesis of Power, the German Army in Politics, by Sir John Wheeler-Bennett (Macmillan, 1953)

Hindenburg, the Wooden Titan, by Sir John Wheeler-Bennett (Macmillan 1936)

The Wreck of Reparations, by Sir John Wheeler-Bennett, 1933 (US Edition Fertig, 1972)

The Economic Recovery of Germany 1933-1938, by C.W. Guillebaud (Macmillan, 1939)

Curzon: The Last Phase, by Harold Nicolson (Constable, 1934)

Conflicts, by L.B. Namier (Macmillan, 1942)

The Decline of the German Mandarins, by Fritz Ringer (Harvard, 1969)

Europe of the Dictators, 1919-1945, by Elizabeth Wiskemann (Fontana, 1966)

Hitler, a Study in Tyranny, by Sir Alan Bullock (Odham, 1952)

Walther Rathenau and the Weimar Republic, by David Felix (John Hopkins, 1971)

Germany, by M. Dill jnr. (Ann Arbor, 1961)

Austria of Today, by V.W. Germains (Macmillan, 1932)

The Economics of Inflation, by Costantino Bresciani-Turroni, translated by Sayers (Kelley, 1937; first published as *Le Vicende del Marco Tedesco*, 1931).

Studies in the Quantity Theory of Money, edited by Milton Friedman (University of Chicago, 1956), which includes Phillip Cagan's essay, 'The Monetary Dynamics of Hyperinflation'.

Index

Aachen 7, 162, 195

Academic hardship 42-3, 110, 155-6, 214-15, 221-2

Acworth, Sir William 153n

Addison, Joseph 46-7, 57-8, 142, 179-80, 188-9, 192, 207, 242

Adenauer, Dr Konrad 37-8, 120

Aircraft, delivery by 163, 175

Allgemeine Elektrizitats G. 62

All Quiet on the Western Front 12, 256

Alsace-Lorraine 13, 15, 127

Amsterdam 11, 163

Anglo-Continentale Guanowerke 118

Anilin u Sodafabrik (Ludwigshafen) 120

Anschluss 17, 94

Anti-Semitism 41-2, 43-4, 59, 69-70, 78-9, 84-5, 95, 119, 192, 201, 234-5

Armistice 6-7, 13-14, 15, 24, 43, 81, 201

Army, German, Supreme Command 6, 8, 27-8, 41-4, 131 (see Reichswehr)

Assassinations 28, 43-4, 43-4, 78-9, 84-5, 94, 131

Assignats 195n, 233

Austria ix, x, 2, 17-26, 40, 59-61, 91-100, 145, 152-7, 181, 208, 223-5, 254

Austrian National Bank 98

'Awakening Hungarians' 225

Baldwin, Stanley 136n, 184

Balogh, Bruno 225

Bankruptcies 66, 66n, 153, 218-19, 227, 229-31

Bankers: banking (German) 5, 18, 46, 53, 75, 138, 144-5, 230, 240-2, (Austrian) 24, 25, 98, 153, (Hungarian) 225

Barmat scandal 238-9

Bartels, Herr 238-9

Barter 110, 113, 139-40

Bavaria 29, 40-1, 44-5, 51, 61, 64, 69, 80, 97, 114, 126, 131, 133, 149, 168, 170, 177-8, 180, 184, 186-7, 191-2, 195, 198, 201-2, 231

Bavarian Separatism 133, 209, 199

Beer 13, 41, 72, 88, 111, 114, 137, 143, 216, 219

Bela Kun 17, 234

Belgium 81, 161

Benes, Edouard 184, 186

Bergmann, Dr Karl 146

Berlin xi, 7-8, 28, 46, 49-51, 57-9, 69, 80, 82, 109, 115-16, 139-40, 149, 151, 180, 252

Berliner Tageblatt 52, 64-5, 112, 118, 133

Berne bankers' conference 46
Bethlen, Count 225
Black Forest 231
Blackett, Sir Basil 54-6, 73
Bochumer Verein 115, 229, 231
Boden Credit Bank 183
Bodenmark 183, 191
Bollo dairy 212
Bonn 120, 195
Börsen Courier 90, 173-4
Bourse 132, 138, 199
Brandenburg 199
Braunschweig 7, 116
Bread 24, 41, 48, 65, 72, 90, 107, 110, 123, 126, 144, 192, 196, 200
Bremen 164, 193-4
Bresciani-Turroni, Costantino 159n, 207-10, 227n, 245, 251
Breslau 130, 149, 200
Brest-Litovsk, Treaty of 6
Briand, Aristide 36, 66-7
British-Hungarian Bank 225
Brussels conferences 33, 35
Buck, Pearl 5, 77-8
Budapest 17, 102-3, 107, 141, 225-6
Budget (Germany) 34, 46, 48, 49-50, 53-4, 64-5, 82, 87, 125, 133, 153, 166,
171, 173-4, 205, 215-227, (Hungary) 103-4
Bullock, Sir Alan 201n
Burgerbraukeller Putsch 201
Butter 66, 72, 113, 115, 119, 139, 165, 212, 216, 219

Cadogan, Alexander 188, 188n
Cagan, Phillip 73n
Cannes conference 66-8
Centre Party 13-14, 147-8, 214, 241
Charitable institutions 221
Cheques 117, 124, 164
Cigars 20, 25, 100, 237
Circulation (Germany) 9-12, 33, 39, 46, 70-1, 90, 111, 117, 123, 132, 142,
146, 151, 164-75, 178-9, 183, 188, 190, 196, 205-13, (Austria) 22, 98,
(Hungary) 100-5
Civil servants (Germany) 32, 34-5, 147, 195, 235, (Austria) 25, 154-6,
(Hungary) 102-3, 103, 141
Class hatred 3, 22-25, 129, 157, 236
Clive, Robert 191-2, 220-1, 250
Coal 10, 20, 76, 78, 121-2, 126-31, 136, 139, 147, 160-2, 184, 190, 198, 203,
228, 253

Coblenz 35, 120, 151, 163, 164
Cologne 7, 37, 57, 114-5, 120, 144, 162-4, 217, 210-11, 219, 231
Commercial bills 81, 146-7, 252-3
Commissioner-General, League of Nations 97, 99, 152-154, 225
Commissioner-General, state 186-7 199
Communist Party (KPD), Communism (Germany) x, 7, 69, 111-12, 116,127, 132, 136, 149, 160, 162, 168, 170, 176-7, 195-202, 213, 254, (Austria) 20, 95
Compiegne 13, 42-3
Corfu 176
Corruption 4, 157, 235-42
Courts of law 226, 230, 246-7
Croydon 177
Crime 139-140, 177, 211, 236
Cumberland, Duke of 195
Cuno, Dr Wilhelm 69, 121, 129, 148, 162, 168-9, 212n
Currency Bank Law (see Rentenbank)
Currency reform (Germany) 206, 228, 249, (Austria) 224n, 224-6, (Hungary) 226
Curzon of Kedleston, Marquess 18, 35n, 50, 61n, 110, 136, 136n, 150-1, 169-70, 188-95, 195n
Czechoslovakia 17, 97-8, 186

D'Abernon, Viscount xi, 33-7, 44, 48, 51, 64, 68, 74-5, 78, 82, 89-90, 91, 117, 135, 165, 171-2, 188, 196, 198, 213, 216, 236, 245-6, 251-2
Daimler 62n, 118
Darmstadt 133, 191
Dawes (Plan) 217, 218, 221, 227-8, 243
Degoutte, General Jean Marie 128, 130, 144-5, 162-3, 190
Democratic Party (DDP) 14, 33, 51
Deutsche Bank 62, 118-19, 158
Deutsche Waffen- u Munitionsfabriken 118
Deutschmark 249, 253
Devisenkommissar 178
Devisenzentrale 96, 105
Die Welt 43
Disarmament Control Commission 64
Dolchstoss 6, 28, 43
Dombois, Herr von 240
Doom 173
Dresden 28, 116, 149, 151, 177, 213, 243
Duisburg 35, 120
Düsseldorf 35, 120, 162, 195, 214
Düsseldorf Landesbank 120

East Prussia 42, 159-60, 177, 202
Ebert, President Friedrich 6-7, 27, 110, 185, 241
Eggs xii, 31, 72, 107, 115, 119, 164, 192, 219
Eichhorn, Arthur 53
Einstein, Albert 112
Eisenmenger, Anna 20-6, 181-2, 223-4, 233, 237
Eitel Friedrich, Prince 41
Elections (1919) 14, (1920) 32-3, (1924) 220-1, 242
Elphick, Mr 193-4, 194n
Enabling Act 189
Erzberger, Mathias 14, 28, 33-6, 78
Essen 7, 54, 115, 130, 136, 162, 214
Experts' committee 112-13

Farmers, farming, peasants (Germany) 41, 108-9, 114, 144, 151, 159, 166, 180-3, 200-1, 205, 219, (Austria) 23, 180-1, (Hungary) 101, 104, 107-9, 225
Fehrenbach, Konstantin 32, 36, 239
Foreign currency (Germany) 49, 56, 93, 113, 134-5, 140, 142-5, 150, 172, 178-9, 211, (Austria) 59, 98-9, 153, 159, 225, (Hungary) 105
Franc (see French franc; Swiss franc)
France, policy towards Germany 15, 53, 65, 67-8, 120, 177, 197
Frankfort-on-the-Main 72, 84-5, 86, 112, 136, 149
Frankfurter Zeitung 66, 80-1, 84
Free Corps 8, 28, 38, 41, 187
French franc 1, 46, 121, 123, 133, 179, 214, 227, 231
Friedlander, Herr 241
Friedrichstrasse 200
Frontkampfertag 43, 77
Furniture 23, 56, 78, 93, 109, 153, 181, 223, 234

Garbo, Miss Greta 18, 25
Gareis, Herr 38
Gasmotorenfabrik Deutsch 231
Geddes, Sir Eric 120
Gelsenkirchen 118, 162, 214, 229, 231
Geneva 33, 38, 51, 97
Geneva Protocols 97, 99, 152, 225
Genoa conference 71, 73, 94
Gerlach, Hello von 43
Germains, V. W. 93
German-American peace treaty 45
German National People's Party (DNVP) 32-3, 43, 131, 187, 198, 242, 246
German People's Party (DVP) (see Volkspartei)
Germania 147-8, 150
Gessler, Dr Otto 42, 185, 187

Gilbert, Parker 243
Gluttony 19, 61, 76, 88-9, 114
Golddiskontbank 218
Gold Loan 134-5, 166-7, 174, 178, 199, 210
Gold reserves 135, 142, 178, 199, 206-7, 253
Goltz, General Count Rudiger von der 41
Gombos, Julian 225
Goode, Sir William 59
Governments, German, fall of 7-8, 15, 37, 117, 168-9, 189, 212, 212n
Gresham's Law 194, 195n
Groner, General Wilhelm 8
Gymnasticism 80, 232

Haldane, Viscount 112
Hamburg 5, 73, 76, 85, 149, 164, 176-7, 195-7, 213, 231
Hanau war material dump 230n
Haniel, Herr von 193
Hanover 177, 193, 195
Hapsburg Empire 17, 92, 100
Harden, Maximilian 44
Havenstein, Dr Rudolf x, 40, 75, 83, 145-6, 151, 165, 167-8, 170-5, 191, 202, 206, 212, 252
Health 48, 72, 106-7, 115-16, 141, 160, 165, 216
Hegedus, Dr 101-2, 104
Heiden, Konrad 202n
Helfferich, Dr Karl 9-11, 15, 43, 78, 187, 191
Hellwig, Herr 230
Hemingway, Ernest 87-8, 136-7, 249
Hermes, Dr Andreas 143, 174
Hilferding, Dr Rudolf 172-4, 189, 191, 212
Hindenburg, Field-Marshal Paul von 8, 27-8, 41, 43, 242, 246
Hitler, Adolf x, 11, 29-30, 77, 127, 131, 133, 136, 168, 170, 176-8, 181, 186-7, 191, 192, 199, 201-2, 202n, 220, 221, 228, 249-50
Hoarding 20, 47, 93, 184, 194, 224, 236
Hodgkin, Howard 37
Hofle, Dr von 241
Hohler, Thomas 103, 103n, 106, 107
Holland 6, 53, 53, 81, 161
Holzmann 239
Horthy, Admiral von 17, 101
Hotelbetriebs Berlin 118
Hotel Bristol, Vienna 59
Housing 56, 77-8, 109, 140, 156, 220, 223
Hummel, Dr 90-1
Hungary x, xii, 1, 17, 100n, 100-107, 140-1, 224-5, 234, 254

Hyperinflation, definition of 73n

Independent Socialist Party (USPD) 14, 33, 44, 129
Insterburg 160
Insurance 55-6, 59, 222-3
Interest rates 124, 167, 214, 227, 239, 244
Italy 23, 46, 94, 97, 99, 113, 120-1, 161

Joyless Street, The 25

Kadar, Janos 201-2
Kahr, Ritter Gustav von 29, 45, 186-7, 191-2, 192n, 201, 221
Kaiser (see Wilhelm, see Karl)
Kallay, Dr 103-4
Kammgarnspinnerei Dusseldorf 118
Kampfbund 176, 186
Kapp Putsch 28-30, 185, 253-4
Kapp, Dr Wolfgang 28-9
Karl, Emperor 17, 101-2
Kautz, Herr 241
Kehl 87-9, 136
Keynes, Professor J. M. 38, 112
Kilmarnock, Lord 30, 163-4
Konigsberg 159
Kolnischer Zeitung 190
Konigsberg University 42, 77, 159
Konigsberger Volkszeitung 160
Kontomark 183
Krupp von Bohlen, Herr 190, 229, 231
Kuczynski, Dr 217
Kurfurstendamm 178-9
Küstrin Putsch 187, 196
Kutisker scandal 238-42

Lampson, Miles 179
Law, Bonar, A., 113, 120, 136n
League of Nations 38, 45, 50, 95-102, 157, 176, 225
Leipzig 31, 134, 149, 226n
Lenin, Vladimir I. 6, 37, 132
Linoleumfabrik-Maximiliansau 120
Linz 181-2
Listowel, Judith, Countess of 141, 141n, 234-5
Lloyd George, David xiii, 36-7, 66-7, 67n, 94-95, 113, 120-2
Locarno, Treaty of 242, 245-6, 248
Loebe, Paul 34-5

London conferences 36, 62, 66, 120-1, 221
London Ultimatum 36-7, 52, 65, 255
Lossow, General Otto von 136, 187, 191-2, 201, 221
Ludendorff, General Erich x, 6, 13, 27-8, 41-4, 127, 129, 176, 178, 186, 220
Ludwig III of Bavaria 7
Luther, Dr Hans 191, 206, 240
Luttwitz, General Freiherr Walther von 28-9

Mainz (Mayence) 120, 130, 195
Majority Socialists (SPD) 13, 33, 44, 51, 168, 172, 239-41
Manchester Guardian 112
Mannesmann 116, 231
Mannheim 133
Mannheimer, Dr Fritz 40
Mansfeld Putsch 37
Marx, Dr Wilhelm 214
Mayence (see Mainz)
McKenna, Reginald 252n
Mehnke, Herr 177
Mendelssohn's Bank 40
Mephistopheles 142
Michael, Jacob 240, 241
MICUM 130, 213
Millerand, President Alexandre 67
Miners, mines 31-2, 122, 162, 190, 213, 230, 231n
Mirabeau, Comte de 233
Monetary laws (1875) 9 (1924) 209
Morgan, J. Pierpont, committee 80
Morgenpost, Der 42
Mortgages 108, 156, 226-7
Moscow (see Russia)
Motor-cars 52, 89, 118, 124, 139, 161, 187, 231
Move, The 225
Münchner Post 192, 192n
Munich 13, 30, 40-1, 45, 62, 72, 77-8, 87, 114, 132-3, 136, 170, 186-7, 191-3, 201, 220-1
Mussolini, Benito 99, 113, 120, 176

National Anthem 132, 176, 176n
Nationalists (see German National People's Party)
National Socialist Party (NSDAP) 45, 77, 127, 131, 176, 201, 220-1, 250
Navy, German 13, 196
New York 24, 84, 138, 145-6, 194, 199, 206
New York World, The 237
Nicholson, Professor J. Shield 194n

Norman, Lord 218
Noske, Gustav 28, 177, 185
Note issue 9, 75, 82, 103, 126, 207
Notgeld 86, 115, 119-20, 119-20, 164, 173, 194, 199, 199-200, 208, 210
Nuremburg 176

Oberammergau 69
Officer Corps, German 6-7, 27-9
Oktoberfest 114
Oldenburg 113
Orgesch 131
Osram 231
Osten, Hans-Georg von der 108-9, 139-140

Pabst, Georg Wilhelm 19
Palatinate 195
Pankow 115
Paris conferences 35, 38, 40, 67, 121
Passive resistance (see Ruhrkampf)
Pawnbroking 76
Petrograd 6, 132, 177
Peuple, Le 43-4
Phillpotts, Owen S. 59-60, 92, 92n
Phoenix 231
Pianos 22-3, 56, 109, 256
Piggott, Mr 37
Plundering 65, 95, 116, 139, 149, 162, 177, 181-2
Poehner, Herr 45
Poincare, Raymond 33n, 67, 85, 91, 120-1, 161, 184, 213, 218, 252
Poland xii, 37n, 38, 50, 199n, 235
Pomerania 109, 177-8, 199, 202
Post Office xiii, 31, 100, 123, 154, 161, 166, 178, 183, 186, 194n, 213, 241-2
Potatoes 65, 72, 119, 127, 139, 162, 178, 204, 205, 216, 219, 256
Printers' strikes 83, 163, 164, 205
Profiteering 10-12, 41, 54, 61, 76, 96, 149, 221-2, 239
Progressive Party 13
Prostitution 236
Prussian State Bank 240-1
Prussian State Mines 190, 231
Pustau, Erna von 5, 77-8, 85, 108, 119, 129-30, 139-40, 173, 237-8
Putsches (Kapp) 28-30, 185, 253-4 (Mansfeld) 37, (Küstrin) 187, 196, (Hamburg) 195-6, 202, (Munich) 201

Quantity Theory of Money 73, 251

Radek, Karl 177

Railways (Germany) 31, 48, 54, 56, 83, 92, 115, 122-3, 130-1, 147, 161-3, 166, 183, 186, 190, 213, (Austria) 100, 153, 153n, (Hungary) 106

Rapallo, Treaty of 71, 72

Rathenau, Walther 38-40, 66, 69-71, 78-80, 85, 94, 104, 148, 252, 255

Red Centuries (see Rote fiundertschaften)

Red Terror 101

Reichsbank, autonomy of 5, 11, 40, 46, 62, 75, 81-3, 145, 151, 172

Reichsbank, credit policy of (under Havenstein)9-10, 75, 121, 132-5, 137, 142, 146-7, 165-166, 173, 206, 251-2, (under Schacht) 210, 215, 227, 240

Reichsbank, general policy of 86, 112, 117, 128, 142, 143-5, 150-1, 163, 167, 183, 188, 194, 206

Reichsmark 209, 227, 249

Reichstag 10, 13, 14, 34, 70, 168, 171, 187, 199, 212, 212n, 214, 246, (Commission of Inquiry) 27-8

Reichswehr 27-8, 127, 136, 185, 199, 247 (see Army, Officer Corps)

Rent restriction Acts (Germany) 56, 73, 222, (Austria) 25, 156

Rentenbank 183, 191, 203, 205-8, 215

Rentenmark 191-2, 198, 203, 206-10, 216-18, 220, 221, 227, 255

Reparations (Germany) 15-16, 27, 33, 46, 49-50, 62, 66-7, 71, 91, 112, 161, 225, 250-2

Reparations Commission (Germany) 33-6, 70, 75, 82, 85, 121, 208-9, 211, 253, (Austria) 59, 96, (Hungary) 225

Restitution 226-7, 227n

Revolution (Germany) 6-7, 13, 29, 116, 238 (Austria) 7, 18, (Hungary) 17, 101, 234, (France) 180, 195n, 233, (Russia) 7

Rheinische Stahlwerke 231

Rhine Ports 35-7, 255

Rhineland 13-15, 168, 198-9 246 (separatism in) 122, 135-6, 161, 177, 195, 203, 218, 220

Rhineland High Commission 30n, 37, 73, 144

Richter, Herr 241

Roggenmark (see Rye)

Rosenberg, Arthur 215

Rosenberg, Friedrirh von 168

Rosenheim 149

Rote Fahne 84

Rote Hundertschaften 132, 160, 177, 199

Roubles 47, 165-6, 249

Ruhe, Geheimrat Dr 240-1

Ruhr 36, 53-4, 115, 120-3, 127-8, 135, 142, 149, 151-2, 162-4, 176,197,199, 212-13, 220-3, 227-8, 231n

Ruhrort 35

Ruhrkampf 122, 129-33, 136, 138, 144, 147, 154-5, 159-61, 168-70, 184-5, 201, 206, 253

Rumania 17
Rupprecht, Field-Marshal Prince 186
Russia xii, 6, 71, 95, 131, 160, 177, 201, 249
Rye bills, rye marks 113, 139-40, 183, 190, 191

Saar 15, 127
St Germain, Treaty of 17-18, 97
Salaries (Germany) 35, 44, 111, 127, 141, 142, 144, 150, 213, 228, (Austria)156, (Hungary) 102, 106
Salzburg 238
Saxony 32, 151, 160, 168, 177, 181, 187, 195, 198-9, 201, 231, 238
Schacht, Dr Hjalmar xii, 11, 109, 148, 191, 205-17, 218, 227, 240, 243, 252n
Scheer, Admiral 41
Scheidemann, Philipp 241
Schlinkmeier, Heinrich 163
Schmolders, Günter 248n, 248-9, 253
Schober, Dr Johann 94-5
Schoneberg 115-16
Schroeder, Franz 146
Schwelmer Eisenwerk 118
Scotsman, The 194n
Seeckt, General Hans von 27, 29, 185, 187, 202, 211, 247
Seeds, William 45, 45n, 62-3, 72, 87-8, 111, 114, 126-7, 132
Seehandlung (see Prussian State Bank)
Seipel, Dr Ignaz 95, 97, 99, 225
Sichel 229
Siemens & Helske 158
Sierks, Stadtbaurat 177
Sklarek Brothers scandal 242
Slump, The 3, 67, 244-5, 248-9, 252-3
Smith, Jeremiah 225
Snowden, Philip 207n
Social Democrats (SPD) (see Majority Socialists)
Societies, reactionary, 'patriotic', secret (Germany) 126-7, 131, 160-1, 168, 170, 184, (Hungary) 103, 107, 225
Solingen 162, 204
Spa conference 33
Spain 176
Spartakists 7, 14 (see also Communists).
Speyer 130
Stabilisation (Germany) 206-16, 219, (Austria) 98-101, 153-7, (Hungary) 225
Stahlwerk Becker-Willich 120
State of Emergency 184-5, 212, 254
Steffeck, Fraulein 211

Stettin 170, 177

Stinnes, Hugo x, 40, 74, 78, 114, 131, 134-5, 139, 160, 162, 172, 190, 197-8, 219, 228-9, 239, 255

Stocks and Shares (Germany) 11, 54, 57-8, 62-3, 117-18, 128, 158-9, 221-2, 227, 227n, 228, 230, 237 (Austria) 21, 24-5, 154, 224 (Hungary) 101, 105

Strasbourg 87-9, 136

Stresemann, Dr Gustav 127, 169-70, 172, 174-6, 176n, 184, 189, 192, 198, 211-14, 237, 243-5

Strikes (Germany) 28-9, 33, 58, 69, 83, 86, 116, 148-9, 162-4, 169, 177, 191, 193, 196, 219-20, (Austria) 92, 95, 155, (Hungary) 104, (Britain) 72, 231

Subsidies 40, 48, 54, 56, 59, 100, 102, 144, 156

Supreme Tribunal (Leipzig) 226

Sweden 6, 42

Swiss franc 20-1, 24, 53, 179

Switzerland 53, 96, 100, 130

Tax evasion 53, 64, 133, 143

Taxis 76, 165

'Ten-day payments' 66, 71

Thelwall, Francis 49, 68

Third Taxation Ordinance 226

Thurstan, Paget 57

Thyssen, Fritz 32, 197, 231

Tiergarten 39

Tirpitz, Grand Admiral Alfred von 41, 77, 129

Toronto Daily Star 87-8, 137, 249

Tourists xiv, 3, 56, 57-8, 69, 95, 114, 244

Trams 106, 165, 167, 173, 179

Thuringia 168, 199-201, 212

Times, The 75

Trade unions (Germany) 30, 32, 45, 73, 83, 110, 116, 189, 197, 198, 215, 247, (Austria) 96, 155, (Hungary) 107

'Transfer Problem' 251-2, 252n

Treasury bills 9-10, 13, 81, 133, 145-6, 172, 178, 206-8 (see also Commercial bills)

Treves 120, 130

Trianon, Treaty of 17, 100n, 104, 106

United States of America xi, 6, 30-1, 40, 54, 71, 69, 89, 123, 238, (US Ambassador) 78, 91

Unter den Linden 139, 178-9, 200

Upper Silesia 15, 36-8, 50, 54, 127

Vaughan, J. C. 200

Versailles, Treaty of 14-17, 27, 33, 35, 40, 43, 67, 120, 124, 160, 186, 246, 248

Vienna 17-18, 19-20, 59-60, 82, 92n, 92-100, 129, 152, 157, 224
Vogler, Dr Albert 198
Volkischer Beobachter 191
Volkspartei (DVP) 169, 189
Volkswehr 154, 237
Vorwarts 172, 239
Vossische Zeitung 12, 89

Waldersee, Field-Marshal Count von 41
War Loan (Germany) 10-13, 55, 118, 138, 207, 227, (Austria) 21-2, (Britain)
55, 207n
Wauchope, General Arthur 246n, 246-7
Weimar Republic 5-7, 14, 15, 27, 84, 147, 174, 188-9
Wheeler-Bennett, Sir John 14, 201n
White Terror 101, 234
Wiesbaden 130, 195
Wilhelm II, Emperor 6-7, 28, 41, 43, 77, 85
Wilhelmstrasse 139
Wilson, President Woodrow 14
Winkelbankiers 138, 144
Wirth, Dr Josef 32, 36, 44, 50-1, 58, 64-5, 89, 91, 94-5, 117, 148, 242
Wittelsbach, House of 7, 78, 186
Working hours 32, 37, 107, 116, 128, 198, 215, 219, 247
Worms 120
Wucheramt 76
Wucherpolizei 178-9

Young, G. M. 18-19

Zeigner, Dr Erich 160, 177, 198-9, 238
Zimmermann, Dr Arthur 99, 99n, 152-4, 225
Zinoviev, Gregory E. 177
Zurich 11, 23-4, 25, 103, 200-1, 204, 224

Acknowledgements

M y thanks are due to the many friends who have given help and advice in the preparation of this book, whose knowledge has prevented some of my errors, and whose recollections and encouragement have to advantage confirmed or dispelled the prejudices I held. For the mistakes and misjudgments which remain the blame is mine.

I am greatly indebted to the staff of the Public Records Office for their help and courage in supplying me from their shelves with more than a hundred heavy files to work through.

And I am grateful to Messrs Constable for permission to reprint extracts from *Blockade* by Anna Eisenmenger; to William Heine-mann for permission to print some lines from *The Truth about Reparations* by David Lloyd George; to the estate of Lord D'Aber-non for permission to quote from his Diaries; and to Allan Wingate for the excerpts from Dr Schacht's *My First Seventy-Six Years*. The extracts from *How It Happens* are reprinted by kind permission of Harold Ober Associates Inc. (copyright 1947 by Pearl S. Buck); and those from Ernest Hemingway's early contributions to the *Toronto Daily Star* by kind permission of Mary Hemingway.

Adam Fergusson